# Vegetarian
# Walt Disney World®
# and Greater Orlando

Vegetarian World Guides™

## Help!

You hold in your hands the first-ever book of its kind—an attempt to pin down the vegetarian scene in an incredibly dynamic, fast-changing tourist center.

We're going to be honest from the get-go and admit that—although every effort was made to ensure accuracy— some of the information in this volume will be imprecise, outdated, and just plain wrong. It's the nature of the game: restaurants close, menus change, chefs move on, and sometimes (but very rarely) sources lie. Because there are so many variables involved, you should always verify our recommendations before you make your own travel plans.

## Submit!

That's why we need to hear from you, whether you've had a bad experience at a restaurant we recommend, or a great experience at a restaurant we missed, or no experience at all because a restaurant, grocery store or hotel closed down between the time of our last visit and yours.

Take a moment to fill out one of the forms in the back of the book and send it to us, or submit your info to our online travel database:

http://www.vegetarianworldguides.com

If we use your tip in our next book, we'll send you a free copy and credit you in the text. In the meantime, we'll check out your submission, verify its accuracy, and possibly include it in our online update page (with a credit, if you'd like).

We can't wait to hear from you!

# Vegetarian Walt Disney World® and Greater Orlando

## First Edition

**Susan Shumaker** and **Than Saffel**

The information in this guide originates with the authors and has not been authorized or endorsed by Disney Enterprises, Inc., Universal Studios, or any other parties whose products, services, and locations are discussed in this book

Walt Disney World is a registered trademark of Disney Enterprises, Inc. Universal Orlando is a service mark of Universal Studios. Some of the attractions, locations, and products discussed in this guidebook are registered trademarks of these and other trademark owners. The use of trademarked names in this work is strictly for editorial purposes, with no claim made by the authors or publisher as to their use, or to imply any form of sponsorship or endorsement of any of the owners of said trademarks. Those words or terms that the publisher has reason to believe are trademarks are designated as such by the use of initial capitalization and trademark symbols, where appropriate. However, no attempt has been made to identify or designate all words or terms to which trademark or other proprietary rights may exist. In addition, nothing contained in this work is intended to express a judgement on, or to affect the validity or legal status of, any word or term as a trademark, service mark, or other proprietary term.

Published in the United States by
Vegetarian World Guides, Morgantown, WV 26508-6206
http://www.vegetarianworldguides.com

© 2000 by Susan Shumaker and Than Saffel
All Rights Reserved. First Edition.

ISBN: 0-9679280-0-1

Library of Congress Card Number: 00-190293

Printed in the United States of America
10 9 8 7 6 5 4 3 2 1

This book and other Vegetarian World Guides are available at a discount for bulk purchases used for sales promotions or premiums. Unique editions—including individualized excerpts and covers—can be created for groups with special needs. For more information write to: Special Sales, Vegetarian World Guides, PO Box 3533, Morgantown, WV 26503-3533.

*This series is dedicated to the memory of*
## Linda McCartney
*whose commitment to compassionate living continues to inspire*
*vegetarians around the world.*

# Table of Contents

# Foreword

by Paul McCartney

*A*s any traveling vegetarian can tell you, this series has been sorely needed for quite some time. Veggies on the road often have to make a special effort to eat right, what with steak houses and fast food chains dominating the landscape.

On our group's last two world tours, I was blessed to have Linda and the great vegetarian chefs we took on the road with us preparing our meals—and every night the catering room was full of beefy riggers wolfing down the fantastic food! But it's a bit difficult to imagine Mum and Dad finding a way to squeeze the luggage, kiddies, Fido, *and* Chef Jacques into the minivan for a holiday at the beach.

That's where these new Vegetarian World Guides come in. With one of these books in your suitcase or glove box, you'll be able to find really great food on the road, without compromising your ideals.

In fact, it was while traveling that Linda and I often reaffirmed our commitment to a vegetarian diet, and to the animals it saves. Driving through the agricultural regions of England and America, passing truckloads of sheep and cows headed for the "processing plant," our hearts were broken again and again. But experiences like those just made it that much more satisfying to tuck into a really delicious veggie meal at the end of the day.

After all, as Linda used to say, "Being vegetarian is about living life, not ending it." And veggies have known for years that it's a lot easier to end the suffering of others if you don't have to suffer yourself to do it! Back in the '60s, you'd order a sandwich at a vegetarian café, and this piece of dried bread with a bit of lettuce on it would come back. You'd be thinking, "*Ooo er, dear me, don't think I could ever go vegetarian!*" But these days, the idea of the vegetarian as some sort of dour, suffering martyr is long gone, thanks to the wonderful variety of food that we veggies can easily prepare or find on a menu.

Not only is it a lot easier to choose vegetarian meals, it just makes a lot of sense. Vegetarianism takes care of so many things in one shot: ecology, famine, cruelty, health—and it's great to see that nowadays more and more people are looking for kinder ways of living.

So if you haven't given vegetarianism a try, now is the time to do it, while you're on a trip and can look forward to really incredible meals prepared by some of the world's best chefs. You're sure to pick up a few great ideas to make your own meals at home more exciting, too. Linda and I often noticed that people who went veggie ended up rediscovering their passion for food, and all the varied and wonderful flavors that they'd lost while stuck in the rut of "meat and two veg."

And for you vegetarians who've bought this guide—I don't need to convince you of the benefits of the veggie lifestyle. But I do want to tell you that this series is a sign that things are getting better—for vegetarians, for the animals, and for the planet.

You've made the right choice. There are more options than ever, more vegetarians than ever, and now there are these great new Vegetarian World Guides. Linda was right when she said, "Going veggie is the single best idea for the new century!" So what are you waiting for? *Get out there and eat!*

**Paul McCartney**
*London, England*

# Preface

*T*his book is based on a radical notion: Vegetarians love food.

When people choose to alter their diet—for health, compassion or environmental reasons—they do not suddenly lose their sense of taste.

In addition to loving food, vegetarians know food. They've been forced to experiment with "exotic" cusines, and to learn how to make great food at home, throwing themselves into the lifestyle with passion. Indeed, many vegetarian diners know more about certain ingredients and techniques than the chefs who cook their meals!

Thankfully, healthful choices have become more commonplace on menus in the last few years, and most restaurants these days offer at least one meatless meal. But with greater awareness comes higher standards, and every vegetarian has a few war stories about pasta with red sauce *again*, or meat dishes with the meat—and all that pesky flavor—removed. If you're not terribly happy to settle for such fare, you still have to do an awful lot of legwork to find a really good meal, whether on vacation at Walt Disney World or in the middle of Manhattan. And wading through listings on Web sites isn't much help—or much fun—when you want to know which Indian restaurant uses the freshest spices, or whose vegan cookies are the consistency of rocks.

That's where we come in.

Vegetarian World Guides are for people who love to travel, but want to maintain their commitment to living well—a demographic that includes over a third of all Americans today. As the first mainstream, internationally-marketed guides devoted to healthful travel, our guidebooks offer a fresh, sometimes irreverent, perspective. And instead of focusing on esoteric retreat centers, we start with a popular travel destination—like Miami Beach or Yosemite National Park—and find the best places for vegetarians to eat, sleep, shop, and spend the day.

Like a conventional travel guide, a Vegetarian World Guide paints a portrait of the destination, but with an emphasis on healthful, veg-friendly attractions and establishments. Unlike a conventional travel guide, a Vegetarian World book will tell you which hotel serves tofu at breakfast, whose "vegetarian" soup is made with chicken stock, and where to buy galangal root for your self-catered Thai stir-fry. And unlike any other vegetarian publication, we rate establishments with our Vegebility Index: a simple but effective method of evaluating the veg-friendliness of mainstream restaurants,  and an indispensable aid when you're dining with folks who eat meat. We provide at-a-glance information grids to help you choose a restaurant as painlessly as possible, with a plethora of information at your fingertips. We help you get to the restaurant with maps. We also give you lots of insider information by including reviews by locals, profiles of master chefs, and introductions to unusual ingredients and culinary techniques.

We approach the researching and recommending of establishments with two aims. First, we want to provide as many options as possible in a given destination, so we recommend outstanding vegetarian options at restaurants which serve meat—as well as tactful ways to let the management know you prefer meatless selections. Secondly, we want to further conscious dining by suggesting completely vegetarian restaurants so good they don't require a cultural paradigm shift on the part of one's meat-eating companions. Many a longtime vegetarian has relished hearing a carnivorous relative wonder aloud, "Are you *sure* this is vegetarian?"

And you, dear reader, can help us! Make your voice heard by posting comments to our web site (www.vegetarianworldguides.com), or by filling out the review grids we've included in the back of the book and sending them to us. It's our hope that, with the publication and wide distribution of this book and its siblings to come, fewer people than ever before will be forced to shell out hard-earned vacation dollars for food they wouldn't tolerate at home.

When you hit the road, we hope you'll always take a Vegetarian World Guide along. We'll be there to help you "go veggie!"

# Acknowledgments

*A* truly great meal is measured not by just the quality of one dish, but by the progression of tastes from one course to the next, gracious service, and exceptional atmosphere. In the same way, our work has benefited from the hands and hearts of many individuals, without whose help and encouragement this book would not exist. An enormous debt of thanks is due to Tim Treharne, for whose advocacy on the other side of the Atlantic we are appreciative. Susan Tauster at *Vegetarian Times* has been a supporter of the project for more years than we care to remember, and has seen us through countless iterations. We are grateful for her advice and her patience. Linda and Paul McCartney were the first to endorse the project, and their commitment to the series kept us going in the worst of times.

A team of researchers and writers worked the phone and the Orlando beat for a number of months. The most important of these was gardenia, our expert on vegan dining in Orlando and at Walt Disney World. Her gentle manner, great sense of humor, and insights into the book's audience contributed enormously to the project and to our enjoyment of it. Thanks also go to Tiffany Shumaker for her work on campgrounds and hostels, to the Luteran family for "beta testing" the manuscript, and to Kelly Diamond for pointing us in the right directions early on.

Susie Albert has, at turns, been our marketing advisor, agent, and biggest supporter. We are grateful for her help, her advice, her friendship—and her connections! Melissa Reed suffered through the birth pangs of a new publishing company as its first advertising rep, a task we would not wish on our worst enemy but which was happily undertaken by one of our best friends. Thanks also to Steve "Shoe Banana" Gelberg for capturing our inner selves in the author photos.

We are grateful to fellow West Virginian Pam Brandon for her enthusiasm, and for hooking us up with all the right people in Orlando; to Suzanne Gerber and Andrea Mather, editors *extraordinaire*, for *Vegetarian Times* assignments that helped underwrite our research; to Karen Haynes and Rhonda Murphy—at Walt Disney World and Universal Orlando, respectively—for their help arranging interviews and checking facts; to Gretchen Van Ness for reassurance in the eleventh hour; and to Karen Woodfork and Chris Van Dyke for lending their ears, advice, troubleshooting talents, and hardware (all Macintosh, of course).

Countless friends and family members deserve thanks and praise for continuing to believe in us and in the project—even after our third year and fourth re-imagining. Geri, Julia, Philip, Jen, Winston, Louise, Gigi, David, Robin, Bob, Dana, and Stephen deserve special mention for their insider advice (and frequent commiseration). Thanks to Heidi for contributing love, support, and the idea for our series logo. Lots of biscuits and long hikes on the Ridge are due to Morgan, Daisy, and Hannah, who gave unconditional love and received too few pats on the head in return. And a big hug to Maya for taking care of the most important stuff.

Rhowyn came on the project at the half way point, bringing more joy than we could have ever imagined. She has helped us keep things in perspective, and reminded us that life is a miracle. And we offer our deepest appreciation, love, and thanks to Beverly and Bob, whose enthusiasm, support, and physical labor made our work possible. We'll spring for the pizzas next time!

Last, but not least, we send shouts out to the chefs in Orlando and around the globe who take vegetarians and others with special diets into consideration when planning their menus. Our tastebuds, bellies, hearts, and souls thank you. And to our colleagues in the promotion of a meatless diet and a compassionate lifestyle: Keep up the good work! We're changing the way the world eats, one plate at a time.

# About this Book

So far as we know, this book is the first ever vegetarian *travel* guide—but let's take a moment to think about what that means. If you're a longtime veg-head, you know that most people of our ilk are nothing if not helpful (maybe even a little bossy!), swapping tips about great restaurants and not-so-great ones, advising each other about where to buy tofu and which grocery has the freshest produce. With the ascendancy of the Web, a profusion of veggie sites has made it easier than ever before to find a decent place to eat. And we know of at least three great books that list veggie restaurants, natural foods groceries, and places to sleep that don't even have wool rugs in the house, much less meat in the freezer.

But in our humble opinion, there's still a void in the array of resources available to traveling veggies, and that's why you're holding this book in your hands. All of the books we mentioned, and an awful lot of supposedly complete Web sites, assume that you're willing to travel out of your way (sometimes far out of your way) to get to a vegetarian restaurant or retreat center.

Now, like many vegetarians—too many, in our opinion—we've been known to drive upwards of three hours just to eat at a restaurant. But we're here to tell you: We're weird. That's our job. It breaks our hearts that so many vegetarians feel they have to go out of their way to eat right, when there may very well be a fabulous meal awaiting them at the café around the corner. With everyday tragedies like these in mind, we've gone the extra mile to provide you with every conceivable tool to find the kind of food you're looking for, *wherever* you are in Greater Orlando. We've done so based upon the firm conviction that a travel guide—like a restaurant—should adapt to you, rather than the other way around.

## Our Methodology

With help from local authors and a few intrepid emissaries, we wrote this guide based upon our own visits to Walt Disney World and Orlando. Like you, we visited these places first and foremost as tourists. On other occasions, we went as journalists, working on two separate articles—one on Walt Disney World, the other on Orlando— for *Vegetarian Times* magazine. We visited most of the restaurants that we recommend twice, and made numerous follow-up phone calls as anonymous diners. When we made these calls, we asked the same questions again, checking for consistency: Do you have any vegan dishes? Are the beans cooked in lard? Does the soup have chicken stock in it? What are the ingredients in the bread? And so on.

In the process, we learned a lot more than we ever thought possible (and perhaps more than we ever wanted to) about vegetarian dining in America's number one tourist destination.

However, our knowledge does have its limits. We are not chefs. We do not claim to be experts in every cuisine or cooking technique. But we do love good food, and we do hate bad food, especially when it's served to vegetarians. And we certainly do claim to have done an enormous amount of research, to care about our readers' experience, and to be a waiter's worst nightmare no matter where we go.

## Our Outlook on Travel, Dining, and Life in General

As you make your way through the text, two things will become clear about the authors:

1. We're obsessive.
2. We're silly.

300 pages on vegetarian dining at a few theme parks? Okay, yeah, we're a little obsessive. Okay, we're a *lot* obsessive. We're this way because we believe that you, as a person hoping for an enjoyable dining experience, shouldn't have to be. We've asked the annoying, nit-picking questions about ingredients in sauces, breads, and just

about everything else so you don't have to, and we stand by our findings as the most complete, accurate information you'll find anywhere (at press time, that is).

However: If you are on a strict diet for medical or ethical reasons, we advise you to double check our research about ingredients yourself. The restaurant world changes rapidly, and a new recipe or supplier could mean the introduction of an animal-based product where none existed before. If you do find an error, please share this new information with us so we can, in turn, share it with others on our website and in future editions of the guide.

We're silly because we have to be. Anyone who has a special diet and doesn't have a good sense of humor is missing out on a good belly laugh at nearly every turn (like the time a server in Connecticut asked us, with a straight face, "But—isn't chicken a vegetable?"). Sometimes if you don't laugh, you just might cry.

## Reader Participation

To the best of our knowledge, all of the information in this guide was correct at press time. But to keep our records current, we need your help.

We've included a few reader surveys in the back of this guide in order for you to tell us about

your own experiences in Orlando. When you find a restaurant, market or lodging that merits mention on our web site or inclusion in the next edition, please let us know. If you were disappointed by a restaurant we recommended, or simply had an experience you didn't expect, we need to hear from you in order to change the review for the next edition, and to let our online community know what to expect.

Send completed surveys to:

Reader Surveys
Vegetarian World Guides
PO Box 3533
Morgantown, WV 26503-3533

If you prefer, you can fill out an online survey at:

http://www.vegetarianworldguides.com

## How to Write the Authors

*Via post:*
Susan Shumaker and Than Saffel
Vegetarian World Guides
PO Box 3533
Morgantown, WV 26503-3533

*Via e-mail:*
susan@stonecircleinc.com
than@stonecircleinc.com

Be sure to include your name and return address in your e-mail or letter, and a phone number if you would like us to respond directly. And please forgive us if you don't hear from us right away. We're probably exchanging knowing looks at a snack stand somewhere in the Yukon.

"Reindeer broth?"
"Yup. Definitely."

## How to Use This Guide

When you're looking for a certain type of establishment—say, a deli that serves vegan items—start with the "At-a-Glance" grids in each chapter. Once you've found a place that has everything you're looking for, check out the map to be sure it's convenient to get to, and then (if it's one of our recommended establishments) read the review for additional information. For each of the theme parks, we've also included brief reviews of restaurants and snack stands that provide one or two options for vegetarians. These "Worth a Mention" reviews are included based upon the notion that guests touring the parks are essentially a captive audience, and would sometimes rather compromise and eat a less-than-perfect meal than trudge halfway across the park in search of a divine repast.

When you just want something quick and convenient, head straight for the maps and work backward from there. That is, check to see what places are closest and use the grid, reviews, and "mentions" to determine whether or not you'll be happy with your choice before you go.

If you find a place we haven't listed on the grids or reviewed, chances are there was nothing fabulous available for vegetarians there at the time of our research. Or, it could be a new restaurant that has opened since the guide was published. If the restaurant looks appealing, check it out! The culinary world is mercurial, and new chefs or new management— many with a vegetarian bent— could be in place.

Again, if you discover a restaurant, inn, or market that hasn't been included, but should be—or if you have a bad experience at one of our recommendations—please let us know. Post to our web site at www.vegetarianworldguides.com, send us a message via e-mail (feedback@stonecircleinc.com) or snail-mail us a completed survey, torn from the back of this book. We'd love to include your findings and comments on-line and in the next edition!

## Symbols

### Maps and At-a-Glance Grids

In each chapter of the guide, a restaurant, inn, or market is assigned a distinct number, repeated in the review, the grid, and on the map for easy reference.

⚑ Indicates a reviewed and recommended location, with ample vegetarian and vegan options available

❶ Indicates a location that provides one or two options for vegetarians and has been included in the "Worth a Mention" section.

## Ratings—Places to Eat

### Vegebility Index
The "vegebility" index provides a quick and accurate indication of a reviewed establishment's vegetarian-friendliness. Ratings are based upon the number of vegan and ovo-lacto choices available, either on the menu or through the willingness of the kitchen staff.

**Excellent:**
More than 8 o/l and 4 vegan choices
**Good:**
4-7 o/l and 2-3 vegan choices
**Fair:**
2-3 o/l choices and 1 vegan choice
**Poor:**
1 o/l choice and no vegan choices

### Dining Prices
The cost of each restaurant has been categorized according to the averaged price of vegetarian entrées or snacks on the menu at breakfast, lunch, and dinner. Please note that non-vegetarian

entrées at the same establishment are often much more costly.

**Inexpensive:**
Breakfast/Lunch: < $5;
Dinner: < $7.50; Snacks: < $1
**Moderate:**
Breakfast/Lunch: $5–10;
Dinner: $7.50–12.50; Snacks: $1-5
**Expensive:**
Breakfast/Lunch: $10-20;
Dinner: $12.50–25; Snacks: $5-8
**Very Expensive:**
Breakfast/Lunch: > $20;
Dinner: > $25; Snacks: > $8

## Places to Stay

### Vegebility Index
After an exhaustive search, we were (sadly) unable to find any self-proclaimed vegetarian lodgings in the Orlando area. However, we *were* able to find a number of veg-friendly establishments that were appealing either because of their cost, location, or sensitivity to environmental and/or health issues. The vegebility index for lodgings is determined according to the following criteria:

**Excellent:**
An entirely vegetarian establishment, within a five minute drive of other recommended restaurants
**Good:**
An inn or hotel that houses at least one recommended restaurant, allows for self-catering, and is within a five

minute drive of at least one other recommended veg-friendly restaurant

**Fair:**

An inn or hotel that serves vegetarian
meals or allows for self-catering, and
is within a ten minute drive of at
least one recommended veg-friendly
restaurant

**Poor:**

An inn or hotel that is within a ten
minute drive of at least one recommended veg-friendly restaurant

### Lodging Rates

The hotels and inns included in the
guide span a wide range of afford-
ability, depending upon amenities,
location, and time of year. Our
classification is based upon the
nightly cost of a double room
with standard amenities, averaged
across low, moderate, and high
seasons. Tax is not included.

**Way Cheap:**

Less than $50

**Inexpensive:**

$50-100

**Moderate:**

$100–150

**Expensive:**

$150–250

**Very Expensive:**

More than $250

## Places to Shop

### Vegebility Index

How many times have you arrived
at your destination, only to find
that you're almost out of your
favorite cruelty-free shampoo? It's
happened to us more times than
we care to admit. Knowing that
people take quick trips to the grocery store for numerous reasons,
we've rated the "vegebility" of markets in four distinct categories:

### Deli/To Go Items

**Excellent:**

More than 8 o/l and 4 vegan choices

**Good:**

4-7 o/l and 2-3 vegan choices

**Fair:**

2-3 o/l choices and 1 vegan choice

**Poor:**

1 o/l choice and no vegan choices

### Produce

**Excellent:**

Exquisitely beautiful produce, at least
75% organic

**Good:**

Nice produce, at least 75 % organic

**Fair:**

Edible produce, with some organic
selections

**Poor:**

Little or no organic selection

### Prepackaged Natural Foods

**Excellent:**

Every healthful prepared item you
might want—from organic chips to
vegan frozen dinners

**Good:**

A nice selection of healthful and
organic items, but not necessarily your
favorite brand

**Fair:**

A small token section of prepackaged health foods

**Poor:**

Very few (if any) healthful prepared items in any section of the store

**Non-Food Items**

**Excellent:**

A large selection of cruelty- and animal-free beauty products, environ-mentally-friendly household supplies, and dietary supplements

**Good:**

A choice of products, and at least one line of dietary supplements

**Fair:**

Few cruelty-free or environmentally-friendly options, no supplements

**Poor:**

Nada

# Planning Your Trip:
# Vegetarian Travel to Orlando

**Walt Disney World General Information:** *(407) 824-4321*
**Universal Orlando Main Number:** *(407) 363-8000*
**Orlando/Orange County CVB:** *(800) 551-0181*

# Introduction

"We can do a whole vegetarian dinner *from start to finish. I can take you through five courses, if you'd like. There are so many things you could do here that you could have a table of six vegetarians, and I could feed you all different courses. We are the king of vegetarians!"*

Your waiter's words ring in your ears as he hustles off to get you a glass of wine, and you take a moment to look around. Fifteen floors in the sky, you notice the view first: a breathtaking panorama of earth and sky through clear plate glass. You manage to pull your gaze from the window and, slowly, you begin to appreciate the sophisticated style of the room itself. Art Deco symmetries remind you of a 1930s ocean liner; a riot of bold forms—square wall panels, circular windows, and tall vases of brushed aluminum—lend an urbane, avant-garde polish.

The crowd this evening is a surprising mix of professional couples, groups of friends out to toast the week's end, and entire families with kids in tow. You order your meal and—at your waiter's suggestion—you take an impromptu tour of the open, "on-stage" kitchen, where sushi counters, pastry stations, and the huge oak-fired grill are abuzz with activity.

Colorful designs, inspired by the abstractions of Klee and Kandinsky, are repeated in the upholstery, the carpets, and the vest of the waiter who returns you to your seat and delivers the first course. If God is in the details, this meal should be divine.

And it is. Chef Clifford Pleau's chilled Gazpacho, spiked with vinegar and topped with fresh guacamole, sharpens your appetite for the savory Brick Oven Flatbread, smothered in grilled mushrooms, roasted garlic, caramelized red onions, and feta cheese. And your companion's Avocado and Vegetable Roll is by far the most delectable sushi you've ever eaten.

You might be content to stop there—and maybe you should—but entrées like Mesquite Roasted Tofu and Summer Vegetable Risotto sound awfully good... And then there's Vegetarian Unplugged: a tempting medley of vegetarian and vegan side dishes arranged, tapas-like, in little bowls on a platter.

As you sip after-dinner drinks, the lights dim and all eyes turn toward the wall of plate glass facing west. Fireworks illuminate the night sky, and uplifting music, in synch with the colorful explosions, is piped into the restaurant.

There aren't many places in the world where food, service, and atmosphere combine to deliver a truly magical experience. Where could you be? On the banks of the Seine? In the heart of tony Manhattan? Perhaps you've died and gone to heaven.

*Surprise! You're at Disney World!*

This scene would have been unthinkable 35 years ago, when Walt Disney first came to sleepy Orlando, Florida and started buying up land southwest of town. Back then, Orlando was still a minor vacation destination—it had been, in fact, ever since the early part of this century, when a Medfly infestation destroyed the orange groves and sent entrepreneurs looking for new income. Before Disney, the hallmark of Orlando was its slow pace, its relative peace and quiet compared with the resort towns on Florida's east coast.

Today, the city is a booming metropolis and the number one tourist destination in the world, thanks entirely to the influence of the Mouse and his ever-expanding House. And the massive influx of tourists in search of merchandise and pleasure has spawned, in turn, every conceivable gimmick, scam, and enterprise to open the pockets of tourists flocking southward. Everywhere you look within a 35 mile radius of the Magic Kingdom there are hotels, motels, timeshares, resorts, ticket scalpers, tour buses, factory outlets, theme parks, water parks, miniature golf courses, movie theatres—and, of course, restaurants.

*Jumpin' Jehosophat, the restaurants!* The sheer profusion of places to stuff your face in the greater Orlando area is truly mind boggling. Disney alone has over 250. Orlando has so many eateries (and so many people to eat in them) that the city has long been a testing ground for new chain restaurant "concepts." The reasoning is obvious: If your corporate restaurant concept flies here, it's generic enough to fly equally well in the suburbs of Minneapolis, Austin, Baltimore, and anywhere else the vast numbers of tourists inundating Orlando originate.

And generic they are, those myriad eateries along Orlando's highways and secondary roads. Sizzler. T.G.I. Friday's. Pizza Hut. The Olive Garden. And on and on and on—a seemingly endless parade of frighteningly similar steakhouses, burger joints, and concept restaurants, intended to simultaneously dazzle and comfort Mr. and Mrs. Carnivorous Malldweller and their ravenous little band of buffet depletion units. Except for a few standouts, vegetarian fare at these places is likely to consist of pasta with cream or tomato sauce, steamed vegetables, fries, salad, and the occasional

## Editor's Picks: The Best of the Best

### Places We Rave About
Artist Point
Baja Burrito Kitchen
Café Allègre
California Grill
Emeril's Orlando
Garden Cafe
The Hollywood Brown Derby
Passage to India
Victoria & Albert's
White Wolf Cafe

### Veggies on a Budget
Baja Burrito Kitchen
Cantina de San Angel, Mexico
Chamberlin's Café
Falafel Cafe
Florida Hospital Cafeteria
Garden Cafe
Taste of India

### Romancing the Shrubberhead
Delfino Riviera
Dux
Palo (Disney Cruise Line)
San Angel Inn
Victoria & Albert's

Portobello Mushroom Something or Other.

That's Orlando's dining scene at first glance: strip malls, franchise restaurants, and theme parks, all

## Editor's Picks, cont'd.

**Most Fun/Wackiest**

50's Prime Time Cafe

Animator's Palate

Café Tu Tu Tango

Confisco Grill (at the character lunch)

Numero Uno (on a weekend night)

Rainforest Cafe

**Strictly Veg**

Florida Hospital Cafeteria

Garden Café

Taste of India

**Vegans' Just Desserts**

Banana Chocolate Mousse
   at Seasons Dining Room

Berry Stack at Narcoossee's

House-made Autumn Sorbets
   at Artist Point

Poached Pear with Vanilla Glaze
   at Café Allègre

Sorbet Berry Parfait
    at Park Plaza Gardens

Vegan Carrot Cake
   at Chamberlin's Café

**Best Use of a Portobello Mushroom**

Portobello Satay at Narcoossee's

**Best Use of an Original Gardenburger®**

Gardenburgers done 22 ways
   at Jungle Jim's

**Most Creative Item on a Children's Menu**

Rice Krispies Sushi at the California Grill

serving carnival food. But scratch the surface, and you'll find more.

"The Mouse shouts so loud, it's sometimes hard to hear us over here," laments Anne-Marie Hennessey, whose husband Michael founded the White Wolf Cafe in Orlando's refreshingly funky Antiques District. But the Mouse hasn't been shouting loud enough to drown out the local and national praise heaped on the White Wolf. Occupying a long, low storefront location on North Orange Avenue, the Café has a devoted following, drawn by its comfortable urban ambience and Chef Robert Tresnor's fresh, deceptively simple café food. The public reception—mostly by locals—has been so positive that the Hennesseys are expanding throughout 2000, replacing the tiny existing kitchen with a full-size workspace.

It's a refreshing story: Guy opens store; serves food. People come. They like the food. More people come. Guy serves more food. No theme; no elaborate business plan; no test marketing. Just a welcoming place with good food.

Compare and contrast this scenario with the life of a restaurant at Walt Disney World, Concept Central, where Imagineers, chefs, menu developers, and interior designers toss around ideas, sometimes for years, before a restaurant actually opens, its storyline and menu focus locked firmly in place.

By the time the first meal is served, the restaurant has been approved and retooled so many times it's difficult to see how any semblance of personality could creep through.

But it does. In the heart of Walt Disney World, at this very minute, Anette Grecchi is undoubtedly hard at work breathing life into someone's meal at Artist Point, the flagship restaurant at Disney's Wilderness Lodge Resort. Grecchi, formerly chef at Narcoossee's in the Grand Floridian resort, switched positions with Artist Point Chef Robert Adams in late 1998. In Adam's Northwest-inspired vegetarian menu, soft cider vinegars were paired with sweet apples and tart berries, and earthy lentils, potatoes, and onions—married with strong seasonings and mellow sauces—transformed comfort food into a high culinary art. Grecchi has taken that menu and expanded it in all directions, including excursions into Native American grain dishes and the Asian influences that pervade the Pacific Rim. Grecchi is a perfect example of the path many talented, inspired chefs take in the Disney organization: seizing the reins of a restaurant concept and injecting her own interests and commitment into the mix, with transcendent results.

It's another chapter in the ongoing paradox that is Disney: Despite being one of the most carefully controlled corporate entities on the face of the earth, the Walt Disney Company knows that its stock in trade is its talent. When that talent is concentrated in the hands of great chefs like Anette Grecchi, the California Grill's Cliff Pleau, and Victoria & Albert's Chef Scott Hunnel, vegetarians everywhere have reason to smile.

And for its part, Disney World has indirectly benefited vegetarians by attracting people to Orlando from all walks of life, and from virtually every world culture. Orlando businesses live and die, at least to an extent, on their ability to siphon off excess consumers from the theme parks, and this is why you will see Indian families, their children wearing Mouse ears, file into Passage to India on International Drive after a hard day of theme-parking, or why you'll find a kettle of miso and tofu soup on the boil at the breakfast buffet of the partially Japanese-owned Dolphin Resort. The sheer quantities of human flesh swarming over Orange County all year long mean there's always a niche to be filled— the vegetarian and health-conscious niche included—and always an industrious entrepreneur trying to fill it.

In fact, almost everywhere you go—on Disney property or off— you'll be able to find a decent meal without a serious drop in standards or a half-hour spent negoti-

# For More Information...

*Wondering about what to do when you're NOT eating? The huge quantity of guidebooks to Walt Disney World Resort and Orlando is surpassed only by the number of Web sites devoted to the subject. These are some of our favorite printed and electronic guides to the World and beyond.*

## Guidebooks

**Unofficial Guide to Walt Disney World (Macmillan)**
An unparalleled attraction-by-attraction guide, with lots of comments from readers, excellent advice and touring plans, and a dry, irreverent sense of humor.

**Walt Disney World for Adults (Fodor's)**
For adults and kids, this guide features full-page reviews of specialty restaurants (great for your omnivorous companions).

**Birnbaum's Walt Disney World, the Official Guide (Birnbaum)**
The official word, straight from Mickey's mouth.

**The Official Visitor's Guide to Orlando (Orlando/Orange County CVB)**
The official guide to the city and surrounding area, published by the Convention and Visitor's Bureau. Includes detailed maps, listings of restaurants and accommodations, money-saving coupons, and brief descriptions of hundreds of area attractions.

## Websites

**The Walt Disney World Information Guide (WDWIG)** *http://www.wdwig.com*
A fantastic website, complete with frequently updated Walt Disney World menus and a section on special diets maintained by our own local author and WDW expert, gardenia.

**Disney Dining Style Restaurant Reviews**
*http://members.aol.com/eatwdw/eatwdw.html*
A write-in site with participation by a lot of users; a good source of information about restaurants, with occasional information about vegetarian choices.

**Disney.com—The Official Website for Families** *http://www.disney.com*
The official Disney website, with information about Walt Disney World, Disneyland, Disney movies, merchandise, and much more.

**Orlando Weekly On-Line**
*http://www.orlandoweekly.com/*
Check out this Orlando alternative newspaper's Web presence for up-to-date dining reviews and great ideas on how to spend your day in town.

**Orlando Sentinel On-Line**
*http://www.orlandosentinel.com/*
The Orlando-area daily newspaper's website, featuring reviews by local chow hound, Scott Joseph.

---

ating with a chef who thinks vegetarians eat only vegetables, preferably boiled. And *Vegetarian Walt Disney World Resort and Greater Orlando* will make your gustatory journey an easier one, with all the information you need, organized the way you need it.

# Chapter 2

# Vegetarian Travel Basics

**Vegetarian Resource Group:** *(410) 366-VEGE; http://www.vrg.org/*
*Publishers of* Vegetarian Journal *and the* Guide to
Natural Foods Restaurants in the U.S. and Canada
**Vegetarian Times:** *(708) 848-8100; http://www.vegetariantimes.com/*
*Check out VT magazine for "Traveling Fare" articles*
**World Guide to Vegetarianism:** *http://www.veg.org/veg/Guide/*
*An on-line guide to vegetarian restaurants the world over*

**W**hether you're flying, driving, staying in a hotel, or visiting with friends, the most important thing a vegetarian can do is be prepared. These pointers will help ensure a trouble-free trip.

## Getting to Orlando

### Flying the Veg-Friendly Skies

The quickest and easiest way to get to Orlando, unless you live in Tampa, is to fly. If your flight includes meal service, you'll need to request a vegetarian meal when making your reservation.

The good news about requesting a special meal is that while everyone else is waiting for the food cart to inch its way down the aisle, you're already tucking in.

The bad news is that, sometimes, you'd rather be tucking into just about anything else—including your seat flotation device.

Let's face it: Keeping vegetarians happy is way down on the priority lists of most airline menu designers, sandwiched somewhere between flavor and freshness. For convenience's sake, many carriers go with a lowest-common-denominator approach, providing a bland, generic meal guaranteed to offend no one: white rice, microwaved vegetables, a packet of chemicals masquerading as soy sauce, and six pathetic irradiated grapes passing for dessert. And to top it all off, the chance of your meal making it on board and to your seat is slim.

Thankfully, all of the above is changing. With vegetarian meals accounting for close to 50% of all special meal requests, the airlines are getting their acts together, hiring internationally-acclaimed chefs like Alice Waters and Todd English to design their menus. Some carriers even serve from five to eight different vegetarian meals each day. Slip-ups in getting your special meal to you do still happen, however. All you can do is remind every official-looking person you see of your dietary preference. And if you're feeling self-conscious about using the V-word over and over again, just think of how self-conscious—and hungry—you'll feel

## If you fly...

**Make your vegetarian meal request when** you book your flight. If you've forgotten to do so, be sure to make it at least 24 hours in advance—a requirement for most carriers. When you request your meal, ask about your options. Vegan, ovo-lacto, "Asian vegetarian" (usually an Indian meal), and kosher dairy meals are sometimes available, especially on international flights.

**Reconfirm your vegetarian meal** when you reconfirm your seat or pick up your boarding pass. And as you board the aircraft, let an attendant know about your special meal. You'll feel like a crank, but the squeeky wheel does get the grease (or, in this case, the vegetable lasagna). Bring along some packed food—fruit, granola, leftover stir fry in some Tupperware—just to be safe.

**If all of the above fails and you're** meal-less at 30,000 feet, talk to the attendants on board. Most will be able to come up with a creative meal of side dishes from the extra first-class and coach meals in stowage. You might even score a piece of that chocolate cake—something you would not have gotten with your health-conscious veg meal!

**Some airlines provide better fare** than others. Our favorite domestic carriers are Delta, American, and Continental. On overseas flights, we try to fly with British Airways, KLM, or Quantas.

on the plane when your meal is nowhere to be seen.

Airport food is almost as bad as airplane food, and Orlando

International proudly carries on the tradition—with the exception of McCoy's restaurant at the Airport Hyatt, located right inside the terminal (see review on page 221). Elsewhere, you're pretty much stuck with the usual suspects with which to fill your unhappy belly: limp fries, iceberg lettuce salads, or coffee and a danish from a kiosk. So if McCoy's menu doesn't appeal to you, you're better off lugging your bags into town for dinner than trying to scrape something appealing together at MCO.

## Taking the Train

If you prefer to experience the landscape as you travel, you might consider heading south via rail. The dining cars in Amtrak's overnight Auto Train and "Silver Service" passenger trains to central Florida provide adequate meals for vegetarians (with the possible exception of breakfast), given 72 hours' advance notice.

### Amtrak Silver Service to Orlando

The Silver Star (train #91 southbound, traveling inland through Raleigh and Columbia, and continuing on to Miami) and the Silver Meteor (train #97 southbound, traveling along the east coast and ending in Orlando) both originate in New York City, with stops in Philadelphia, Baltimore and Washington, D.C. Both are over-

night affairs, so you'll definitely need to eat while on board.

The customary vegetarian dinner on a Silver Service train is the "Veggie Medley": a plate of sugar snap peas, corn on the cob, and a choice of sweet potato casserole or garlic mashed potatoes. With some advance nudging, Amtrak food service will put some other goodies in the larder just for you, including fixin's for veg stir fry over rice or a penne pasta primavera. Gardenburgers® are available at lunch time, too—but all of the above require at least 72 hours' advance notice, company policy.

Breakfast is another story. Despite a host of egg dishes, grits, pancakes, and a selection of cereals for vegetarians who eat eggs and dairy, practically nothing is available for vegans (unless you count dry cereal). And here's some more bad news: The hash browns served on board all Amtrak trains contain bacon.

### Amtrak's Auto Train to Orlando

The largest passenger train in the world, Amtrak's Auto Train originates just south of Washington, D.C. in Lorton, Virginia, and ends in Sanford, Florida, about 23 miles north of Orlando on Interstate 4. Auto Train is a popular way for retirees from the northeast to move south in the wintertime. Meals are included in the ticket price and, because of its older clientele, Amtrak's Auto Train tends to feature more healthful fare.

Auto Train sports two dining cars—one for first class sleeping car passengers, the other for riders in coach. In the former, a vegan dinner of vegetarian lo mein and vegetable spring roll is available upon request. Stir fried vegetables over rice and a very dairy vegetarian lasagna constitute the choices in coach. And again, Wholesome and Hearty saves the lunch hour with its ubiquitous Gardenburger®.

Strict vegetarians fare better at breakfast on Auto Train than on any other long-distance rail route. Choose between blueberry and corn muffins (both vegan) or any number of offerings in the train's fresh fruit basket. Amtrak attendants are unable to offer access to the refrigerators in their kitchen, but if you bring along some small drink boxes of soymilk, you can tuck into some cereal as well. Be sure to avoid the bacon-infested hash browns here, too.

## Staying Healthy on the Highway

Like most conscious diners, we long for a day when healthful fast food restaurants dominate the nation's highways, every off-ramp yielding a veritable cornucopia of meatless—and convenient—dining options. Although rumours abound, and one startup in San Francisco is reported to be gaining momentum, the dawning of that happy day seems far off.

In the meantime, it is possible to find good vegetarian restaurants while traveling, with some help from *Vegetarian Journal's Guide to Natural Foods Restaurants*, available from Avery Publishing Group (see contact information for the Vegetarian Resource Group in the "If you drive..." sidebar, opposite

## If you take the train.....

**Make your vegetarian meal "special** service request" when you book your seat, or—at a minimum—72 hours in advance, by calling (800) USA RAIL. For the Auto Train, call (877) SKIP I-95. When you request your meal, ask about your options. If they don't give you a choice, mention the meals listed in the text, all of which were confirmed by Amtrak's public affairs office and their central food service division at press time.

**Reconfirm your vegetarian meal** when you reconfirm your seat and when you pick up your ticket at the station. As you board, you might take a quick trip down to the dining car, too, just to be safe.

**Bring along some packed food in a** small cooler. Cups of ice from the onboard snack bar will keep your veggies crisp and your other goodies fresh and cool.

**Don't count on grabbing more than** a snack in a train station along the way. Most have vending machines only.

page). Over 2000 restaurants, delis, and juice bars across the U.S. are listed in the guide. If you're willing to plan your mealtimes accordingly, you're sure to find a healthful option somewhere along your route. Be sure to call ahead to verify opening times and get directions, and to keep a good atlas handy for locating the restaurant while driving.

For a speedier, and just as delicious, meal, find out if a natural or organic food store is on your route. Many have in-store deli counters or restaurants where you can pick up fabulous healthful salads and prepared foods. An excellent source for finding natural groceries with deli counters is *The Tofu Tollbooth*, available from Ceres Press/Ardwork Press, PO Box 87, Woodstock, NY 12498; Tel. (888) 804-8848. Most of the co-ops and organic markets it lists are within a few miles of the highway.

Thanks to a shift in America's eating habits, more and more fast food chains are providing meatless options. We like to think of these as "compromise foods"— they aren't necessarily healthful, or haute cuisine, but at least they don't contain meat!

Unless you've taken a quick detour to the United Kingdom, you won't find any veg burgers on the menus at Burger King or McDonald's. But you will find tossed garden salads, veg-friendly

**If you drive...**

Know ahead of time which fast food restaurants serve truly vegetarian and vegan meals. Booklets listing fast food establishments that serve vegan fare are available from the Vegetarian Resource Group for $4.00 and can be ordered from VRG's Web site at www.vrg.org/catalog/ or via mail at The VRG, PO Box 1463, Baltimore, MD 21203. Excerpts from the booklet can be found on-line at http://www.vrg.org/journal/vj98jan/981fast2.htm

**Again, bring along some packed food** JUST IN CASE you can't find anything. You won't be sorry, and think of all that time you're saving by not having to stop!

french fries (animal fats are no longer used in the frying process, much to Julia Child's chagrin), and even a vegan Apple Pie.

One of our favorite highway fast food options is Blimpie's VegiMax™: a hot sub made with a whole grain and vegetable patty (courtesy of Morningstar Farms) on a whole wheat sub roll. Topped with lettuce, tomato, pickle, onion, and more, the 12" sub is enough for two adults to share. If pizza is more to your liking, the introduction of a vegan pie at all national Sbarro locations will have you shouting for joy. Made with dairy and egg-free shells, and topped with low fat, vegan pizza "cheese" from Orlando's own Galaxy Foods, the pizzas can be topped with a riot of veggies, including broccoli, onion, mushrooms, peppers, and green and black olives. The corn and flour tortillas at Taco Bell are vegan, as are the pinto beans, taco sauces, and Cinnamon Twists. But according to the Vegetarian Resource Group, all pizza sauces served at Pizza Hut contain either a beef base or chicken fat. You're much better off at Pizzeria Uno, Shakeys, or Sbarro.

## Eating Out in Orlando

Orlando, blessed by year-round sunshine, abundant rain, and a temperate climate, is a paradise of produce. From citrus of all kinds to fresh local vegetables, just about everything a vegetarian could want is grown within a 100 mile radius of the city. Heck, there's even a soyfoods company—Galaxy, manufacturers of Veggie™ and Soyco Foods—in the city limits.

And the fruit—*aye carramba*, the fruit! A person could become a fruitarian down here! Papaya, kumquat, kiwi, and star fruit all thrive in the state's lush acreage. Tropical and citrus fruits—relegated to garnish status in colder climes—are celebrated in Florida. They're sliced, diced, squeezed, and mashed into salads and relishes, and they add flavor and freshness to dishes both savory and sweet.

As a direct result of the state's agricultural abundance and the eclectic mix of ethnic cultures, a specialty of the Orlando area is New Florida or "Floribbean" cuisine: an innovative fusion of Florida's native produce with spicy Caribbean flavors. Distinctive Cuban and other Latin American restaurants are scattered throughout the city, as well, along with a growing number of Asian eateries—Vietnamese, Thai, Chinese, and Japanese—especially in the streets clustered around East Colonial Drive.

Don't miss a chance to try hearts of palm, an epicurean delicacy served raw or cooked, usually in a salad drizzled with a tangy vinaigrette, and available fresh only in Florida. Its local nickname— "swamp cabbage"—doesn't do justice to this gourmet treat, similar in flavor to artichokes. Another Floridian salad is "gaspachee." Based loosely on Spanish gazpacho, this regional goodie consists of hard tack biscuits soaked in water and topped with sliced tomato, cucumbers, onion—*and mayonnaise* (didn't see that one comin', now did ya?).

If you're looking for an authentic Floridian dessert, try key lime pie, a mixture of sweetened condensed milk, eggs, and the juice of small, yellow limes native to the Florida Keys: a jewel-like chain of islands that begins some 250 miles south of Orlando. Key lime pie is frequently topped with meringue, and is served in a crumb or pastry crust. If you see a fluorescent green variety, watch out; the authentic key lime pie is a cool shade of lemon yellow, and is *dee-lish*!

## Hidden Ingredients and Other Bugbears

Orlando and Walt Disney World offer a plethora of dining options for folks with special diets. However, some care is needed when "traveling the world" of culinary delights. Take heed: Hidden ingredients are everywhere! The following list will give you a rough idea of what to look out for in Orlando's ethnic eateries, but always ask your server about hidden meats and stocks in whatever you order, just to be safe.

### Chinese

Chinese restaurants, as with all Asian eateries, can be treasure troves for vegetarian diners, if you know what to ask for, and what to avoid. Egg roll wrappers are made of wheat flour, water, and—as one might guess—egg; spring roll wrappers, however, are usually comprised of wheat flour and water only. Most Asian soups start with a meat base; egg drop soup, for instance, is often made with chicken stock, and hot and sour soup typically has a beef base. When asking about stocks at Chinese restaurants, use the word "broth," a term more commonly used in Asian cooking.

Certain noodle and rice dishes—including the ubiquitous Chinese fried rice—are often simmered in a meat broth as well, whether they are listed on the "vegetarian" menu or not. Many Chinese noodle dishes, including vegetarian lo mein, are made with oyster sauce, a popular Cantonese table and cooking condiment made by reducing oysters, water, and salt to a thick concentrate.

One major drawback to eating at a Chinese restaurant are the high levels of fat, cholesterol, and sodium in typical menu items, including lo mein, mu shu, and fried rice. To eat healthfully, order meals that are more like those you'd find on a typical dinner table in China: steamed or "dry wok" vegetables over plain rice (and ask your server to please hold the M.S.G.). If you have the chance, sample some *fu yu*: wine-fermented soybean curd that tastes remarkably like cheese.

### Cuban

There are two ubiquitous hobgoblins for vegetarians in all Hispanic restaurants: chicken stock in the rice and pork in the beans. Sadly, this is true in the vast majority of Cuban restaurants in Orlando, as well. We'd love to sample *plato* after *plato* of *moros y cristianos*

# Tips for Getting the Meal You Want

**If possible, try to score a menu ahead of time** (via FAX or the internet), so you know which dishes are likely to be vegetarian. Then, call the restaurant and speak with the chef, preferably around 3 PM when the restaurant isn't too busy. If the chef tells you there's nothing available, ask if a menu item can be altered to your liking, or see if the kitchen is flexible enough to create something new just for you. If you meet resistance on all these fronts, it's time to ask whether the restaurant is one you want to patronize.

**However, let's say your entire extended** family has been looking forward to eating at a specific (not necessarily veg-friendly) restaurant since your great-great-grandmother overheard a passerby recommend it during a parade in 1902 when she saw Bismarck ride through town on a white horse. You're eating at that restaurant whether you like it or not! If you don't see an entrée that's appealing, ask if the kitchen will make an entrée-sized portion of an appetizer that is. Or try combining two or three appetizers as your meal.

**If you want to avoid meat, eggs, or dairy,** but aren't sure if you trust the kitchen, state that you're "allergic" to the ingredient in question. Chefs are much more likely to worry about your special diet if they think you might be carried out of their restaurant on a stretcher!

**If you know you don't trust the kitchen** to tell the truth, it sometimes helps to act as though you *want* to find ingredients like *nam pla* and *bonito* in your sauces and stocks (of course, if your server is that unscrupulous, who knows what you're getting?).

**If you want something on the menu that** normally features a meat item, and you're just not getting any help from the kitchen, try to think of a creative substitution yourself. For example, suggest to the kitchen staff that they try portobello mushrooms in a steak salad, or fresh spinach leaves in place of the Canadian bacon in Eggs Benedict.

**To cut down on fat and cholesterol, ask** if your dish can be steamed, or cooked in a very small amount of oil.

**Never be afraid to ask about ingredients** and techniques, no matter how vegetarian-friendly—or unfriendly—a dish appears to be. Who knows—you might get a yummy bowl of *pho* in return for your tenacity!

---

("Moors and Christians," better known as black beans and white rice), but a Cuban restaurant that serves a vegetarian version is devilishly hard to find.

Another fabulous Cuban specialty is the *sandwich cubano*: a half loaf of French bread filled and grilled in a sandwich press until its contents are hot. Most contain generous amounts of ham, pork, and cheese, but there are a few places in town that will make meatless versions to order. Just be sure to check that the bread doesn't contain lard. *Ai yai yai!*

### French

With its emphasis on meats and heavy cream sauces, traditional

French cooking wasn't typically associated with healthful dining. But with the explosion of nouvelle cuisine in the early 1970s—thanks to chefs like Paul Bocuse and Roger Vergé, and more recent missionaries like Patricia Wells —French food suddenly became lighter, fresher, simpler, and much more vegetarian-friendly. It even inspired our most favorite of food revolutionaries, Alice Waters, to craft California produce into a full-fledged cuisine.

When dining at a French restaurant, be on the lookout for the use of meat glazes on vegetables and for meat-based reduction sauces. French onion soup—a staple of French cooking and a great way to use up that stale baguette— is always made with a beef stock. Quiche lorraine, a savory egg and cream tart, contains bacon. Strict vegetarians who eat no eggs or dairy should ask about the use of egg washes on breads.

### Greek & Middle Eastern

Middle Eastern restaurants are among the most enjoyable places for vegetarians to dine. Vegetable and salad dishes usually take up a large portion of the menu, and high-protein legumes and whole grains have been a staple of the Greek and Middle Eastern diet since the dawn of civilization.

A Greek appetizer not to be missed is *dolmadakia* or *dolmades*: savory stuffed grape leaves. Ask for the vegetarian version, traditionally served cold (meat-filled dolmades are usually hot). If you're concerned about sodium, ask if the grape leaves are fresh or from a can or jar (canned grape leaves are often packed in brine). A wonderful and simple meatless Greek entrée is *fava*: a purée of yellow split peas blended with onions and garlic, popular among Hellenes during Lent. One warning: Greek rice is often cooked in chicken stock; ask to be sure.

Vegetarian stuffed grape leaves are a common item on Middle Eastern menus as well, often part of a meze or appetizer platter that includes *hummus bi tahina* (a creamy, garlic-laced purée of chick peas and tahini), *baba ghanoush* (roasted eggplant dip), and *tabbouleh* (a lemon-infused salad of bulghur wheat, onions, tomatoes, and lots of parsley). Another staple of the meze platter is *falafel*: deep fried chick pea and fava bean balls seasoned with onions, cilantro, garlic, and cumin. Pita sandwiches stuffed with falafel, some sort of salad, and tahini are popular not only in the U.S., but also in Israel, where they are referred to jokingly as "Israeli hot dogs."

If you make it to a Moroccan restaurant, be sure to try vegetarian couscous. But again, check to see that the grain is not cooked in a chicken or lamb stock.

## Indian

Thanks to the influence of the Hindu and Jain religious traditions—which regard *ahimsa*, or non-violence, as a major virtue—Indian cuisine is very vegetarian friendly. Over 50% of all South Asians eschew meat and eggs, but do eat dairy products, often in abundance. If you are on a low-fat or vegan diet, ask about the preparation of sauces and breads; many contain cheese, milk, or *ghee* (clarified butter). A good example is *naan*, a north Indian bread that's flash baked in the clay tandoor oven. Naan is usually vegan (though some cooks add yogurt to the dough), but is frequently topped with butter just before being brought to the table. And in America, mulligatawny—a spicy lentil soup—often contains pieces of chicken and a meat broth. Ask your server to be sure.

## Italian

An old standby for healthful dining, Italian restaurants do warrant a mention here, particularly for diners who avoid eggs and dairy. Traditional hard or dried pastas, made with semolina (durum wheat flour) and water, are 100% vegan, but many hand- or house made fresh pastas—ravioli, fettucine, and others—are made with eggs instead of water. Another staple on Italian menus, minestrone is a thick vegetable soup that typically contains pasta and sometimes peas or beans, and often chicken or beef stock. It's also frequently served topped with freshly grated parmesan or pecorino romano cheese.

Richly flavored stock—but not always one derived from meat—is a key ingredient in risotto, an Italian rice specialty, as well. Another warning for vegans: The arborio rice used in risotto is traditionally sautéed in butter before simmering in cup after cup of stock or wine. Polenta, an Italian cornmeal mush similar to grits, was a daily staple of the Roman legions. It's been rediscovered by vegetarians looking for a flavorful, hearty main course, in combination with roasted vegetables and topped with butter or cheese.

## Japanese

As with Southeast Asian cuisine (see below), the primary bugaboo for vegetarians interested in traditional Japanese cooking is *dashi*, a broth that's usually based on flakes made from the flesh of the bonito tuna. Dashi provides flavor for a number of concoctions, including otherwise vegetarian delicacies like *hijiki*—a mild black seaweed dish, often prepared with carrots and tofu—and miso soup, a staple of Japanese breakfasts.

Even if you're a vegetarian who doesn't eat fish, it's worth taking a moment to check out the sushi menu. To please American palates, many sushi bars are starting to offer bite-sized pieces of vegetable *nori maki*, the most common of which is *kappa maki*. Made with sticky rice and cucumber slices, this mild and refreshing sushi is named for Kappa, a water goblin in Japanese mythology.

## Mexican

The main thing to look out for at Mexican restaurants is rice and beans, often cooked in chicken broth or with lard, respectively. Your best bet is to steer toward Cal-Mex cuisine, with its emphasis on big burritos stuffed with salad ingredients and rice, as well as more health-conscious versions of classic Mexican favorites. Be warned, however, that the flour tortilla wraps that hold burritos together sometimes contain lard. Corn tortillas typically do not, but may be deep fried in lard prior to serving. Be sure to ask your server what kind of cooking fat is being used. Sauces, like *mole poblano*, often contain chicken, turkey, or other meat stocks as well.

## Southeast Asian (Burmese, Thai, Cambodian, Vietnamese, Filipino, and Malaysian)

Generally light and healthful, Southeast Asian food is among the most vegetarian friendly cuisines, except for one small and very pun-gent problem: fish sauce. It is used in everything, it seems—at least all things labeled "vegetarian."

Popular throughout Southeast Asia, fish sauce can be any number of mixtures based on the juices from salted and fermented fish. This distinct, strongly-flavored condiment and seasoning is as ubiquitous in Southeast Asian cooking as soy sauce is in Japan. To compound the problem, fish sauce goes by a variety of names, including *nam pla* (Thai), *nuoc mam* (Vietnamese) and *patis* (Filipino).

Once you manage to steer clear of the nam pla, many Thai dishes, especially curries, are vegan—they're made with coconut milk in place of dairy. The mildest of the vegetarian Thai curries is Massaman, followed in BTUs by red curry, and reaching their final gastrothermal glory in the green Panang curries: the hottest of the hot, equivalent to Indian vindaloo. The two most common desserts in American Thai restaurants—*sang ka ya*, steamed pumpkin custard made with coconut milk, and *kha niew mamuang*, sticky rice flavored with coconut cream, sugar, and topped with sliced mango—are vegan as well.

In Vietnam, it's practically a punishable offense to serve a spring roll without a little jar of *nuoc cham*, the national table condiment. Akin to the classic Indian pairing of onion chutney and sweet tamarind sauce, or Chinese duck sauce and hot mustard, nuoc cham usually contains *nuoc mam*—an anchovy-based version of fish sauce. Consisting of nuoc mam, vinegar, sugar, chiles, lime juice, and shredded carrot, nuoc cham is utterly delicious—and off limits to strict veggies. So when you order *cha gio chay* (vegetable spring rolls), ask for soy sauce instead. OK, it doesn't have the same *je ne sais quoi*, but it is vegetarian. You'll also want to look out for Vietnamese and Cambodian salads and noodle dishes, which are frequently dressed with fish sauce, or peanut sauce (which uses fish sauce as a primary ingredient). Be sure to let your server know ahead of time about your wish to keep your meal fish—and fish sauce—free.

Perhaps the greatest contribution of Vietnam and Cambodia to the culinary world is a delicacy too often denied vegetarians: the enticing, steaming bowls of white vermicelli noodles and utterly fresh vegetables in broth that the Vietnamese call pho. Sadly, a bowl of noodles and broth without—yes, you guessed it, fish stock— is unthinkable to most Vietnamese chefs, and the cook who will work with you on this subject is rare indeed. However, the other flavors and textures in a bowl of pho are so yummy, so comforting on a chilly day, so spicy and exhila-

rating on a baking hot Orlando afternoon, that it's certainly worth a try. If you do manage to talk your way into some faux pho, you can bring it closer to the real thing by supplementing a half-hearted vegetable broth with soy sauce to taste, a dash of chili sauce, and a squeeze of lime at the table. It's not exactly authentic, but a decent substitute on the fly.

Once you get past all the pescatory finagling, a Southeast Asian meal can be sublime, with flavors drawing on the fabulous veggie cuisines of East Asia—tofu, soy sauce, noodles, stir frying—and of the Indian subcontinent, with its curries, chilies, rices, and spices. Toss in the sweet, hot sauces of Burma and Malaysia, and you've got a galaxy of flavors that employ veggie-friendly practices galore... except for all that fish sauce.

If you have a great deal of trouble explaining your avoidance of meat in a Southeast Asian restaurant, one possible solution is to tell your server that you're a Buddhist. Most Vietnamese Buddhists are vegetarian, and certain dishes common to Buddhist kitchens have made their way into the Southeast Asian repertoire. Among the Vietnamese dishes that are usually vegetarian are *cari rao kai*

(curried vegetables), *mi don xao chay* (tofu, vegetables, and crispy noodles), and *rao xao* (tofu with mixed vegetables). As always, ask to be certain.

### Spanish

In the United States, Spanish cuisine is frequently confused with Mexican and other Latin American cooking. This is unfortunate, for they have little in common. Spanish dishes are usually mild, and closer to the foods of Mediterranean France and Italy. You won't find many tortillas in a traditional Spanish kitchen (unless you count tortilla española, a potato omelet), nor will you find tacos or enchiladas.

There is one major similarity: Spanish rice, like Mexican, is frequently made with a chicken stock base. But other than that, Spanish cuisine, which rarely includes cream or butter, is as low-fat and healthful as the peasant cuisines of Italy and southern France. If you do find yourself in a tapas bar or restaurante, be sure to order a cup of gazpacho andaluz: a cold soup of puréed tomatoes, cucumbers, sweet green peppers, garlic, bread crumbs, and olive oil. American chefs often interpret gazpacho as a chunky, fresh tomato and cucumber salsa suspended in its own juices, but it's wonderful in the Andalusian style. Puréed so finely it's almost creamy, and reeking of

fresh garlic, it's the perfect way to escape the Orlando heat!

# Eating "In" in Orlando

One of the best ways to ensure that your dietary needs are accommodated—and to save a little cash—is to cook for yourself. With seven Chamberlin's natural food markets and a Whole Foods Market all in the greater Orlando area, you'll find plenty of organic and vegetarian fixin's for your feast. But be warned: After a long day in the theme parks, the idea of cooking a meal from scratch may not sound as appealing as it did when you were planning your trip! Thank goodness, then, for the growing selection of healthful, vegetarian convenience foods. A huge selection of prepared foods is available at all Chamberlins and Whole Foods locations, and—in more limited quantities—at most other Orlando area supermarkets.

The list below outlines some of your options for "eating in" while on vacation, and offers a few tips for each approach.

## Self-Catering Apartments, Homes and Suites

Vacation rental homes and villas furnish a home away from home, including fully-equipped kitchens and, often, swimming pools—a definite plus in sweltering Orlando.

There are literally thousands of condos and homes available for rent in the Orlando/Walt Disney World area, from one-bedroom apartments to massive 10-bedroom villas. If you're renting a home, you'll also want to rent a car: most rental properties are located in residential areas of Kissimmee and beyond. But even with the added expense of a rental car, homes are often the most cost-effective solution for a large family or group—especially off-season, when rates on smaller condos start at $70/night.

Can't decide whether you want the convenience of a hotel room or the added comfort of your own apartment? Another option is to stay in a hotel suite with a simple kitchenette. Suites vary widely in price and amenities, and their "kitchens" can be anything from a microwave and mini fridge to a fully-outfitted room sporting all the major appliances. Be sure to find out exactly what amenities you're getting before you make your reservations.

For a listing of self-catering condos, homes, and hotels featuring in-room kitchens, get a copy of the Official Accommodations Guide to the Orlando area from the Orlando and Orange County Convention & Visitors Bureau at (800) 551-0181. On-line, visit www.go2orlando.com, or check out www.orlando.com's "Orlando Vacation Guide." Both are good general sources of information about area attractions, as well.

## Camping Out

Another option for dining in (or perhaps we should say "dining out," as in "under the stars") is to pitch your tent or park your R.V. at one of greater Orlando's campgrounds. A few Kissimmee campgrounds are just 10 minutes from Walt Disney World's Main Gate, and one—Fort Wilderness—is an official WDW Resort, located just a stone's throw (okay, a cannon shot) from the Magic Kingdom. Far from forcing you to rough it, Walt Disney World and Orlando area campgrounds offer deluxe amenities like cable TV, voice mail, and daily housekeeping service—not to mention pools, horseback riding, evening campfires, and movies. Just park, hook up, and relax in your mobile air-conditioned pleasure palace.

On the other hand, if you're carrying your palace (and all your provisions) on your back, think about bringing along some pre-packaged vegetarian camp food to lighten your load. Some of the best is made by Packlite Foods.

All Packlite dinners are 100% natural, one-pot vegetarian meals that are ready to eat in eight to ten minutes. Some are surprisingly delicious, like Meals with Wheels: vegetarian "wagon wheel" pasta combined with sweet garden peas, onions, green pepper, and mushrooms, cooked in a cheddar cheese sauce. A double serving provides 1410 calories, and weighs in at just 14 ounces. Just as good is the Bountiful Bean & Lentil Chili—a mix of red, black, and pinto beans, garbanzos, and lentils, combined with julienned tomatoes, red and green bell peppers, and leeks in a dairy-free tomato sauce. Vegans will want to leave off the sprinkling of parmesan cheese. A double serving of the chili provides 872 nutritious calories to keep you moving through the parks, and weighs just 10.8 ounces (to keep you from dragging on the trail!).

If you're car camping and weight isn't as much of an issue, bring along staples—rice, beans, spices, and oil, for instance—in plastic containers and bottles. To avoid confusion, be sure to label everything and to jot down basic instructions (cooking times and measurements). And don't forget to bring camp kitchen essentials: a frying pan, saucepan, wooden spoons, a good knife and cutting board, a cooler, and a camp stove, not to mention a few hot pads, dish scrubbies, and dishwashing liquid. You might pick up some deli food at an Orlando natural foods store, too, just in case your open hearth is dampened by a sudden downpour!

## Staying in a Hostel

A great way to stay on the cheap and still be able to cook your own meals is to stay in one of Orlando's youth hostels. No longer just for kids, hostels are gaining popularity not only because of their low cost, but also because of the clientele they attract: interesting, friendly folks who don't mind sharing kitchen facilities or conversation over a communal meal.

Getting a space in one of Orlando's hostels isn't always easy, especially in Kissimmee, where a convenient, top notch hostel draws theme park visitors in large numbers. Be sure to call ahead and make a solid reservation. If you're hoping to snag a private room for yourself and your sweetie (the majority of hostellers bed down in same-sex dorms), make your reservation a few months in advance— even longer if you're visiting during the summer or holidays. Also, remember to bring your own linens; hostels charge $1 or more per night to provide these (and they're often pretty threadbare).

At all hostels in this country and abroad, guests are responsible for serving and cleaning up after themselves. Kitchen facilities are yours to use, but remember to be courteous to fellow travelers. Before you put that package of vegan burgers or container of hummus in the fridge, be sure to mark it with your name and check-in date. And never ever help yourself to a fellow hosteller's grub, no matter how tempted you are! Make your meal with your own ingredients, and those on the refrigerator and pantry shelves marked "free food." If you're not sure what's up for grabs and what isn't, ask the hostel management.

To find out more about hostelling, contact Hostelling International—American Youth Hostels, the oldest and largest hostelling organization in the country. You can get their official guidebook, *Hostelling USA*, by calling (202) 783-6161, or writing HI-AYH at 733 Fifteenth Ave. NW, Suite 840, Washington, D.C. 20005. Our favorite guidebook to hostelling, however, is *Hostels U.S.A.* by Evan Halper and Paul Kerr—a frank assessment of 340 hostels across America. It's published by Globe Pequot Press, and available at bookstores throughout the country and online.

## Staying with Friends

Seeing old friends and family who no longer live nearby is one of the joys of traveling. But if you're vegetarian and your friends aren't, staying with them can sometimes end in disaster. When you bed down with omnivores, follow these tips for saving your vacation—and your friendship!

### Communicate

Be sure to tell your hosts well in advance that you're vegetarian. Spell out for them what being vegetarian means to you (for example: "I don't eat any meat products—including stock or bouillon—any dairy products, or any eggs;" "I don't eat meat, but I do eat fish;" and so on). You'll also want to be absolutely sure that your diet won't present a problem. If they seem put out—well, let's just say that sometimes it's better to shell out some money for a hotel room or sleep in your car than to deal with a hostile environment! Try and find tactful ways to keep reminding your hosts about your diet during the vacation planning stage, especially right before your arrival.

### Pitch In

Tell your hosts that you love to cook, and that you'd love to make them some scrumptious meals as a thank you for their hospitality. On nights when you're not cooking, offer to help out, even if you're not technically making the meal. That way you'll be sure to have something suitable to eat.

If you're only staying a night or two, suggest that you all go out to a neutral restaurant. Tell your friends that you've been reading about a restaurant nearby that you'd really like to try. Then head to one of the veg-friendly places reviewed here; that way you'll know there will be something on the menu you can eat.

## Be Prepared

Bring along some food, or stock up at a grocery store on the car trip from the airport. You'll want to have an emergency stash, and you'll also want your hosts to know that you don't want them to knock themselves out trying to deal with this wacky kick you're on. If they're having turkey and mashed potatoes, pull an okara patty out of the freezer and zap it in the microwave. When your hosts whip up pancakes and sausage, offer some Morningstar Farms Breakfast Patties for comparison. Who knows... they might even be surprised at how good your version of the meal tastes!

## Roll with the Punches

If all else fails, just smile and eat the side dishes; hopefully by the next meal, your hosts will have remembered what you can and can't eat. Above all, don't apologize for being vegetarian! You have a right to make your own choices about the foods you eat. Don't bring up the subject, though, unless asked. And remember: It isn't polite to talk about downed cows at the dinner table!

# The Mouse Takes the Cheese: Walt Disney World Resort

**Walt Disney World General Information:** *(407) 824-4321*
**Priority Seating Arrangements:** *(407) WDW-DINE (939-3463)*
**WDW Switchboard:** *(407) 824-2222*
*Call the switchboard to be transferred to a chef
at the restaurant where you'd like to dine.*

# Walt Disney World

**Walt Disney World General Information:** *(407) 824-4321*
**Priority Seating Arrangements:** *(407) WDW-DINE (939-3463)*
**WDW Switchboard:** *(407) 824-2222*
*Call the switchboard to be transferred to
a chef at the restaurant where you'd like to dine.*

**D**ieter Hannig is a man with a mission. He and his staff have been charged with the awesome task of making Walt Disney World a dining destination to rival the world's great resorts—while ensuring that hungry toddlers, weary parents, picky teenagers, and people with esoteric diets can all find some delightful culinary treat as they traipse across 7,000 acres of theme parks and resorts. It's a mammoth undertaking, but if anyone is up to the task, it's Hannig.

You might even say Dieter Hannig, Walt Disney World's Vice President of Food and Beverage, is obsessed with the challenge before him. One can easily picture him arguing passionately on behalf of a tub of frozen yogurt, his thick German accent liberally sprinkled with American idioms, his expressive eyes widening meaningfully as he drives home each point. Flavor. Freshness. Quality. The Guest Experience. As he talks, Hannig's small marathon runner's frame seems enlarged by the power of his convictions.

A self-described "part-time vegetarian," Hannig was tapped to create and open more than 20 unique American restaurants at Disneyland Paris over ten years ago, having left a position at Hilton International as a Director of Food Research.

# Strategies for Great Veggie Dining at WDW

**1) Book early**

Make your Priority Seating arrangements for the restaurant of your choice at least 24 hours in advance—we recommend a week's notice for vegetarian meals—by calling (407) WDW-DINE (939-3463). Priority Seating arrangements can be made up to 120 days in advance for most restaurants, although Victoria & Albert's Chef's Table reservations can (and should) be made 180 days in advance.

**2) Ask and ye shall receive**

If you're a vegan or on a strict low-fat diet, call the Walt Disney World main switchboard at (407) 824-2222 and ask to be transferred to the restaurant of your choosing. Once connected, ask to speak directly with a chef and explain your dietary needs. Have fun brainstorming with the chefs about your special meal. If you give them enough advance notice (usually a week will do), Disney chefs are more than happy to purchase special items like rice milk, kamut, or seitan to make your meal memorable. Remember to get your chef's full name and to let him or her know the date and time of your dining arrangements.

**3) Be a (well-mannered) pest**

Check in at the restaurant as soon as the park opens and tell the host that you've made prior arrangements with Chef X for a special vegetarian meal. Be sure the host verifies this before you head off to enjoy the park. If you haven't made prior arrangements, do so now.

**4) Be presidential: stay on message**

Upon being seated at the restaurant, let your server know about your special dietary needs. If you've made arrangements with the chef for a meal not usually on the menu, tell the server your name and the name of the chef with whom you spoke.

**5) Roll with the punches**

If you have not made any special prior arrangements, a meal can often be prepared for you "on the fly" at table service restaurants. Ask your server if you can speak with a chef at your table. Find out what ingredients are on hand in the kitchen, and have fun being creative with Disney's culinary talent!

**6) Remember: the squeaky wheel**
   **gets the monounsaturated fats**

If you're at a quick service location and one of the newer castmembers tells you that special meals and substitutions cannot be made, ask to speak with a manager. Nine times out of ten, your needs will be accommodated.

**7) Mickey helps those who help themselves**

If you have a very strict diet and simply can't risk a goof-up with your special meal, feel free to bring a small cooler of goodies into any of the parks with you (only guests with special dietary restrictions are allowed this privilege). To avoid lugging your cooler around all day, stow it in a rental locker, located near the entrance to each park.

Hannig was disillusioned in his role at Hilton, attempting to direct chefs and restaurant managers in over 100 locations and 42 countries by telephone and memo. "We had people sitting up in the corporate offices telling chefs and managers what to do. You just cannot do this!" he says. "If a chef can't do in her restaurant what she wants to do, and I have to send her a memo, I'm wasting my energy."

At Disneyland Paris, Hannig was able to implement a simple approach to foodservice that had a revolutionary effect on the WDW diner's experience. He and his whole management team simply gave autonomy to chefs and restaurant managers, and in return, they got restaurants which won praise even from French critics.

"It's not really that we did something very revolutionary," says Hannig. "It's all about great people and talent. You put people in a place, you 'paint the big picture' of what the guest experience should be, and you tell them, 'That's your restaurant. Go with it.' The food and beverage teams make your idea better, they make their guests happy, and they get the credit and recognition for a job well done."

His unique approach in Paris earned Hannig the respect of his peers and those who worked under him. In fact, after he came to Walt Disney World in 1992, many of the chefs and managers who worked with him at Disneyland Paris eventually joined him. His team has ushered in a sea change in the quality of food throughout the property, from snack bars to resort dining rooms.

"Ten years ago, there wasn't much to talk about," concurs Franz Kranzfelder, Manager of Menu Development and Culinary Standards. "But now we have about 15 top chefs on Disney property, with great talents. The whole mentality about leadership has changed. We no longer have executive chefs, we have working chefs—you'll see them in the kitchen on a daily basis. They are passionately involved in cooking. That was a big change for this company. We don't have kitchen generals anymore, we have missionaries: people who are standing up for what they believe in."

## What to Expect at Walt Disney World

Despite Hannig's revolution, many people who haven't visited Walt Disney World in recent years (or ever) still think of it as a big expensive carnival, with expensive carnival food: popcorn, cokes, burgers, and hot dogs. To a certain extent, they're right, especially in the World's four theme parks where the emphasis is on portability, economy (the Disney version), and the satisfaction of the Vacationing Hordes. But to merely offer one type of food—at one set of price points—to the bewildering melting pot of tastes that

*Continued on page 34*

# A Conversation with Dieter Hannig

*Dieter Hannig, Walt Disney World's Vice President of Food and Beverage and czar of all things culinary, is passionately devoted to making sure that guests at the Resort get the best food he can provide—to exceed diners' expectations, even in fast food venues on property. Hannig was brought in 12 years ago after a string of successful restaurant openings at Disneyland Paris, including the original California Grill. His ultimate aim at Walt Disney World has been not only an increase in customer satisfaction, but increased awareness of what he sees as the most important aspects of food: simple preparation of superior ingredients. In the process, he has presided over an unprecedented increase in vegetarian options at the Resort's restaurants. It's a fitting role for a former vegetarian whose colleagues called him the "Tofu King." We spoke with Hannig in June, 1999.*

**Vegetarian World Guides:** *You have a strong commitment to simplicity, in food and in life. What aspects of your upbringing and your education influenced that?*

**Dieter Hannig:** Growing up in the German countryside, food was always an important part of life. It was more than just eating because you're hungry. Food was always the big thing—the way to get together with the family every day and talk.

We learned as children to appreciate where food comes from. It just doesn't come out of the supermarket in plastic wrap. In the fall I had to pull the potatoes, and in the spring I gathered the first berries. It's just part of living in the country and understanding the circle of life.

Everybody respected food because it's directly related to a lot of work. Cooking, preserving, living off the land was all a pretty basic part of our life cycle. It made us self-sufficient; it made us independent. That's a pretty good feeling!

Great cooking in any culture is based on a very few ingredients. The fewer ingredients, the more challenging it becomes. And then you just really focus on the perfect quality and freshness, and the seasonal availability of each product. A lot of chefs are in the fusion—and confusion—business these days; you know, mixing a whole bunch of flavors. But when was the last time people got excited because they had a really great carrot, that tasted like a carrot? Now, in the springtime we get all these huge, huge strawberries, but when was the last time you had a really great strawberry that tasted like a strawberry? I think if you watch great restaurant chefs today, they're focusing a lot more time on getting great products. Some of them have come to the conclusion, "Well, if I cannot get them, then I'll start growing my own."

In the big farming industry, everything has to have a longer shelf life, and things need to be safe from a sanitation point of view. But these processes also have an influence on the taste. So I'm trying to do the opposite: to go back to the basics and focus on simplicity.

**VWG:** *Tell us why your colleagues gave you the nickname "The Tofu King?"*

**DH:** That haunted me for quite some time! Again, it's really a matter of simplicity, and of personal preference. My refrigerator probably has more tofu and tempeh than anybody else's in this business. But this is just a pure personal choice I make when I'm not on duty. I find great flavor there. I had a beautiful tempeh dinner just last night!

**VWG:** *What accomplishments during your tenure as head of Food and Beverage at Walt Disney World have made you most proud?*

**DH:** There are a lot of success stories which, on the surface, might appear to be small, but are a real sea change for this industry. For example, in the Magic Kingdom today, all the fresh salads are tossed to order. A couple of years ago, you would find what I call "the polyester of salads:" iceberg lettuce. Today, people have seasonal greens, and mixes including oak leaf and arugula. To someone who runs a fancy restaurant in New York or San Francisco, this might not give a sense of accomplishment. But to me this is something that goes pretty deep.

**VWG:** *How have you and your team worked to ensure options for vegetarians at the theme parks?*

**DH:** In each theme park , there is a key person who is expert in special diets, and they can handle any request, and help with itinerary planning.

On all of our menus, there will always be at least one meatless sandwich or entrée, and lots of fresh fruit and veggies scattered throughout the parks. We have been staying away from labeling meals as "heart healthy" or vegetarian on menus because it has aggravated a lot of people, making them feel that we look at them as merely a minority.

It's virtually impossible to have food available to take care of every special diet at every location. If you made it mandatory, you would have some locations that would sell maybe one or two products a day, and you end up with a guest eating something that shouldn't even be around. So, instead of having every restaurant suit everyone's preferences, we're really trying to take care of what we call itinerary planning. And there, I think we've been very successful.

**VWG:** *Gallup recently did a consumer poll of restaurant goers, and 33% said they would order a vegetarian item if it were listed on the menu. Is that true of guests dining at Walt Disney World?*

**DH:** We do a lot of guest surveys, and healthy alternatives or vegetarian selections are always in the top five requests. However, I think what people tell you on a survey—versus their actual buying habits—can be two different things. People tell you, "Oh, you know, I really should have this..." But the moment they sit down and smell the sizzle of steak on the grill, they sometimes go back in the other direction!

**VWG:** *One of the culinary trends that you've predicted is that healthier choices influenced by lots of cultures and nations will  replace many of your established quick service options. Can you give us some examples of the food you're envisioning?*

**DH:** In Epcot, one of our best sellers is freshly made pita bread with tabbouleh. Anything that is bean- or flatbread-influenced, anything that is from Latin America, especially from Mexico, is becoming a staple today. So, you'll probably see a lot more of that.

We have to be careful not to lose sight of the real product, though. We don't want to have food from all over the world fusing into a sort of "New World Cuisine," because in just a few years, the beauty and the differentiation of those ethnic foods can become totally diluted.

But, I suppose this is the evolution of dining, and you cannot stop it. For our part, we are constantly listening to the guests to see what can be done intelligently in quick service. It's an evolution. You have to see what the people are buying and if they like it. Hopefully it will continue to get better and better.

*Continued from page 31*

makes up Walt Disney World's clientele would be missing a tremendous opportunity, and not just in terms of sales.

Hannig elaborates: "The point is to change the guests' perceptions so that, all of the sudden, they go to a quick service operation, and *Hey!* There is a freshly tossed salad! And it's not prepackaged, and chilled. And suddenly you have a Caesar Salad which is, like, *edible*, and you say, 'Ooo! That's pleasantly surprising!'"

To delight and surprise the teeming masses into handing over their hard-earned cash with a smile, Dieter Hannig and his band of menu designers have come up with an astonishing array of dining opportunities, distributed among the following categories:

## Food carts and Snack Shops

The cuisine offered by the food carts and snack shops you see all over the theme parks is definitely closer to Food Court than Carnival. You can't turn a corner without running into one of these thirst slakers and pang assuagers, hawking Mall-ish fare like spring water, soft drinks, cappuccino, cookies, fruit, popcorn, nuts, and frozen delights, in addition to decidedly non-vegetarian items.

For the most part the carts and snack shops are veg-friendly, if you ignore the hot dog stands—particularly the egregiously fleshy smell coming from the one right outside the Animal Kingdom's feelgood-fest, Conservation Station (well, after all, they don't make the hot dogs out of those cute pigs in the petting area). However, if you have a question about the fare offered at a cart (i.e., are any of the cookies offered vegan?), you might not be able to get a definitive answer. Snack shops, on the other hand, usually offer a wider range of goods and often keep ingredient lists on hand for your reference.

## Counter Service and Buffet Restaurants

For the mobile consumption units known as families, there are fast food (or, in the genteel dialect of Disneyspeak, "quick service") restaurants galore, as well as "all-you-care-to-eat" buffets. These eateries are designed to handle the bulk of the food business in the parks, with an approach that's closer to military precision than culinary finesse. According to Franz Kranzfelder, the menus of these quick service restaurants is largely dictated by the public's tastes: if an item doesn't sell, it's substituted with something that does. Despite the fluidity of the menus, these are the toughest places to find something decent as a vegetarian, primarily because there are no chefs waiting to whip something up if you don't like what you see on the menu board. That having been said, quick-service food at Disney can be surprisingly decent, and a few oddball items—like veggie burgers and vegetarian roll-ups—do find their way onto the occasional menu. Use our grids and recommendations to help you find the spots that do the best job catering to vegetarians.

## Table Service Restaurants

It is in the table service restaurants that vegetarians will find the widest selection and the best preparation of vegetarian entrées. Organic produce, low-fat meals, and even tofu frequently grace the menus at many of Walt Disney World's finer establishments.

The one thing all eateries on Disney property have in common is their relaxed dress code (with the exception of the exceedingly tony Victoria & Albert's). Whether it's in the pocket of your camouflage shorts or an Armani suit, your dollar is welcome. But even though it isn't strictly mandatory, you might want to clean up a bit before hitting one of the fine dining destinations in Walt Disney World's resort hotels. You certainly won't be turned out if you show up for dinner in a tank top and cut-offs, but you might feel a bit underdressed at stylish showcases like the California Grill or the Flying Fish.

# Chapter 4

# The Magic Kingdom

Walt Disney World General Information: *(407) 824-4321*
Priority Seating Arrangements: *(407) WDW-DINE (939-3463)*
WDW Switchboard: *(407) 824-2222*
*Call the switchboard to be transferred to*
*a chef at the restaurant where you'd like to dine.*

In Biblical Palestine, all roads may have led to Damascus. But in end-of-the-Millennium Central Florida, all roads lead to the Magic Kingdom—or at least three lanes of I-4 do.

When most people say "Disney World," they're really thinking of the Magic Kingdom, subconsciously envisioning Cinderella's Castle at its heart. The first park at Walt Disney World, the Magic Kingdom is *the* main draw for the under-six set, with lots of characters and an entire area  of the park devoted just to them. But the Magic Kingdom is not just for kiddies. Adult rides like Space Mountain and Alien Encounter make this park a treat regardless of age. And surprise: The Magic Kingdom is not too bad for health-conscious diners.

Since 1994, the Disney Company has made a commitment to providing healthful meals and snacks throughout Walt Disney World. Vegetarians, vegans, diabetics, and others with special diets will have no problem finding plenty of good food to eat in the Magic Kingdom. Vegan burgers, veggie wrap sandwiches, and some creative salads can be found at counter service venues, and no less than three fresh fruit markets are distributed around the park. There are even a couple of places to enjoy creative, delicious, and healthful meals in a relaxing, sit-down setting. Whether it's a result of good planning or just a measure of Disney magic, the end result is a park that even the pickiest eater could love.

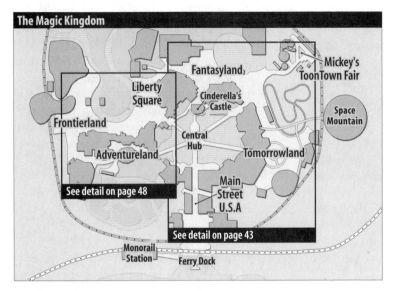

The Magic Kingdom

Fantasyland

Mickey's ToonTown Fair

Liberty Square

Cinderella's Castle

Space Mountain

Frontierland

Central Hub

Adventureland

Tomorrowland

See detail on page 48

Main Street U.S.A

See detail on page 43

Monorail Station

Ferry Dock

## Main Street, U.S.A.

### The Best of the Best on Main Street, U.S.A.

⭐ **Tony's Town Square Restaurant**
**Vegebility: Good**
**Price: Expensive**
Casual Italian
Table Service
B, L, D
Main Street, U.S.A.
The Magic Kingdom
(407) 939-3463
MC/V/AE

It's anything but a dog's life for vegetarians at Tony's Town Square Restaurant, a beautiful Main Street establishment that takes its theming from Disney's animated classic *The Lady and the Tramp*. With more special dietary options than any other restaurant in the Magic Kingdom, you'd do well to take a tip from the Tramp and head here for lunch. The best time to eat at Tony's is between 2 and 3 PM, after the lunch rush is over but before the restaurant closes for its afternoon break (which, depending upon park hours, is between 3 and 4 PM or 3 and 5 PM daily). After the break, a more expensive—and less vegetarian-friendly—dinner menu kicks in.

The mid-day menu is packed with options for ovo-lacto veg-

*For* a comprehensive guide to our ratings system, see page xviii.

**At-a-Glance Grid**

# The Magic Kingdom: Best of the Best

**Key to Categories and Abbreviations**

**O/L, V: Ovo-lacto and vegan selections**

• - Always available    + - Available upon request    A - Request in advance

**Es: Type of establishment**

T - Table Service    C - Counter service    S - Snack stand or cart

**$: Average price for a single vegetarian entrée**

| | | |
|---|---|---|
| 1 - under $10 | 3 - $16 - $20 | 5 - $31 - $40 |
| 2 - $10 - $15 | 4 - $21 - $30 | 6 - over $40 |

**Meals:**

B - Breakfast    L - Lunch    D - Dinner    S - Snacks

| Main Street, USA | O/L | V | Es | $ | Meals |
|---|---|---|---|---|---|
| ❶ Tony's Town Square Restaurant | • | + | T | 3 | L, D |
| ❷ Center Street Produce | • | • | S | 1 | S |
| **Tomorrowland** | | | | | |
| ❾ Cosmic Ray's Starlight Café | • | • | C | 1 | L, D |
| **Mickey's ToonTown** | | | | | |
| ❿ Mickey's ToonTown Market | • | • | S | 1 | S |
| **Fantasyland** | | | | | |
| ⓬ Cinderella's Royal Table | • | A | T | 3 | L, D |
| **Liberty Square** | | | | | |
| ⓯ Columbia Harbor House | • | + | C | 3 | L, D |
| ⓰ Liberty Square Potato Wagon | • | • | S | 1 | S |
| ⓱ Liberty Square Produce Wagon | • | • | S | 1 | S |

etarians. Try the marinated grilled eggplant and portobello panino topped with goat cheese and pesto, or the Pasta Primavera, with Gorgonzola and wild mushrooms adding a welcome and delicious twist. Or how about the mouthwatering Insalata Mediterranea con Pasta: a cool combination of orzo, kalamata olives, and bell peppers, tossed with parmesan, basil, garlic, and sun-dried tomatoes.

For vegans, the Insalata can be made without parmesan, and "Joe"—a.k.a., the team of professionals in the kitchen—is more than happy to whip up a wild mushroom or sautéed vegetable pasta dish (all hard pastas at Tony's are eggless). Even more tempting is the Pizza con Verdura: an assortment of roasted vegetables atop

# A Vegetarian Tour of the Magic Kingdom

*Make your day in the Kingdom magical by selecting one of our tried-and-true itineraries. Be sure to make your Priority Seating reservation at least 24 hours in advance by calling (407) WDW-DINE. To order a special meal, call the WDW switchboard (407/824-2222) a few days ahead and ask to speak with a chef at the restaurant where you wish to dine. And don't forget to check the times of the Magic Kingdom parades and fireworks before scheduling your meals.*

### Itinerary One

**9 AM:** Enter the park. Stop at Tony's Town Square Restaurant on you way in to reconfirm your lunch arrangements, and proceed to Character Breakfast at Cinderella's Royal Table.

**9:15 AM:** On your way to the castle, pick up some fresh fruit and vegetables at the Center Street Produce Wagon on Main Street, U.S.A. to enjoy later. You won't want to traipse all the way back here when your tummy starts to grumble! Spend the morning and early afternoon exploring Fantasyland, Mickey's ToonTown Fair, and Tomorrowland.

**12 NOON:** Now's the time to tuck into that fruit and veggie pack!

**2:15 PM:** Lunch at Tony's after the crowds die down, exiting in time to catch the mid-afternoon parade. After the parade, take a stroll down Main Street, and spend the rest of the day in Adventureland, Frontierland, and Liberty Square.

**7:30 PM:** Small dinner from the Liberty Square Potato and Produce Wagons, seated in view of the Main Street Electrical Parade.

**Or:**

**7 PM:** Exit the park; boat launch to Wilderness Lodge for dinner at Artist Point.

### Itinerary Two

**9 AM:** Enter the park; quick breakfast on Main Street, U.S.A. (fruit from Center Street Produce Wagon; pastries and muffins from Main Street Bake Shop). Spend the morning exploring Main Street, Mickey's ToonTown Fair, and Tomorrowland.

**12 NOON:** Lunch at Cosmic Ray's Starlight Cafe in Tomorrowland. After lunch, head over to Fantasyland and Liberty Square.

**3 PM:** Snack at the Liberty Square Potato and Produce Wagons, in view of the mid-afternoon parade. Spend the rest of the afternoon in Frontierland and Adventureland.

**6 PM:** Exit the park. Take the monorail to the Contemporary Resort for dinner at the California Grill.

**Or:**

**5 PM:** Exit the park; return to your room for a nap and shower before dinner.

**8 PM:** Dinner at California Grill (request a window table for a good view of the Magic Kingdom's "Fantasy in the Sky" fireworks, if scheduled).

---

freshly-made tomato sauce and a crispy vegan shell. Tony's house marinara contains cheese, but the chefs will prepare a strictly veg version with plum tomatoes, fresh herbs, and garlic on the fly.

If you want something special (and who doesn't?), your best bet is to give Tony's 24 hours' warning. But, former chef Dee Fondoukis assures us, "If a guest comes in and they have not made Priority

Seating arrangements, that's not a problem either. We can have a chef come to the table and they can cater to whatever the guest wants. Of course," she admits, "it's easy with Italian cooking: you throw it in a pot, sauté it in some olive oil, and it tastes grrreat!" Wait a minute... Which Tony are we talking about here?

For folks with other special diets, Tony's keeps gluten-free pasta on hand, and can make gluten- and sugar-free pizza shells and cakes with advance notice. For fun, order the extra-long spaghetti and share it with your sweetheart. Who knows—maybe one of those noodles will end in a kiss!

---

⚑  **Center Street Produce Wagon**
**Vegebility: Excellent**
**Price: Inexpensive–Moderate**
Snacks
Main Street, U.S.A.
The Magic Kingdom

**"Our pizza shells are made with just flour, water, and a little olive oil.**

We can top a pizza shell with roasted or grilled vegetables of any assortment. We can do anything a guest wants with vegetables tossed with pasta in any kind of sauce. We can make a tomato sauce, we can make a garlic and herb sauce, just an herb sauce alone. We can do anything on the menu without cheese. Just ask to speak with a chef, say, "This is what I want," and I guarantee 100% that, at Tony's, you'll get what you want!"

✳  *Dee Fondoukis*
*Former Chef, Tony's Town Square*

---

When you're sick of cotton candy, buttered popcorn, and ice cream, head for one of the Magic Kingdom's three produce stands. The first is located near the park entrance, on the corner of Main Street and Center; the second is in the center of Liberty Square; the third is in Mickey's ToonTown Fair, the Magic Kingdom's newest "land." Each stand offers more than ten varieties of only the freshest whole seasonal fruit, pre- washed for immediate enjoyment. Also available are mixed fruit cups, crisp barrel-cured pickles, and, in the cooler months, carrot sticks. Healthful libations include a selection of juices, bottled water, and— for when your feet are really beginning to drag—Powerade.

## Worth a Mention on Main Street, U.S.A.

The Fresh Vegetable Sandwich at the ❹ **Plaza Restaurant** is a cool combination of sliced cucumber, tomato, squash, and Swiss cheese, piled high on multigrain bread and topped with a fresh dill spread. If you're vegan, the sandwich can be made without the cheese and dill spread. There's no price reduction for removing the cheese, but at $7.75 the sandwich is still the cheapest entrée on the menu. The in-house Ice Cream Parlor features old-fashioned floats, sodas, and sundaes—and a new-fangled, low fat, sugar-free chocolate shake.

The character meals at the ❺ **Crystal Palace** are adequate for an ovo-lacto vegetarian who's hankerin' to mingle with Pooh and friends, but don't expect a lot for your $15 lunch buffet (prices subject to change). The menu changes

*Did you know.*
*that Walt Disney's father*
*owned the first soy*
*dairy in Pasadena?*
*Of course you didn't, because it's*
*not true! But wouldn't that have*
*been neat?*

# Veg Burgers in Paradise?

*From frozen Boca Burgers® to garlic chickpea burgers made on the spot, meatless patties are scattered around Walt Disney World— sometimes listed on the menu, sometimes not. Be sure to ask for a veggie burger everywhere their meaty counterparts are sold. Disney's menu planners really do listen to you! Here are a few places to find them now:*

**Magic Kingdom**
   Cosmic Ray's, Tomorrowland
**Epcot**
   Le Cellier Steakhouse, Canada (lunch only)
**Disney-MGM Studios**
   Rosie's All-American Cafe
   50's Prime Time Cafe
   Sci-Fi Dine-In Theater Restaurant
**WDW Resorts**
   Beaches & Cream, Yacht and Beach Club
   Cabana Bar, Dolphin (lunch only)
   ESPN Club, Disney's Boardwalk
   Yacht Club Galley, Yacht and Beach Club
**Downtown Disney**
   Planet Hollywood, Pleasure Island

weekly, and chefs are happy to work with people on special diets, but typical meatless dishes include grilled vegetables, rice, roasted or mashed potatoes, and an assortment of salads.

If you've got a sweet tooth, stop by the ❸ **Main Street Bake Shop** to sample an assortment of cookies,

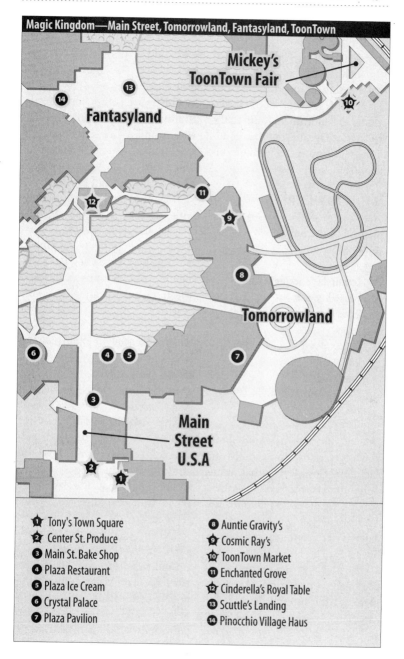

**Magic Kingdom—Main Street, Tomorrowland, Fantasyland, ToonTown**

Mickey's
ToonTown Fair

Fantasyland

Tomorrowland

Main
Street
U.S.A

1 Tony's Town Square
2 Center St. Produce
3 Main St. Bake Shop
4 Plaza Restaurant
5 Plaza Ice Cream
6 Crystal Palace
7 Plaza Pavilion

8 Auntie Gravity's
9 Cosmic Ray's
10 ToonTown Market
11 Enchanted Grove
12 Cinderella's Royal Table
13 Scuttle's Landing
14 Pinocchio Village Haus

cakes, and pastries. If you're vegan, ask for the strawberry fruit cup, or ask to see the ingredient list kept behind the counter (the list was missing at the time of our last visit). If it's too hot for baked goods, continue down Main to the ❺ **Plaza Ice Cream Parlor** for hand-dipped ice cream (including non-fat and sugar-free varieties).

# Tomorrowland

## The Best of the Best in Tomorrowland

✪ **Cosmic Ray's Starlight Cafe**
**Vegebility: Fair**
**Price: Moderate**
Casual American
Counter Service
L, D
Tomorrowland
The Magic Kingdom
MC/V/AE

One of the best fast food joints for vegetarians in the Magic Kingdom, Cosmic Ray's has something on its menu that others don't: a vegan burger! Dubbed the "Earthly Delight," this meatless patty is actually an original Boca Burger®. The meal comes with a side of baby carrots or french fries and your choice of condiments at the topping bar, all for less than $6—a pittance by Disney standards. A person could make a pretty mean veggie sandwich at the topping bar alone, with the usual lettuce, tomatoes, pickles, and condiments joined by notable additions like mushrooms and grilled onions.

Other selections include the Country Vegetable soup (100% vegan) and a Greek salad, which can be had separately or combined as a classic "soup and salad combo" for around $7. If you're vegan, be sure to ask for the Greek without feta cheese. A refreshing Vegetable Salad, featuring diced yellow squash, tomato, cucumber, and zucchini tossed in a light vinaigrette, rounds out the meatless selections on Cosmic Ray's very veg-friendly menu.

## Worth a Mention in Tomorrowland

If you need a refreshment break after the high-tech excitement of *Alien Encounter*, stop by ❻ **Auntie Gravity's Galactic Goodies**. A selection of ice cream treats are balanced by fresh fruit cups and strawberry "smoothies." Vegans should note that the latter are made with Auntie's vanilla soft serve ice cream.

When you're in the mood for pizza, the ❼ **Plaza Pavilion** serves up individual cheese pies for less than $5. For vegans, small and large tossed salads are also available, as are peanut butter and jelly sandwiches for the meat-free munchkins in your group.

# Mickey's ToonTown Fair

## The Best of the Best in Mickey's ToonTown Fair

⑩ **ToonTown Market**
**Vegebility: Excellent**
**Price: Inexpensive–Moderate**
Snacks
Mickey's ToonTown Fair
The Magic Kingdom

Even when you don't have toddlers in tow, consider a quick trip to ToonTown to stock up on healthful snacks at the ToonTown Market. Modeled after an open-air farmer's market, this large permanent stand offers more than five varieties of fruit, washed and ready for snacking, and a selection of juices, bottled water, and other restorative drinks. Crisp barrel-cured pickles and beautiful Florida citrus are among the more tempting offerings on a hot, hazy, and humid Disney World day.

As you wend your way through ToonTown, be sure to notice the miniature vegetable garden plots alongside Mickey and Minnie's Country Houses and beside The Barnstormer at Goofy's Wiseacre Farm. These verdant patches don't just look great—they also provide daily fresh produce for the chefs at Tony's Town Square Restaurant on Main Street, U.S.A.

# Fantasyland

## The Best of the Best in Fantasyland

⑫ **Cinderella's Royal Table**
**Vegebility: Fair**
**Price: Expensive**
Casual American
Table Service
B, L, D
Fantasyland
The Magic Kingdom
(407) 939-3463
MC/V/AE

*"I think over the last couple of years, with the right people in the right place, we have created a couple of beautiful stages.*

*And it's because we have people here who are totally committed, and have a passion for this business. You can have an incredible set. You can build great restaurants and attractions. But, at the end of the day, you're only as good as the last meal you serve."*

– Dieter Hannig
*VP of Food and Beverage, Walt Disney World*

Cinderella's Castle is one of the most magical dining "sets" on Disney property. Lit by torches and stained glass, the main banquet hall has been carefully crafted with high vaulted ceilings and stone archways reminiscent of medieval castles. Leaded glass windows provide lords, ladies, and their progeny with a storybook view of Fantasyland.

For the littlest family members, nothing is more wondrous than a Character Breakfast at Cinderella's Royal Table, with the fairytale princess herself presiding. This "all-you-care-to-eat" feast is great for both vegetarians and strict vegans, provided you've given the chefs plenty of notice. Call a week ahead to arrange for home-made vegan pancakes served with 100% pure maple syrup and vegetarian sausage, a Brobdingnagian fresh fruit platter, or home-made muesli with your choice of rice or soy milk—and that's just what the chef *we* spoke with dreamed up on the spot. Request what you like, and it shall be yours. After all, when you're seated at Cinderella's Table, *you are royalty*! One warning: the royal breakfast potatoes on the menu are cooked with bacon. At your request, the chefs will prepare seasoned hash browns, cooked only in canola oil.

When the lunch and dinner hours roll around, Cinderella's Castle begins to seem more like a dungeon for vegetarians. There's hardly a meatless item on the menu. But with 48 hours' advance notice, Chef Lenny DeGeorge and his team will make anything your heart desires.

If you've forgotten to call in advance, head straight to the Castle as soon as the park opens and make Priority Seating arrangements. Tell the cast member who takes your reservation that you're vegetarian and would like the "Vegetable Plate." Back when Cinderella's Royal Table was called King Stefan's Banquet Hall, this scrumptious vegan concoction was listed on the menu as the "Fairy Godmother's Vegetarian Plate." And despite being yet another pasta n' veggies medley, it's better than most. Vegan cavatelli pasta is tossed with fresh and oven dried tomatoes, garlic, raisins, pine nuts, a bit of fresh spinach, and crimini mushrooms, then drizzled very lightly with olive oil. If you eat dairy, a side dish of Parmesan cheese adds a savory bite.

Another tempting Cinderella's entrée—this one on the menu—is the Salad of Field Greens: a mix of baby mesclun, romaine, and red leaf lettuces topped with sautéed crimini, portobello, and button mushrooms, finished with chunks of Gorgonzola and a light Raspberry Vinaigrette.

Our favorite appetizer at any restaurant in the Magic Kingdom

## Join the Lunch Bunch

*For the past few years, Walt Disney World has been giving guests the option of swapping the ubiquitous (and not-so-healthful) side dish of french fries for a small bunch of seedless grapes or carrot sticks. According to Franz Kranzfelder, Disney World's Manager of Menu Development and Culinary Standards, diners at quick-service restaurants have responded favorably, choosing the fresh goodies over french fries at least 18% of the time.*

is Gus's Artichoke and Spinach Dip, served hot with crispy home-made pita chips. Roasted red peppers, artichoke hearts, Parmesan and American cheeses, and a healthy dose of white pepper and Cajun seasonings make this lip-smackin' appetizer well worth the extra calories.

## Worth a Mention in Fantasyland

For a quick meal in Fantasyland, try ⓮ **The Pinocchio Village Haus**, directly opposite the Carousel. The meal-sized veggie garden salad, the scaled down tossed salad—both freshly tossed—and the assorted fruit cup make this one of the most healthful fast food options in the park. A nice twist at this location, and elsewhere: a side order of carrots can be had in place of

french fries. A vegan children's meal of peanut butter and jelly sandwich, chips, and a child-size beverage is also available.

The sliced Granny Smith apples topped with warm caramel at ⓭ **Scuttle's Landing** are a perfect way to put a skip back into your stride, especially on a cool winter evening. For a lighter treat, sample the Landing's shaved ice in grape, cherry, strawberry, and "blue raspberry" flavors. Lemonade slushes and assorted juices are also available at the ⓫ **Enchanted Grove**, right next to Ariel's Grotto.

## Liberty Square

### The Best of the Best in Liberty Square

⓯ **Columbia Harbour House**
**Vegebility: Fair**
**Price: Moderate**
Casual American
Counter Service
L, D
The Magic Kingdom
Liberty Square
MC/V/AE

Antiques, model ships, tie-back curtains, and low-beamed ceilings make Columbia Harbour House—located near the entrance to Fantasyland—one of the nicer "quick service" establishments in the Magic Kingdom. It also features three meatless entrées for

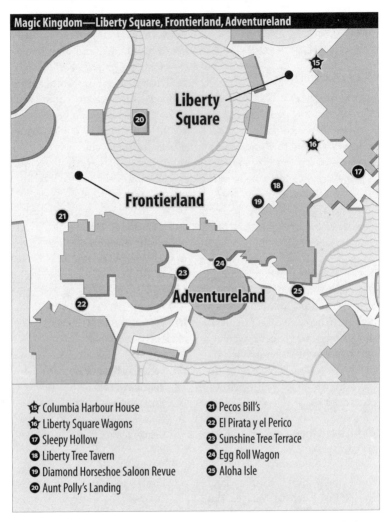

Magic Kingdom—Liberty Square, Frontierland, Adventureland

Liberty Square

Frontierland

Adventureland

🔞 Columbia Harbour House
🔞 Liberty Square Wagons
🔞 Sleepy Hollow
🔞 Liberty Tree Tavern
🔞 Diamond Horseshoe Saloon Revue
🔞 Aunt Polly's Landing

🔞 Pecos Bill's
🔞 El Pirata y el Perico
🔞 Sunshine Tree Terrace
🔞 Egg Roll Wagon
🔞 Aloha Isle

health-conscious diners, more than any other fast food restaurant on property.

At Columbia Harbour House you'll find the Coral Reef Sandwich. Slathered with hummus and broccoli slaw and topped with heirloom tomatoes, this sub-stantial repast will only lighten your wallet by about five bucks. Also available for under a fiver is the hearty vegan chili, served in a bread bowl. Ask for the Garden Galley Salad without the chicken, and you'll receive a price reduction and an unconventional mix that includes pecans, pineapple, and feta cheese. Side orders of french fries, potato chips, and coleslaw are also on offer, as is "fresh baked" apple pie for dessert.

---

🏵 **Liberty Square Potato and Produce Wagons**
**Vegebility: Excellent**
**Price: Inexpensive–Moderate**
Snacks
Liberty Square
The Magic Kingdom

---

The humble potato wagon, parked inconspicuously in Liberty Square, has won the hearts of many a visitor to the Magic Kingdom. Its simple offerings of baked white and sweet potatoes (the latter are offered seasonally) are a welcome hot lunch on a cool winter afternoon, providing hearty sustenance without all the grease, sugar, or chemical additives. A variety of toppings, including margarine,

*Food facts*

*Wondering why those Walt Disney World french fries taste so light and yummy? They're 100% vegetarian, deep fried in nothing but pure vegetable oil. Enjoy!*

butter, sour cream, and chives, are available.

Right next to the potato wagon is the Magic Kingdom's third produce stand. Your choice of apples, bananas, citrus fruits, or sliced melons make a tempting and nutritious dessert. A selection of juices, baby carrots, and crisp barrel-cured pickles are also on hand. Sit under the Liberty Tree and enjoy the lightest, most nutritious—and least expensive—lunch the park has to offer.

---

## Worth a Mention in Liberty Square

🔞 **The Liberty Tree Tavern's** menu is forbiddingly meaty—don't they know Ben Franklin was a vegetarian?—but there is one entrée on the lunch menu for the vegetarian patriot at the table. The Capitol Idea is perhaps a bit expensive for dressed-up red beans and rice, but if you're in the mood for a Colonial dining experience, it's certainly better than nothing. Character dinners at the Tavern are served "family style" by cast members dressed in Revolutionary War costumes, and usually include flank steak, honey-roasted ham, and roasted turkey breast. With advance notice and a Priority Seating booking, the Capitol Idea can be had in place of the meat—but be prepared to pay the same big price as your companions for that, a salad, and a few (ovo-lacto) side dishes.

Return visitors to the Magic Kingdom may remember when ❶ **Sleepy Hollow** featured an entirely meatless menu—an idea that, according to Disney VIPs, was before its time. Today, Sleepy Hollow is loaded with sweet snacks—caramel corn, brownies, and seasonal fruit cobblers—but the veggie entrées are history. Still, the shady and secluded brick patio to the right of the food counter is a lovely spot to rest your feet and enjoy an iced cappuccino, espresso, or specialty coffee.

# Frontierland

## Worth a Mention in Frontierland

At the ❶ **Diamond Horseshoe Saloon Revue**—Frontierland's Old West dinner show—you'll find the Magic Kingdom's ovo-lacto version of the "wrap" sandwich: cole slaw and cheddar cheese topped with ranch dressing and rolled up in a green spinach tortilla. The other meatless offering is a simple tossed Garden Salad. Vegans should bring their own packets of salad dressing, since only two—Ranch and Caesar—are offered; the former contains dairy, the lat-

ter: anchovy paste. For the kiddies, a peanut butter and jelly sandwich is also available.

'Bout the only things available at ❷ **Aunt Polly's Landing** for vegetarian Tom Sawyers (and their Aunt Pollys) are pint-sized peanut butter and jelly sandwiches, apple pies, chips, and pickles. Reckon that'll have to do.

Food wranglers at ❷ **Pecos Bill's Tall Tale Cafe** are happy to make the Kit Carson Chicken Salad sans fowl, resulting in a zippy combination of jicama slaw, lettuce, assorted vegetables, and cheese in a lime vinaigrette (for vegans, cheese can be omitted as well).

# Adventureland

## Worth a Mention in Adventureland

On a hot day, head to the ❷ **Sunshine Tree Terrace** for one of the best thirst-quenchers around: frozen orange juice. Transform your beverage into a classic treat by mixing the juice with non-fat vanilla yogurt in a Citrus Swirl. Voila— an almost guilt-free Dreamsicle! Non-fat chocolate yogurt, floats, coffee, and sodasare also on hand.

All things pineapple can be found at ❷ **Aloha Isle**, including mouthwateringly fresh pineapple spears.

If it's Mexican food ye be wantin', swashbuckle across the way from Pirates of the Caribbean to

# Veggie Kids in the Magic Kingdom

*Sticking to the meatless options offered kids at many Walt Disney World restaurants could be pretty monotonous—and not necessarily healthful. If you'd like your tots to have a little more variety, you might just skip the kiddie menu and share some adult meals around the table.*

## Vegetarian Kids' Meals at Table Service Restaurants

**Cinderella's Royal Table (Fantasyland)**
Jaq's Macaroni and Cheese, served with mashed potatoes

**Liberty Tree Tavern (Liberty Square)**
Yankee Doodle Noodles (Stouffer's macaroni and cheese), served with fruit

**Plaza Restaurant (Main Street, U.S.A.)**
Grilled cheese sandwich, served with a small portion of ice cream

**Tony's Town Square (Main Street, U.S.A.)**
**Breakfast:**
Italian toast with syrup; waffles; cold cereal; fruit
**Lunch and Dinner:**
Pasta topped with tomato sauce or butter; cheese ravioli

## Kid-Friendly Vegetarian Meals at Counter Service Restaurants

**Aunt Polly's Landing (Frontierland)**
Peanut butter and jelly sandwiches

**Columbia Harbour House (Liberty Square)**
Hummus and broccoli slaw sandwiches; vegan chili

**Cosmic Ray's Starlight Cafe (Tomorrowland)**
Boca Burger; vegetable soup; baby carrots

**Diamond Horseshoe Saloon Revue (Frontierland):**
Peanut butter and jelly sandwiches

**El Pirata y el Perico (Adventureland):**
Nachos (request without chili)

**Liberty Square Potato Wagon (Liberty Square):**
Stuffed baked potatoes

**Pinnochio's Village Haus (Fantasyland):**
Peanut butter and jelly sandwiches

**Plaza Pavilion (Tomorrowland):**
Individual cheese pizzas;
Peanut butter and jelly sandwiches

## Healthful Snacks

**Aloha Isle (Adventureland):**
Fresh pineapple spears

**Auntie Gravity's Galactic Goodies (Tomorrowland)**
Fresh fruit cups; strawberry smoothies

**Center Street Produce Wagon (Main Street)**
Fruit; carrot sticks; pickles

**Liberty Square Produce Wagon (Liberty Square)**
Fruit; baby carrots; pickles

**Main Street Bake Shop (Main Street, U.S.A.)**
Strawberry fruit cup

**Scuttle's Landing (Fantasyland)**
Sliced Granny Smith apples topped with warm caramel

**Sunshine Tree Terrace (Adventureland):**
Frozen orange juice; non-fat vanilla and chocolate yogurt; Citrus Swirls

**ToonTown Market (Mickey's ToonTown Fair):**
Fruit; carrot sticks; pickles

❷ **El Pirata y el Perico.** Nachos can be made without chili and the Taco Salad can be made without ground beef. The lip-smackin' churros—traditional Spanish and Mexican doughnut-like spirals, sprinkled with cinnamon and sugar—contain dairy but no egg. The opposite is true of the vegetarian egg roll at the ❷ **Egg Roll Wagon**, parked just outside the Swiss Family Treehouse.

# Chapter 5

# Epcot

- - - - - - - - - - - - - - - - - - - - - - - - - - - - - - - - - - - - - -

**Walt Disney World General Information:** *(407) 824-4321*
**Priority Seating Arrangements:** *(407) WDW-DINE (939-3463)*
**WDW Switchboard:** *(407) 824-2222*
*Call the switchboard to be transferred to
a chef at the restaurant where you'd like to dine.*

*T*he theme park that visitors now know as Epcot (formerly EPCOT Center) bears little resemblance to the Experimental Prototype Community of Tomorrow that Walt Disney imagined in the early sixties. In Disney's original vision, EPCOT was at the heart of Walt Disney World, and it wasn't just an educational theme park. EPCOT was to be a full-fledged Utopian community of 20,000 people—a spanking new, technologically advanced, meticulously planned solution to the terrible problems of America's cities. At the city's center would be a vast climate-controlled shopping and office district: a showcase for the most advanced technology of the day, with a towering hotel shooting more than twenty stories into the sky. EPCOT citizens would live and work near the center of their futuristic city, using monorail transportation to run errands and go to work. The Magic Kingdom and other theme parks would fulfill their need for wholesome, beardless family entertainment.

Less than a year after he introduced his plans in a film screened at a Winter Park movie theatre, Walt Disney passed away, and with him died his fantastic vision of EPCOT. Over the next few years Disney executives and imagineers tinkered with the original concept in an attempt to reconcile Walt's grandiose plans with the economic realities of the late seventies.

The result is the two-part leisure and education complex visitors know today. Epcot may not be what Uncle Walt wanted it to be, but

## At-a-Glance Grid

# Epcot: Best of the Best

**Key to Categories and Abbreviations**

**O/L, V: Ovo-lacto and vegan selections**

• - Always available    + - Available upon request    A - Request in advance

**Es: Type of establishment**

T - Table Service    C - Counter service    S - Snack stand or cart

**$: Average price for a single vegetarian entrée**

1 - under $10    3 - $16 - $20    5 - $31 - $40
2 - $10 - $15    4 - $21 - $30    6 - over $40

**Meals:**

B - Breakfast    L - Lunch    D - Dinner    S - Snacks

| Furure World | O/L | V | Es | $ | Meals |
|---|---|---|---|---|---|
| ❶ The Garden Grill | • | A | T | 3 | B, L, D |
| ❷ Sunshine Season Food Fair | • | • | C | 1 | B, L, D, S |
| ❸ Pure and Simple | • | • | C | 1 | B, L, D, S |
| ❺ The Electric Umbrella | • | + | C | 1 | B, L, D, S |
| ❼ Fountainview Espresso & Bakery | • | • | C | 1 | B, S |
| **World Showcase** | | | | | |
| ❽ San Angel Inn Restaurante | + | + | T | 2 | L, D |
| ❾ Cantina de San Angel | + | + | C | 1 | L, D |
| ❿ L'Originale Alfredo di Roma | • | + | T | 3 | L, D |
| ⓬ Marrakesh Restaurant | • | A | T | 2 | D |
| ⓴ Les Chefs de France | • | A | T | 1 | L, D |
| ㉓ Le Cellier Steakhouse | • | • | T | 2 | L, D |

it is awfully fun—particularly for an older crowd that can appreciate the educational exhibits throughout Future World and the semi-immersive environments of the World Showcase.

Dining in Epcot is without a doubt the most varied of any of the parks, due primarily to the abundance of eateries in the pavilions of the World Showcase. In addition to these and other year-round dining venues, Epcot hosts two massive food-oriented parties annually. The Epcot International Food and Wine Festival, held each Autumn, is a month-long celebration of the cuisines and cultures of over 30 nations. Food Among the Flowers, a springtime

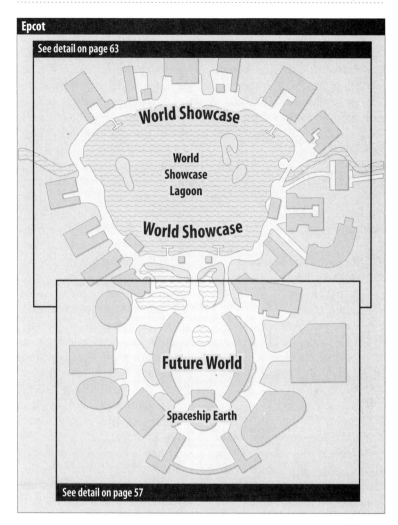

event, is a succession of mid-Saturday brunches featuring freshly prepared foods and a series of guest speakers, including gardening editors from Southern Living magazine. Both events are very vegetarian-friendly, making those times of year ideal for a visit.

From October, 1999 to January 2001, Epcot hosts Disney's millennium celebration. Its theme, "Celebrate the Future Hand in Hand," is embodied each day in spectacular events like IllumiNations 2000, Disney's fireworks, music, and laser display, or the Tapestry of Nations: a "movable street festival" that makes its way around the World Showcase twice each evening. The culinary centerpiece of the celebration, located in the new Millennium Village Pavilion, is "The Gifts of Cuisine"—eight kiosks offering food and beverage from all corners of the globe.

# Future World

## The Best of the Best in Future World

⭐ **The Garden Grill Restaurant**
   **Vegebility: Fair**
   **Price: Expensive**
   Casual American
   Family Style Table Service
   B, L, D
   The Land, Future World
   Epcot
   (407) 939-3463
   MC/V/AE

There are numerous possibilities for sampling the cuisines of faraway places in Epcot's World Showcase. But if you're on the Future World side of the park and want a sit-down meal (one attended by Farmer Mickey and a cast of Disney characters, to boot), head to the Garden Grill Restaurant, located upstairs in The Land. An all-you-can-eat meal served "fam-ily style" at your table, the Grill offers a revolving view of the Living with the Land attraction and is a wonderful spot for family dining. Vegetarians who pay for the restaurant's skillet selection can help themselves to side dishes, in addition to a special Vegetarian Plate of couscous topped with lightly grilled vegetables—many of which are grown in the Land's greenhouses. Don't miss the buffet's dense, chewy sunflower bread, also vegan and wonderful. The salad is accompanied by a creamy ranch dressing on the buffet, but the kitchen stocks oil and vinegar, too.

The character breakfast at the Grill provides ovo-lacto vegetarians with a wealth of choices, including an oven baked potato casserole rich with cheddar cheese and onions and topped with cornflakes (yes, cornflakes—this is breakfast, after all), and delicious buttery grits. And with a week's advance notice, chefs at the Grill can provide goodies for guests on a more restricted diet, including vegan pancakes, cholesterol-free vegetarian breakfast meats, and bounteous fresh fruit platters. *—Thanks to gardenia for her help with this review.*

⭐ **Sunshine Season Food Fair**
   **Vegebility: Good**

*F*or a comprehensive guide to our ratings system, see page xviii.

Price: Inexpensive–Moderate
Casual American
Counter Service
B, L, D
The Land, Future World
Epcot
MC/V/AE

Thanks to its food court-like selection and emphasis on products of the land, the Sunshine Season Food Fair—a dining complex occupying much of the pavilion's ground floor—is more veg-friendly than most quick service venues at Walt Disney World. Three main shops provide a plethora of options.

At the Pasta and Potato Shop, vegetarians who eat dairy would be crazy to miss the Fresh Vegetable Lasagna—a Food Fair signature dish featured in Bon Appetit magazine and made on the premises. Don't worry, those meat-like morsels folded into the layers of pasta are the chef's secret ingredient: dehydrated mushrooms. Eggplant parmesan, cheese tortellini, and an egg-based fresh fettuccine are also available, but be sure to request marinara sauce. Potatoes are available topped with broccoli, cheese or margarine—or, for the true spud lover, nothing at all.

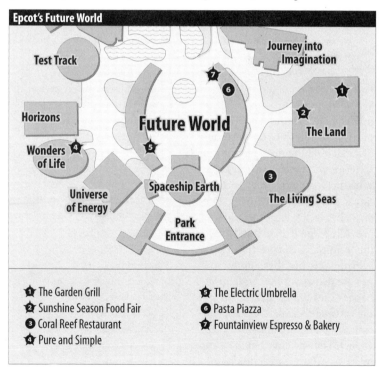

**Epcot's Future World**

Test Track

Journey into Imagination

Horizons

Future World

The Land

Wonders of Life

Universe of Energy

Spaceship Earth

The Living Seas

Park Entrance

① The Garden Grill
② Sunshine Season Food Fair
③ Coral Reef Restaurant
④ Pure and Simple
⑤ The Electric Umbrella
⑥ Pasta Piazza
⑦ Fountainview Espresso & Bakery

A delightful portobello mushroom wrap is available at the Sandwich and Salad Shop. Thin strips of portobello are tossed with assorted vegetables and wrapped in a green spinach tortilla, slathered in a tart cream cheese and radish spread. If you don't do dairy, the spread can be omitted. A garden salad with a choice of nonfat Italian or balsamic vinaigrette dressing is also available.

---

✪ **Pure and Simple**
   **Vegebility: Good**
   **Price: Inexpensive–Moderate**
   Casual American
   Counter Service
   B, L
   Wonders of Life, Future World
   Epcot
   MC/V/AE

---

With the pavilion's emphasis on fitness and health, you'd expect the fast foodery in the Wonders of Life to be a cut above the rest in terms of veg-appeal. And it is! With no less than four possibilities for a vegetarian lunch, Pure and Simple lives up to its name, providing "guilt-free goodies" to the teeming Future World masses.

The heart-healthy oat bran waffles are delish, topped with strawberries or (if you're extra nice to the castmember behind the counter) a little dollop of fat-free frozen yogurt. They're served all day, and make a yummy breakfast, snack,

## It's a Wrap

*From bean burritos to portobello mushroom lavosh to hummus and tabbouleh strollers, "wrap" sandwiches have gone from being a craze to an institution in the last ten years. That's good news for vegetarians, since flatbread-based cuisines are usually veggie-friendly. It's even better news for vegans, since the unleavened tortillas, pita, and flat breads used as wrapping are typically dairy- and egg-free. Wraps at WDW are no exception.*

**Magic Kingdom:**
   Diamond Horseshoe Saloon Revue,
   Fronteirland *(request without chicken)*
**Epcot:**
   African Outpost, World Showcase
   Electric Umbrella, Innoventions East
   Liberty Inn, American Adventure
   Pure & Simple, Wonders of Life Pavilion
   *(request without chicken)*
   Sunshine Season Food Fair, Land Pavilion
**Animal Kingdom:**
   Chakranadi Chicken Shop, Asia
   *(request without chicken)*
**Resorts:**
   Grand Floridian Café, Grand Floridian
   *(lunch only)*
   Reflections, Disney Institute
   Spoodles, Disney's BoardWalk
   *(breakfast wrap)*
   Food Courts, Disney's All-Star Resorts
**Downtown Disney:**
   FoodQuest, DisneyQuest, West Side
   *(request without chicken)*
   Gourmet Pantry, Market Place

or dessert. For lunch, tuck into a roasted vegetable salad or a veggie wrap (both can be requested without chicken) or an oversized baked potato topped with meatless chili. The vegetable pizza is prepared with a vegan shell, and can be ordered without cheese. And for dessert, Pure and Simple serves fruit cups, non-dairy pineapple and strawberry smoothies (unlike the ice-cream based "smoothies" in the Magic Kingdom), and (very dairy) low-fat sugar free cheesecake, plain or topped with strawberries.

*Mmm, mmm good...* but guilt free? No matter how lowfat the cheesecake, we find it hard to feel entirely guiltless sitting at a table munching, watching other folks burn up the calories on their excercise bikes.

---

**5  Electric Umbrella**
  **Vegebility: Fair**
  **Price: Moderate**
  Casual American
  Counter Service
  L, D
  Innoventions East, Future World
  Epcot
  MC/V/AE

If you need a quick bite before heading into the World Showcase, stop at the Electric Umbrella, located on your left as you pass through Innoventions Plaza. Inside, in addition to cheeseburgers and chicken sandwiches, you'll find a delicious veggie wrap. In fact, the Umbrella was Disney's testing ground for this then-new concept in meatless fast food, and the wrap's popularity here stimulated Food and Beverage higher-ups to place it on a few other menus around the property (see "It's a Wrap!" on the opposite page for more info).

Stuffed full of tabbouleh, hummus, and chopped tomatoes and bundled together in a pita, this Mediterranean-inspired wrap is almost entirely vegan. A small amount of cream cheese holds the sandwich together; if you don't do dairy, ask the cast member taking your order to leave it off. Sit on the terrace and enjoy your refreshing wrapper sandwich... and the amazing dancing waters of the Fountain of Nations. French fries and fruit salad are also available. —*Thanks to gardenia for her help with this review.*

---

**7  Fountain View**
  **Vegebility: Fair**
  **Price: Moderate**
  Casual American
  Counter Service
  B, Snacks
  Innoventions West, Future World
  Epcot
  MC/V/AE

*Ah, coffee!* What else could keep you going after an exhausting morning of chasing the kids

# A Vegetarian Tour of Epcot

Eat your way through Epcot at our favorite veg-friendly restaurants. Be sure to make your Priority Seating reservation at least 24 hours in advance by calling (407) WDW-DINE. To order a special meal, call the WDW switchboard (407/824-2222) a few days ahead and ask to speak with a chef at the restaurant where you wish to dine. Don't forget to confirm the times of the Tapestry of Nations and IllumiNations 2000 (Oct. 1999 to Jan. 2001) before scheduling meals.

**Itinerary One**

**9 AM:** Enter the park. Stop at Guest Relations on your way in to reconfirm your lunch arrangements and special meal at L'Originale Alfredo di Roma Ristorante or Les Chefs de France Restaurant. Proceed to Pure & Simple in the Wonders of Life Pavilion for a quick breakfast of oat bran waffles and fruit. Spend the morning exploring Future World.

**12:30 PM:** Start you way around the World Showcase in Canada, and pop into the Millennium Pavilion for a snack. One of the delicious vegetarian "gifts of cuisine" is bound to appeal!

**2:30 PM:** Lunch at L'Originale Alfredo di Roma or Les Chefs de France after the lunch rush has abated.

**8 PM:** Leisurely dinner at Cantina de San Angel on the shores of the World Showcase Lagoon. As you eat, check out the Tapestry of Nations Parade (one of the emerging points is behind the Mexico Pavilion). Linger at your table for dessert, drinks, and a view of IllumiNations 2000.

**10 PM:** Exit the park, profoundly satisfied.

**Itinerary Two**

**9 AM:** Enter the park. Stop at Guest Relations on you way in to reconfirm your dinner arrangements and special meal at Les Chefs de France Restaurant or the San Angel Inn Restaurante, and dessert at the Rose & Crown Pub and Dining Room (subject to availability). Proceed to Character Breakfast at the Garden Grill Restaurant in the Land Pavilion.

**1 PM:** After spending the morning in Future World, grab a veggie wrap at the Electric Umbrella in Innoventions East, or cruise back by the Land for a vegetable lasagna or a portabello wrap from the Sunshine Season Food Fair. Grab dessert and coffee at Fountain View in Innoventions Plaza. Sit outside on the café terrace for a spectacular view of the Fountain of Nations, then head over to the World Showcase.

**6:30 PM:** After checking out the 6 PM Tapestry of Nations Parade, enjoy a romantic dinner at Chefs de France or the San Angel Inn.

**8:30 PM:** Dessert and drinks on the terrace at the Rose & Crown Pub (subject to availability), in time for IllumiNations 2000.

**10 PM:** Exit the park ready for a good night's sleep and another day of vegetarian touring.

around Future World? And there's still the entire World Showcase to get through before dinner! It's times like these when you could really go for an iced cappuccino. What's that... you don't do dairy?

NEVER FEAR! Fountain View, perched on the margin between the World Showcase and Future World, serves the only non-dairy iced cappuccino we've found in Orlando... make that anywhere (although we're not saying it's *natural*). Sit on the terrace and enjoy your faux cappy while watching the mesmerizing Fountain of Nations, or recharge your batteries with a cold granita or a strawberry slush (no caffeine, but lotsa sugar), also dairy-free.

One warning: the tiramisu at Fountain View contains gelatin. Fruit tarts and tulips do not.

## Worth a Mention in Future World

Meaty pizzas and hoagies are made for the masses at ❺ **Pasta Piazza Ristorante** in Innoventions West. The only entrée for vegetarians is cheesy eggplant parmigiana, not recommended for those on a low-fat, low-cholesterol diet. Garden salads and fruit cups are available.

Seafood is the focus of the ❸ **Coral Reef Restaurant** in the Living Seas, but many a vegetarian has been known to eat there—if only to catch a glimpse of the spectacular aquatic creatures living right next door. An eight-inch-thick, eight-foot-high sheet of acrylic separates diners from one of the largest saltwater aquariums on earth, holding more than 5.7 million gallons of seawater and nearly 8,000 inhabitants. Other than an appetizer-sized salad, there's only one vegetarian item on the Coral Reef menu, but it's a good one: a deliciously savory phyllo dough strudel stuffed with fresh sautéed

vegetables and spinach Boursin cheese, baked golden brown, and served with a lentil salad. With a few hours' notice, Chef John Clark can also make a vegan version of the dish, or something altogether different, like a roasted

*Facts for foodies*

ike portobello mushrooms today, **eggplant** *was the star player in vegetarian menu items of the 1970s. Eggplant parmigiana—sautéed breaded eggplant slices baked with tomato sauce, parmesan, and mozzarella cheese— was, it seemed, everywhere. Eggplant can be prepared in a variety of ways, but because of its sponge-like ability to absorb liquids, care must be taken when cooking eggplant with oil or other fats.*

*s a member of the nightshade family, eggplant is most closely related to the tomato and the potato. Although commonly considered a vegetable, eggplant (like the tomato) is actually a fruit—a berry, to be more specific. There are many varieties of eggplant, from the thin, straight Japanese or Asian eggplant, to the delicate and delicious Italian or baby eggplant, to the large deep purple variety most common in the United States.*

market vegetable and portobello mushroom salad. Seasonal fruits and deliciously fresh, house-made sorbets are always featured on the dessert menu.

# The World Showcase

## The Best of the Best in the World Showcase

⑧ **San Angel Inn Restaurante**
**Vegebility: Fair**
**Price: Expensive**
Casual Mexican
Table Service
L, D
Mexico Pavilion, World Showcase
Epcot
(407) 939-3463
MC/V/AE

The San Angel Inn Restaurante, located inside the Mexico pavilion, is consistently ranked as one of the most romantic dining spots on Disney property. Guests enter the restaurant in "twilight" through the courtyard of a Mexican village and are led to candlelit tables beside a murmuring indoor river. A huge Pre-Columbian pyramid looms overhead, surrounded by grass huts, and backed by an ominous smoking volcano. If it sounds kitschy, well…it is, a little bit. But the dim lighting, the babbling brook, and the good food make the San Angel Inn a great place to enjoy an evening with that special someone.

The restaurant's menu can best be described as Mexican regional, with an emphasis on traditional flavors and ingredients. Americans used to the light, fresh Baja cuisine common in chain restaurants can expect darker, smokier flavors here than they may be accustomed to.

Sadly, gone are the days when the San Angel Inn offered vegetarians their own eight-item *Menu Vegetariano*. But the restaurant's rice and beans are made without lard or meat stock, so just about any non-veg menu item can be made meatless. The real bargain here, though, is the Vegetarian Combination, featuring an oversized black bean burrito, an enchilada (your choice of cheese or bean), and a medley of sautéed green pepper, red pepper, and red onions. Not too shabby—but we sure wish they'd bring back that vegetarian menu!

⑨ **Cantina de San Angel**
**Vegebility: Fair**
**Price: Inexpensive–Moderate**
Casual Mexican
Counter Service
L, D
Mexico Pavilion, World Showcase
Epcot
MC/V/AE

Wandering by the Mexico Pavilion, you can't help but notice a waterside cantina offering frozen margaritas and authentic Mexican food. "What a perfectly lovely place to stop for lunch!" you say to yourself. As you approach the menu board, your heart sinks: chicken tacos, beef burritos, tacos al car-

bon... *Egad!* Even the salad contains meat!

What the menu does not reveal, however, is the willingness of your amigos in the cantina to cater to people like us. Cantina de San Angel's black beans are completely vegetarian; lard is not used in the preparation of the refried bean side

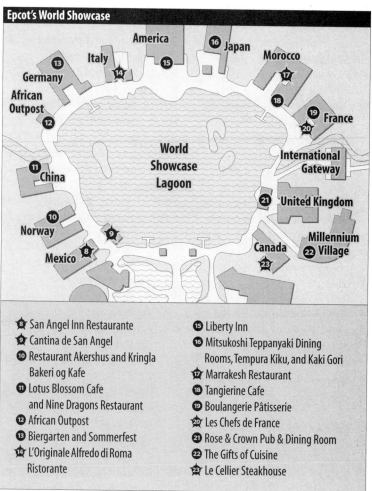

**Epcot's World Showcase**

🏮 San Angel Inn Restaurante
🏮 Cantina de San Angel
🔟 Restaurant Akershus and Kringla Bakeri og Kafe
⓫ Lotus Blossom Cafe and Nine Dragons Restaurant
⓬ African Outpost
⓭ Biergarten and Sommerfest
🏮 L'Originale Alfredo di Roma Ristorante

⓯ Liberty Inn
⓰ Mitsukoshi Teppanyaki Dining Rooms, Tempura Kiku, and Kaki Gori
🏮 Marrakesh Restaurant
⓲ Tangierine Cafe
⓳ Boulangerie Pâtisserie
⓴ Les Chefs de France
㉑ Rose & Crown Pub & Dining Room
㉒ The Gifts of Cuisine
🏮 Le Cellier Steakhouse

## A Foodie Festival

A highlight for food lovers each Fall is the Epcot International Food and Wine Festival. The outdoor festival around the World Showcase celebrates the authentic cuisines and wines of more than 30 nations.

Visitors to Epcot can witness cooking demonstrations, drop in on wine seminars, and (best of all) indulge in "tastings"—appetizer-sized samples of ethnic dishes priced at $1 to $3. Vegetarian offerings abound, with nearly every nation's booth featuring at least one meatless morsel. Tastebud tantalizers include Brazilian vegetable pasteles, Alsatian caramelized onion tart, spanakopitas with a tangy tzatziki sauce, and vegetable sushi.

More than 200 vintages of wines can be sampled in special marketplaces, featuring wineries from South Africa, Argentina, Austria, Portugal, Australia, and Chile. But the festival isn't just for oenophiles. Beer lovers can visit Beer Gardens throughout Epcot where they can sample more than 30 microbrew and boutique beers.

For a special evening, treat yourself to a Grand Tasting—the best of 16 wineries paired with cuisine from celebrated American chefs and live entertainment—or a "Winemaker Dinner," where a Disney chef and a "guest" chef collaborate on an exquisite five-course meal. Check out the schedule on the Disney Web site (www.disney.go.com) to see which dinners are best for vegetarians, and call ahead to discuss the evening with a Disney chef. Even if nothing is listed on the menu, chefs should be willing to work with you to create a memorable meal.

dish, or the black beans used to stuff burritos and tacos. Combine this with two additional distinctions—the rice contains no chicken or meat stocks, and the red sauce used to smother burritos is vegan—and you've got a wealth of options for creating a great vegetarian meal. And, if you omit cheese, it's possible to enjoy a low fat, totally vegan lunch or dinner. Portions are big, but the price tag isn't: the Plato Combinacion—a bean taco, vegetable and bean burrito, and a quesadilla served with refried beans and Mexican salsa—is less than $7.

For dessert, tuck into a sticky fried churro (Mexico's answer to the cinnamon doughnut) or a creamy caramel flan, both of which contain dairy and/or egg. And don't forget to sample a refreshing frozen margarita: a 100% vegan Cantina treat.

---

☆ **L'Originale Alfredo di Roma Ristorante**
**Vegebility: Good**
**Price: Expensive**
Casual Italian
Table Service
L, D
Italy Pavilion, World Showcase
Epcot
(407) 939-3463
MC/V/AE

L'Originale Alfredo di Roma Ristorante, located in the World

Showcase's Italian Pavilion, is distinguished by its association with Fettuccine Alfredo, the invention of original owner Alfredo de Lelio. Apparently our man Alfredo, unable to coax his pregnant wife into eating anything at all, mixed freshly churned butter and fine Parmesan cheese with his fresh pasta, discovering a combination so irresistible that she broke down and ate the whole thing—and suffered a coronary on the spot.

That last part isn't true. But there's no question that Alfredo's delightfully rich concoction did have an impact on the world. Today there are four L'Originale di Alfredo Ristorantes in America serving up the official recipe, along with an abundance of other tempting Italian fare.

The entryway to L'Orlando Alfredo is decorated with signed photographs of international celebrities who've dined at the original Rome restaurant. The elegant dining area, with its stylish mauve velvet chairs and bright pink tablecloths, enjoys a relaxing view of the courtyard at the center of the pavilion.

For the most part, vegetarian selections are limited to salads and pasta variations. Most of the pastas served are of the hard, eggless variety—only the fresh fettuccine used in the restaurant's signature dish contains egg. Ovo-lacto veggies should try the Tricolore di

Pasta—a sampler of Fettuccine Alfredo, vegetable lasagna, and linguine with pesto—or the fabulous Ziti alla Mediterranea: ziti pasta with fresh mozzarella, Sicillian olives, fresh tomatoes, and basil. Vegans can enjoy this dish without the mozzarella. Just be sure to save room for an order of Alfredo's out-of-this-world (and gelatin-free) tiramisu!

---

### ✡ Marrakesh Restaurant
**Vegebility: Fair**
**Price: Expensive**
Casual Moroccan
Table Service
D
Morocco Pavilion, World Showcase
EPCOT
(407) 939-3463
MC/V/AE

Serving dinner only, the Morocco Pavilion's Marrakesh Restaurant may be the best place on Disney property for a table of four vegetarians to grow closer by eating exactly the same thing together.

Mysteriously, that's just what hordes of vegetarians seem to enjoy—or accept—since Marrakesh offers only two vegetarian selections, but remains popular among veggie types. Admittedly, the food is well prepared. Jasmina's Salad plate offers an assortment of traditional Moroccan salads, and the vegetable couscous is light, fluffy, and well seasoned. Both

## An Idea for the Imagineers...

Everyone who loves American food—especially post-1970s American food—can't help but cringe as they walk past the American Adventure in Epcot's World Showcase. Perhaps providing fast food in the midst of culinary portraits like Les Chefs de France and the German Biergarten is *apropos* for America. But now that we do have a national cuisine worth celebrating, thanks to visionaries like Alice Waters, Dean Fearing, and Larry Forgione, one can't help wondering: can't we do better than this?

Fortunately, things may be about to change (emphasis on *may*). Rumor has is that the American Pavilion is scheduled for a facelift. Wouldn't it be great if the renovations included a new dining complex stressing seasonality and simplicity, and featuring three or four vegetarian items? That would make the American restaurant *the most vegetarian-friendly spot in Epcot*—a great statement about the culinary landscape of America today.

come in large enough portions for a couple to share. But vegetarians who would like to try vegetable shish kebab or a meatless version of the harira soup (tomatoes, lentils, and lamb) are out of luck. *Too bad! No soup for you!* Vegans can't even enjoy the couscous, since it's made with butter. And the recent addition of family style "feasts" make no concessions for vegetarian diners.

Apparently the lack of variety is outweighed by the restaurant's stunning interior and fun stage show, featuring accomplished belly dancers and outstanding traditional musicians. Soaring ceilings, tall, thin columns, and just about every other surface of the exotic, multi-tiered room is beautifully painted or tiled in intricate Islamic calligraphic designs.

But if you can take or leave the couscous, the décor, and the enter-

tainment, there's more interesting Middle Eastern food to be had just a short walk or boat ride away at Spoodles, on Disney's BoardWalk. As far as we're concerned, it's a no-brainer.

---

☆ **Les Chefs de France Restaurant**
**Vegebility: Fair**
**Price: Moderate**
Elegant French
L, D
France Pavillion, World Showcase
Epcot
(407) 939-3463
MC/V/AE

Les Chefs de France offers vegetarians an all-too-rare opportunity to enjoy *la nouvelle cuisine végetarienne*, prepared by three of France's reigning culinary monarchs. Nouvelle cuisine pioneers Paul Bocuse and Roger Vergé and pastry artist Gaston Lenotre have

designed a menu that draws upon the best culinary traditions of France, to be savored in the bustling, elegant dining room or on the tiled veranda overlooking the streets of the World Showcase's France Pavilion. While veggie selections aren't exactly legion (there's only one entrée on the dinner menu), a vegetarian couple can enjoy a romantic meal by sharing a few of the excellent appetizers and splitting the *Plat Végetarien*—a delicious gratin of zucchini, eggplant, and tomato, topped with cheese and a drizzling of olive oil. Try the vegetarian vichysoisse soup, a wonderful salad of warm cheese and field greens, or our favorite, the tarte a la tomate: a savory fresh tart of yellow and red tomatoes with fresh basil and goat cheese on a thin crust.

The lunch menu also features a terrific grilled vegetable sandwich on a baguette, served with pommes frites (french fries). Pay close attention to the fries: although french fries are named for the cutting technique of "frenching" and not for France, French chefs are traditionally judged by their ability to produce fries that are crisp, golden, and tender.

True sorbets, made with fresh fruit, are always available on the dessert menu. But if you eat dairy, you owe it to yourself—no, you owe it to France—to finish your

meal with a sweet, rich crème caramel or an impossibly light millefeuille pastry, accompanied by a glass of champagne or a cappucino. *C'est si bon!*

## Millennial Munch

When Disney throws a party, it throws a BIG party. And when a big opportunity—like, say, the turning of the millennium—presents itself, Disney throws a GARGANTUAN party.

For foodies, the centerpiece of the Epcot celebration will be Millennium Village, a new World Showcase pavilion located between Canada and the United Kingdom. Amidst 65,000 square feet of artisans, storytellers, and exhibits from over 35 countries, a modest row of food kiosks will be dishing out ❷ **The Gifts of Cuisine** from around the world. In addition to ethnic foodstuffs, the eight kiosks—representing Asia, the Pacific Rim, Europe, the Caribbean, Africa, the Middle East, South and Central America and North America—will feature traditional and regional beverages, like Arabica coffee from the Middle East and Red Stripe beer from Jamaica. Veg selections include a crispy Vietnamese spring roll and a deliciously savory European sandwich, with grilled vegetables, Greek feta cheese, and olive tapenade on Italian focaccia bread. A Middle Eastern platter of Lebanese hummus, tabouleh, and baba ghannoush", served with whole wheat pita wedges, provides an entirely vegan meal.

⭐ **Le Cellier Steakhouse**
**Vegebility: Fair**
**Price: Moderate–Expensive**
Casual Canadian
Table Service
L, D
Canada Pavilion, World Showcase
Epcot
(407) 939-3463
MC/V/AE

So you're schlepping around the World Showcase with your Uncle Melvin and he says, "Oy! I've gotta have a nice steak right now or I'm going to drop!" You stifle your smart-aleck comment about how he may drop if he does pile another steak onto that sack of mushrooms he calls a body and you all saunter over to Canada's Le Cellier Steakhouse for a look at the dinner menu.

Uh-oh, this doesn't look so good… Cheese soup with bacon… New York Strip Steak… Venison Osso Buco… *Venison?! Bambi!?!?!* "Fantastic!," beams Uncle Melvin. You roll your eyes and file in for another evening of salad and dinner rolls.

Or so you think. Le Cellier may not be the best destination on Disney property for a vegetarian, but your meal can be pretty darn good if you plan ahead and ask the right questions. With 24 hours' advance notice, the chefs at Le Cellier will make you anything—yes, *anything*—your little heart desires. Vegetarian Shepherd's Pie? Certainly. Lemongrass Tofu with stir-fried vegetables and sticky rice? It's not exactly Canadian, but why not?

The secret to the restaurant's flexibility is a willingness to use Epcot's vast array of dining venues as a multiethnic market, borrowing Asian ingredients from Japan, fruit sorbet from the nearby Living Seas restaurant, or vegan sandwich buns from the French pavilion—again with plenty of advance notice. Not that the menu is so spartan you need to go to those lengths. The lunch menu features a house-made roasted garlic chickpea burger, with your choice of potatoes and a garlic-infused jicama slaw. It's an all-vegan meal except for the bun (and you can always request a different bread in advance). Dinner's standout entrée is the yummy vegan Napoleon of portobello mushrooms, zucchini, squash, pepper, oven dried tomato, and black bean spread. Again, it's not exactly Canadian… but what vegetarian specialty *is*?

## Worth a Mention in the World Showcase

The assortment of salads on the koldtbord buffet at ❿ **Restaurant Akershus** in Norway is large, but not especially veg-friendly; fish and meat are primary constituents in most selections. The kitchen will make a grilled vegetable plate that has garnered raves from vegetarian diners for less than $10, and friendly servers will sometimes let guests sample a few meatless items from the buffet free of charge. Head across to the ❿ **Kringla Bakeri og Kafe** for traditional Norwegian desserts like waffles, cinnamon rolls, "kringle"—sweet pretzels with raisins and almonds—or a fresh fruit cup.

Choices are limited at the two restaurants in the China Pavilion. ⓫ **The Lotus Blossom Cafe**, China's counter service restaurant, serves just one veg item: cold sesame noodles and marinated vegetable salad. The Cafe's vegetable lo mein is made with chicken stock; a meatless version cannot be special ordered. The separate "vegetarian" menu at ⓫ **Nine Dragons Restaurant** contains three meals—Eggplant Sauteed in Garlic Sauce, Stir Fried Seasonal Chinese Vegetables, and Ma Po Tofu—all of which are made with a chicken stock. According to a castmember at the restaurant, "We can't use M.S.G., so we have to use *something* for flavor!" Be sure to ask for your selection without chicken stock, and without oyster sauce—another potential hidden ingredient. And keep your fingers crossed that your meal will arrive with some flavor intact!

In the Fall of 1999, a new ⓭ **Biergarten** opened in Germany under the watchful eye of Chef Christine Weissman (formerly of Seasons Dining Room at the Disney Institute). An 84-foot buffet provides authentic, but lighter, modern German cuisine. About ninety percent of the salads on the buffet are vegetarian, with standouts like Weissman's spelt salad—infused with white balsamic, cucumber, and fresh dill—always available. Other items, such as a hearty lentil soup, rotate with the seasons. Red cabbage, spaetzle, and assorted seasonal vegetables can be found on the hot bar. And with advance notice, Germany's chefs can create goodies like potato pancakes or dumplings in a mushroom stock sauce.

Beck's beer (guaranteed 100% vegetarian, thanks to Germany's centuries-old purity laws) and soft pretzels are available at ⓭ **Sommerfest**, the small outdoor café at the rear of the Germany pavilion. Look for the introduction of a salad in the near future. Right now, you can tuck into one of the vegetarian wrap sandwiches available on property at the ⓬ **African Outpost**. Marinated, roasted vegetables are seasoned with African spices and rolled up in a white flour tortilla.

If you missed the veggie wraps at the Electric Umbrella and the African Outpost, you can still pick one up at the ⓯ **Liberty Inn** in the American Adventure. A mix of hummus and tabbouleh wrapped in a tortilla shell, the sandwich makes a great walk-about meal. If you're vegan, be sure to ask for the sandwich without cream cheese.

*Facts for foodies*

Chewy, light, and pleasantly tart, **tabbouleh** has made its way onto lots of American menus in recent years, and vegetarians everywhere have been the happy beneficiaries. Tabbouleh is a traditional salad in Middle Eastern countries, and has at its base bulghur—wheat berries that have been steamed, dried, and crushed. The tender and fluffy grain is mixed with chopped tomatoes, mint, parsley, onions, olive oil, and a generous amount of lemon juice to make tabbouleh. The best tabbouleh is bright green and moist, indicating a generous amount of parsley in the dish, and is usually served chilled with lavosh—a thin Armenian bread—or pita.

Japan's traditional cuisine is diverse, beautiful, and very vegetarian-friendly, so the paucity of meatless entrées at its World Showcase eateries is surprising. The main draw at the ⑯ **Mitsukoshi Teppanyaki Dining Rooms** is the Benihana-esque experience of watching stir fry chefs prepare meals tableside on a teppan grill. Unfortunately, your veggies are likely to be stir fried right along with your neighbor's Kobe beef. No area of the grill is reserved for vegetables, and no separate utensils are used.

At Japan's ⑯ **Tempura Kiku**, the house specialty is tempura—batter-dipped and deep-fried pieces of chicken, shrimp, and vegetables. Although vegetable tempura is not listed on the menu, the kitchen is happy to prepare some upon request, but it will have been fried in the same oil as the batter-coated meat. If you decide to eat here, try the hiyayakko: simple and refreshing chilled tofu, served with green onion and fresh ginger. As you walk through the Japan Pavilion on a hot day, grab a refreshing ⑯ **Kaki Gori**: shaved ice topped with fruit syrup.

In search of a delicious and light Mediterranean meal? Stop at Morocco's brand new ⑱ **Tangierine Cafe** for a "vegetarian platter" of hummus, tabbouleh, and other traditional Middle Eastern salads, perfect for sampling on the outdoor terrace. The platter is totally vegan, with the exception of a small amount of mayonnaise in the lentil salad—easily omitted in favor of a bit more of another platter component. The cafe also features Moroccan breads and desserts, including a dairy-free almond pastry, all baked on the premises; if you're vegan, ask about the contents of each item before ordering. A wider—and more fattening—selection of baked goods is available next door, at France's ❿ **Boulangerie Pâtisserie**, including napoleans, palmiers, mousses, soufflés, and the occasional vegan tarte or turnover. If you don't eat eggs or dairy, ask to see the ingredient list kept behind the counter to help decide between too many delicious choices.

# Veggie Kids at Epcot

*Child-size offerings at Epcot are more diverse than those available in the Magic or Animal Kingdoms: vegan pancakes, couscous, sushi, hummus, and real Norwegian macaroni and cheese are all available. If you don't see something on the kid's menu you know your little shaver will like, you'd do well to share a couple of sure-fire hits from the adult menu.*

## Vegtarian Kids' Meals at Table Service Restaurants

**Alfredo's (Italy):**
Kid-sized portions of Spaghetti Al Pomodoro (ask for it without meatballs) or L'Original Fettuccine All' Alfredo

**Coral Reef (The Living Seas):**
Triton's Pasta (pasta with marinara sauce)

**Garden Grill (The Land):**
Character breakfast of vegan pancakes, cholesterol-free vegetarian breakfast meats and fresh fruit (by advance arrangement only)

**Restaurant Marrakesh (Morocco):**
Child's portion of vegetable couscous

**Restaurant Akershus (Norway):**
Ovnsbakt Makaroni og Ost (baked macaroni and cheese)

**San Angel Inn (Mexico):**
Two child sized bean burritos, served with rice (request the burritos without beef)

## Kid-Friendly Vegetarian Offerings at Counter Service Restaurants

**African Outpost (between Germany and China):**
Roasted vegetable wrap sandwich

**Electric Umbrella (Innoventions East):**
Hummus and tabbouleh wrap sandwich

**Liberty Inn (American Adventure):**
Hummus and tabbouleh wrap sandwich

**Pure and Simple (Wonders of Life):**
Oat bran waffles topped with strawberries; baked potatoes stuffed with meatless chili; veggie wraps; vegetable pizza (available without cheese by special order); fruit cups; non-dairy pineapple and strawberry smoothies.

**Sunshine Season Food Fair (The Land):**
Vegetable lasagna; baked potatoes; cheese tortellini

## (Sorta) Healthful Snacks

**Fountain View Espresso and Bakery (Innoventions West):**
Fruit tarts and tulips

**Kaki Gori Stand (Japan):**
Kaki Gori (shaved ice, topped with fruit syrup)

**Kringla Bakeri og Kafe (Norway):**
"Kringle" (sweet pretzels with raisins and almonds); fruit cups

With some estimates placing the number of vegetarian or almost-veg Britons at 38%, England is a paradise for meatless diners. But ❹ **The Rose & Crown Pub and Dining Room**, catering to an American crowd, offers only one meatless (but dairy-rich) meal: vegetable curry, a holdover from the British Raj. Starters include creamy wild mushrooms in puff pastry, an assortment of English cheeses and fruits, and a garden salad. For our money, though, you'd be crazy not to save your visit to the Rose and Crown until after dinner, when you can enjoy IllumiNations 2000 with some sherry trifle, a lovely cuppa tea, or a pint of Bass Ale on the terrace. On busy nights, however, the terrace is reserved for guests eating dinner only.

# Chapter 6

# Disney-MGM Studios

------------------------------------------------

**Walt Disney World General Information:** *(407) 824-4321*
**Priority Seating Arrangements:** *(407) WDW-DINE (939-3463)*
**WDW Switchboard:** *(407) 824-2222*
*Call the switchboard to be transferred to
a chef at the restaurant where you'd like to dine.*

ack in 1985, when mega media mergers were big news, company CEO Michael Eisner made a deal with MGM Studios to license its back catalog and its name as the basis for a new theme park. The idea was sheer business brilliance, simply because it worked on so many levels. MGM's grown-up movie catalog was great fodder for a theme park, and another successful theme park meant more visitors for the whole Disney complex. More parks to see meant guests would likely book for longer stays—and duration of stay, in the theme park business, is what it's all about.

Hollywood and the movies also make a great backdrop for the Studios' wildly diverse and very veg-friendly restaurant scene. Four full-service restaurants (the 50's Prime Time Cafe, Mama Melrose's Ristorante Italiano, The Sci-Fi Dine-In Theater Restaurant, and The Hollywood Brown Derby) are complemented by a popular Character Buffet (Hollywood & Vine) and a plethora of quick service restaurants, stands, and snack windows.

The Hollywood Brown Derby is the park's culinary standout, with a refined atmosphere and an educated staff capable of stretching beyond the restaurant's not-terribly-veg-friendly menu. Ahead of the Derby in popularity and veg-friendliness—but not always quality—is Mama Melrose's Ristorante Italiano, tucked away in a far corner of the park. The vibe at "Mama's" is bustling but relaxed and the food is classic New York trattoria fare with a few Californian twists: don't miss the gar-

**At-a-Glance Grid**

# Disney-MGM Studios: Best of the Best

**Key to Categories and Abbreviations**

**O/L, V: Ovo-lacto and vegan selections**

• - Always available    + - Available upon request    A - Request in advance

**Es: Type of establishment**

T - Table Service    C - Counter service    S - Snack stand or cart

**$: Average price for a single vegetarian entrée**

| | | |
|---|---|---|
| 1 - under $10 | 3 - $16 - $20 | 5 - $31 - $40 |
| 2 - $10 - $15 | 4 - $21 - $30 | 6 - over $40 |

**Meals:**

B - Breakfast    L - Lunch    D - Dinner    S - Snacks

| Echo Lake | O/L | V | Es | $ | Meals |
|---|---|---|---|---|---|
| 50's Prime Time Cafe | • | • | T | 2 | L, D |
| Echo Park Produce | • | • | S | 1 | S |
| **Sunset Boulevard** | | | | | |
| The Hollywood Brown Derby | • | + | T | 3 | L, D |
| Anaheim Produce | • | • | S | 1 | S |
| Rosie's All-American Cafe | • | • | C | 1 | L, D |
| **Commissary Lane** | | | | | |
| Sci-Fi Dine-In Theater Restaurant | • | + | T | 2 | L, D |
| **New York Street** | | | | | |
| Studio Catering Company Nut Wagon | • | • | S | 1 | S |
| Mama Melrose's Ristorante Italiano | • | + | T | 2 | L, D |

gantuan Panino sandwich, a massive amalgam of roasted vegetables, portobello mushrooms, and chewy ciabatta bread topped with Boursin cheese.

Disney-MGM Studios also boasts what may be the wackiest dining experience in any Disney park—the Sci-Fi Dine-In Theater Restaurant, where guests eat in mini automobiles facing a huge movie screen showing '50s horror flicks. You needn't recoil in horror at the menu, though. With some creativity, it's possible to fashion four vegan entrées from the choices on the lunch menu. And since most seats face the movie screen, no one is really encouraged to chat—something that might be welcome after a morning spent enduring your little brother's antics.

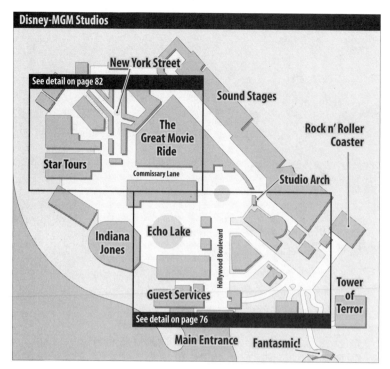

**Disney-MGM Studios**

New York Street

See detail on page 82

Sound Stages

The Great Movie Ride

Rock n' Roller Coaster

Star Tours

Commissary Lane

Studio Arch

Indiana Jones

Echo Lake

Hollywood Boulevard

Guest Services

Tower of Terror

See detail on page 76

Main Entrance    Fantasmic!

# Echo Lake

## Best of the Best around Echo Lake

⭐ **50's Prime Time Cafe**
**Vegebility: Fair**
**Price: Expensive**
Casual American
Table Service
L, D
Echo Lake
Disney-MGM Studios
(407) 939-3463
MC/V/AE

If you've ever dreamt about stepping into an episode of Leave It to Beaver or My Three Sons, you owe it to yourself to check out 50's Prime Time Cafe. Diners sit in a series of rooms decked out like 1950s suburban kitchens, complete with space-age linoleum patterns, chrome appliances, and black and white TVs playing clips from vintage sitcoms. Cast members—Cousin Bill or Sister Sue—have a lot of fun ribbing guests, especially when they don't clean their plates.

*F*or a comprehensive guide to our ratings system, see page xviii.

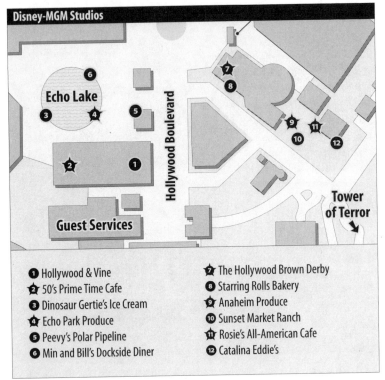

**Disney-MGM Studios**

Echo Lake

Hollywood Boulevard

Guest Services

Tower of Terror

❶ Hollywood & Vine
❷ 50's Prime Time Cafe
❸ Dinosaur Gertie's Ice Cream
❹ Echo Park Produce
❺ Peevy's Polar Pipeline
❻ Min and Bill's Dockside Diner
❼ The Hollywood Brown Derby
❽ Starring Rolls Bakery
❾ Anaheim Produce
❿ Sunset Market Ranch
⓫ Rosie's All-American Cafe
⓬ Catalina Eddie's

A glance at the all-American menu, featuring meatloaf and fried chicken in the starring roles, reveals relatively few options for vegetarians, even fewer for vegans, and virtually nothing for those who are watching their intake of saturated fat and cholesterol. But the good news is that you won't find Uncle Charley in the kitchen. Chef Michael Senich (referred to variously as "Uncle Mike" or "Dad" by the waitstaff) has been cooking all day, and he's got a lot of good stuff for the vegetarian members of the family, too.

In addition to a yummy penne pasta—tossed with garlic, olive oil, spinach, crimini mushrooms, and oven-roasted tomatoes—and a traditional vegetarian lasagna, the menu includes a statement asking diners to tell their server of special dietary concerns. When you do, Senich or another talented Prime Time chef comes to the table, armed with a list of items like Boca burgers and Tofutti, and a bunch of questions to help them whip up a customized, "home-cooked" meal just for you. Menu favorites like Dad's Onion Rings,

# A Vegetarian Tour of Disney-MGM Studios

*Tour the Studios with one of our tried-and-true itineraries. Be sure to make your Priority Seating reservation at least 24 hours in advance by calling (407) WDW-DINE. To order a special meal, call the WDW switchboard (407/824-2222) a few days ahead and ask to speak with a chef at the restaurant where you wish to dine. And don't forget to confirm the times of the Disney-MGM Studios parades and Fantasmic! before scheduling your meals.*

**Itinerary One**

**9 AM:** Enter the park. Stop at Guest Relations on your way in to reconfirm your lunch arrangements at 50's Prime Time Cafe and your dinner at Mama Melrose's Ristorante Italiano.

**9:30 AM:** Breakfast of pastries, fruit, and muffins at Starring Rolls Bakery. Spend the morning exploring Hollywood Boulevard, the Animation Courtyard, and Mickey Avenue.

**12 NOON:** Snack time! Grab a bag of carrots or a deliciously sour pickle at Anaheim Produce. Be sure to leave lots of room for lunch. Time to hit those big attractions on Sunset Boulevard.

**2:00 PM:** Lunch at 50's Prime Time Cafe, exiting in time to catch the mid-afternoon parade as it cruises down Hollywood Boulevard. Spend the rest of the day around Echo Lake, Commissary Lane, and New York Street.

**6:30 PM:** Dinner at Mama Melrose's .

**8 PM:** Exit the park.

**Itinerary Two**

**9 AM:** Enter the park. Stop at Guest Relations on you way in to reconfirm your Fantasmic! Dinner Package arrangements (subject to availability) at The Hollywood Brown Derby.

**9:30 AM:** Breakfast on the shores of Echo Lake with fruit from Echo Park Produce -OR- at The Writer's Stop (great coffee!). Spend the morning on Sunset Boulevard.

**12 NOON:** Lunch at Rosie's All-American Cafe or at Starring Rolls Bakery. Afterward, tour Animation Courtyard, Mickey Avenue, and New York Street.

**2:30 PM:** Snack on a bag of roasted nuts at the Studio Catering Company Nut Wagon, and wander back toward Commissary Lane for a view of the mid-afternoon parade. After the parade, hit the big attractions around Echo Lake (Star Tours and Indiana Jones), and spend some time in the shops on Hollywood Boulevard.

**5:45 PM:** Dinner at The Hollywood Brown Derby. As your server gives you the bill, don't forget to get your ticket for special seating at Fantasmic! (subject to availability).

**7:15 PM:** Fantasmic!

**8 PM:** Exit the park.

---

for example, can be made with an eggless breading with no advance notice, and a fabulous roasted vegetable soup can be on your table ten minutes after you order.

If only our own dads and uncles were always so well-prepared!

**✿ Echo Park Produce**
**Vegebility: Excellent**
**Price: Inexpensive–Moderate**
Snacks
Echo Lake
Disney-MGM Studios

As you enter the Studios, check your backpack. Don't worry if you forgot to stash that banana on your rush to get out to the park. Echo Park Produce, located on the shore of Echo Lake as you reach the end of Hollywood Boulevard, stocks plenty of bananas, apples, pears, and much more—over ten varieties of fresh fruit. The market also offers pre-cut chunks of watermelon, grapes, barrel-cured pickles, and, in wintertime, an assortment of fresh veggies. To slake your thirst, you can pick up ice cold bottled water, sports drinks, and sodas.

## Worth a Mention on Echo Lake

Just a couple of years ago, ❻ **Min and Bill's Dockside Diner** was one of the best places in the park to get low-fat vegan fast food. A Mexican restaurant sunk into the hull of a cartoonish fiberglass ship, the old Diner served up beans made without lard, guacamole with no sour cream, and taco salads you could live with, if not die for. Sometime in 1998 all that changed, and the little tramp steamer became a purveyor of milk shakes. For those of us in search of a quick but nutritious bite, it was a sad day indeed.

Around the same time, Hollywood & Vine Cafeteria was re-imagineered as the ❶ **Hollywood & Vine Cafeteria of the Stars**, a Disney character buffet. Serving breakfast, lunch, and dinner, the buffet is sufficient for ovo-lacto vegetarians, with items like spinach and jack cheese frittata, rigatoni with pesto, and macaroni and cheese scattered among the meaty offerings. If you're on a more restrictive diet, tuck into the roasted veggie fried rice, topped with portobello mushrooms. But if you want something beyond that, call ahead and speak with a chef. Special arrangements can be made with 24 hours' advance notice, making the $15–16 price tags more palatable.

On the far side of the lake, ❸ **Dinosaur Gertie's Ice Cream of Extinction** offers a selection of soft serve ice creams. Closer to Hollywood Boulevard on the backside of Keystone Clothiers is ❺ **Peevy's Polar Pipeline**, dishing out frozen Coca-Cola and Minute Maid concoctions.

# Sunset Boulevard

## Best of the Best on Sunset Boulevard

☑ **Hollywood Brown Derby**
**Vegebility: Good**
**Price: Moderate–Expensive**
Casual American
Table Service
L, D
Sunset Boulevard
Disney-MGM Studios
(407) 939-3463
MC/V/AE

What happens to a wonderful restaurant when your favorite chefs leave and a new team comes in and mixes things up? When that team includes Shawn Kane, what happens is magic.

Kane is a restaurant chef at the Brown Derby under Chef Rob

*Facts for Foodies*

*In the summertime, a number of Walt Disney World menus—including the Hollywood Brown Derby's—feature* **"toybox tomatoes."** *If you're like us, you're probably wondering what, exactly, toybox tomatoes are, and how they got their playful name.*

*According to our sources, a few years ago a group of California farmers produced a surplus of small tomatoes. Miniature cherry tomatoes, Cherokees, red and golden pear tomatoes, Sunbursts, Sweet 100's, and grape tomatoes were packed together in small boxes— "toyboxes"—and sold to chefs in the San Francisco Bay area. The mixed tomatoes looked so great in the boxes—like toys just waiting to be played with—that they were immediately successful.*

*But remember—you're really not supposed to play with your food.*

Millner. His history at WDW (including a stint under Cliff Pleau at the California Grill) has put him in the position of learning from the best while also allowing him to stretch his own creative limits and take a few chances— something with which the former professional motorcycle racer is well acquainted! Kane describes his culinary style as "contemporary, with a nutritional and vegetarian consciousness." That consciousness—combined with Millner's ability to please even the prickliest of diners—makes a world of difference at the Brown Derby.

As at most places on Disney property, there are only a few vegetarian offerings on the menu, mostly concentrated in the appetizer section. But with little or no advance notice, Kane or Millner can create great meatless lunches or dinners out of thin air. In one example, quinoa is topped with savory tamari-marinated tofu. In another, delicate strands of capellini are inundated with Greek olive chutney, peppers, and capers in a Mediterranean taste explosion.

The Brown Derby's signature Cobb Salad typically contains turkey, bacon, and egg, in addition to chopped greens, tomatoes, blue cheese, avocado, and chives. But the kitchen will make a vegan or ovo-lacto version on the fly. The menu changes daily according to what's in season, but one frequent inclusion not to be missed is the grilled portabello mushroom sandwich with red and yellow tomatoes, roasted red peppers, asparagus, and field greens, topped with pesto aioli and accompanied by crispy shoe string potatoes or a medley of julienned veggies. Another tempting salad is the toy-box tomato medley (see "Facts for Foodies," previous page), accompanied by fresh mozzarella, pesto, and baby greens all drizzled with aged balsamic vinegar. And the earthy mix of woodland mushrooms with fresh pasta and chèvre is simply wonderful.

If you can find room, don't miss the grapefruit cake. But don't even think about riding the Rockin' Roller Coaster afterwards!

—*Thanks to gardenia for her help with this review.*

---

🏛 **Rosie's All-American Cafe**
**Vegebility: Fair**
**Price: Moderate**
Casual American
Counter Service
L, D
Sunset Boulevard
Disney-MGM Studios
MC/V/AE

Disney's theme parks are littered with fast food joints serving nothing but burgers and fries, chicken and fries, and hot dogs and fries. Suddenly, into that bland, unadventurous mélange comes Rosie's:

the only place at the Studios where you can get a fat-free vegan Boca Burger®—and fries, if you want them—without ordering at a table service restaurant.

It takes a few extra minutes to cook the burger, but it's well worth the wait. The burger is served un-adorned, allowing you to decorate it however you wish at an expansive condiment bar. Pick up a baked potato at Sunset Ranch Turkey Legs or some grapes at Anaheim Produce for a healthful side dish. Or indulge in some fat free yogurt topped with fresh fruit at Catalina Eddies. All are located in the same outdoor food court complex as Rosie's. —*Thanks to gardenia for her help with this review.*

---

⭐ **Anaheim Produce**
**Vegebility: Excellent**
**Price: Inexpensive–Moderate**
Snacks
Sunset Boulevard
Disney-MGM Studios

Farmers' markets like those of sunny California seem to have sprung up everywhere in recent years—including at Disney-MGM Studios. Disney-MGM has capitalized on the trend toward healthful snacks at a number of spots throughout the park, including Anaheim Produce. Named for the Disney Company's southern California hometown, this simulated farmer's market offers the same variety of fruits and vegetables as other stands in the park, but in greater abundance. In addition to fresh produce, Anaheim also sells granola and power bars, as well as a selection of juices and other natural beverages.

## Worth a Mention on Sunset Boulevard

One of the best places to grab a meal on the run is ❽ **Starring Rolls Bakery**, right next to the Hollywood Brown Derby on the corner of Hollywood and Sunset Boulevards. In addition to fresh cookies, pies, pastries, and other typical bakery fare, Starring Rolls offers sugar-free pies and strudels, fruit cups, and a small selection of fresh fruit. The bakery shares a kitchen with the Brown Derby, making vegetarians the grateful beneficiaries of upscale treats like a 100% vegan sandwich topped with grilled veggies, made to order... and to go! Pick one up on your way to the long lines for the Tower of Terror.

In Sunset Boulevard's open-air food court sits ⓬ **Catalina Eddie's**. If you're craving pizza (or if the vegetarian burger at Rosie's next door just doesn't appeal), sink your teeth into one of Eddie's plain cheese pies. ❿ **Sunset Market Ranch** offers a baked potato and a variety of toppings.

"*The whole motivation is to create a better experience for our guests.*

*And that means having the best chefs. The whole mentality about leadership has changed. We no longer have executive chefs; we have working chefs. You'll see them in the kitchen on a daily basis. We don't have kitchen generals anymore. We have missionaries— people who are passionately involved in cooking.*"

*— Franz Kranzfelder*
Walt Disney World Food & Beverage

# Commissary Lane

## Best of the Best on Commissary Lane

✿   **Sci-Fi Dine-In Theater Restaurant**
  **Vegebility: Good**
  **Price: Moderate–Expensive**
  Casual American
  Table Service
  L, D
  Commissary Lane
  Disney-MGM Studios
  (407) 939-3463
  MC/V/AE

The ultimate in Disney restaurant theming, the Sci-Fi Dine-In scores big on atmosphere. It feels more like an attraction than a restaurant: diners eat in diminutive versions of 1950s American automobiles, watching vintage science fiction film clips and cartoons on a drive-in movie screen and waiting for their server to roller skate by with the check. Sound scary? It could be, if it weren't so darn Disney!

Although the vegetarian food doesn't compare to that in Disney's resort restaurants, the Sci-Fi Dine-In makes a great compromise for a vegetarian visiting the park with meat eaters, or a family with children (large or small) craving a theme dining experience. The surprising fact about this fictional restaurant is that it offers no fewer than four vegan main dish possibilities... with some last-minute ingredient omissions, of course.

The Vegetable Club is a tantalizing sandwich stacked high with smoked portobello mushrooms, roasted red peppers, yellow tomatoes, and onion on grilled vegan focaccia, with (or without) tangy pesto and parmesan cheese. An anise-flavored mix of French tarragon and vegetables over cavatelli shell pasta can be ordered sans parmesan, as can the spicy roasted red pepper sauce—which has Bloody Mary mix as its secret ingredient—served over short twists of *gemelli*

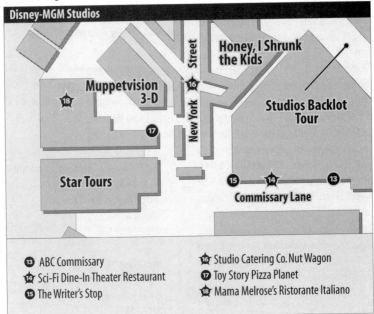

Disney-MGM Studios

Muppetvision 3-D
New York Street
Honey, I Shrunk the Kids
Studios Backlot Tour
Star Tours
Commissary Lane

⓫ ABC Commissary
⓬ Sci-Fi Dine-In Theater Restaurant
⓭ The Writer's Stop
⓰ Studio Catering Co. Nut Wagon
⓱ Toy Story Pizza Planet
⓲ Mama Melrose's Ristorante Italiano

pasta. Order the latter two without chicken or shrimp. Hiding out in the back with the creepy monsters and space aliens are always one or two Original Vegan Boca Burgers®; your server will be glad to resuscitate one, if you say the word. A selection of salads and appetizers round out the menu's veg-friendly selections. And Sci-Fi's chefs will make just about anything according to your specifications, given a day's advance notice.

That's not so scary, now, is it?

## Worth a Mention on Commissary Lane

Down Commissary Lane from the Chinese Theater, near the Great Movie Ride, the ❸ ABC Commissary offers fast food with few concessions to vegetarians, but it is a good place to grab a snack before heading out to watch the Studios' afternoon parade. The Commissary serves up the Vegetarian Salad: an oversized bowl of mixed greens, cheeses, and your choice of dressing. If you're vegan, the salad can be made without cheese. French fries and a pasta salad served with soy sauce round out the meatless selections.

One of the best things about Disney's obsessive attention to detail is the recipe book most quick service and snack stands keep behind the counter for cranks like us. You can deconstruct any recipe

you want at ❶ The Writer's Stop, a good place to get a sweet treat, a frozen natural fruit drink, a sparkling water or a cuppa Joe. Most of the rotating assortment of snacks are vegetarian, but to get the skinny—or the chubby—on ingredients, ask to see the recipe book.

Around the corner at the entrance to New York Street, ❶ Toy Story Pizza Planet serves up surprisingly decent cheese-and-tomato pies. Order Buzz's Meal Deal and you'll also get a small salad (lowly iceburg lettuce and tomato, but at least it's freshly tossed) and a drink. Patrons dine in the noisy, megasized arcade—complete with lots of crane machines—that adjoins the restaurant, and Toy Story characters Buzz Lightyear and Woody put in the occasional appearance for the fans.

# New York Street

## Best of the Best on New York Street

⓱   **Mama Melrose's
Ristorante Italiano
Vegebility: Good
Price: Moderate–Expensive**
Casual Italian/Californian
Table Service
L, D
New York Street
Disney-MGM Studios
(407) 939-3463
MC/V/AE

Tucked into one of the farthest corners of the Studios off the back of New York Street, sits Mama Melrose's Ristorante Italiano. Despite its out-of-the-way location, Mama Melrose's is one of the most popular restaurants in the park, and it's easy to see (and smell) why: the heavenly aromas wafting out the doorway speak volumes about the delicious California-inspired comfort food waiting inside.

Those who are able to get a table will be rewarded by Mama's oak-fired pizzas, including at least three meatless pies at any given time. A delicious cheeseless pizza is featured on the menu, topped with vine-ripened tomato and sweet basil, and brushed with virgin olive oil. These simple ingredients highlight the delicate, earthy flavors of the vegan pizza shell—a flatbread that holds up wonderfully on its own. Chefs in the open kitchen are happy to leave the Boursin cheese off the oak roasted vegetable pizza at a moments notice—meaning vegan diners can order a record-breaking two (2) vegan pizzas at any time! Mama's menus change approximately every two weeks, however, so be sure to ask about the pizzas when you make your reservation.

A standout on the lunch menu is the panino sandwich. When former chef Glen Golcher introduced the roasted vegetable panino in the Fall of 1997, it sold so well

## A Fantasmic Meal

If you're planning to see Fantasmic!, the elaborate musical-cum-sound-and-light-show playing nightly in the Hollywood Hills Amphitheater, consider the Fantasmic! Dinner Package, which may be available during your visit. The package includes Priority Seating at one of the Studios' table service restaurants and entrance to a special reserved section of the amphitheater, substantially reducing your wait to get in. While other guests stand in line up to 90 minutes, you'll be able to show up a mere 15 minutes before show time and still have a seat.

There's no extra charge for the package. Simply mention that you'd like to participate when making your Priority Seating, order from your restaurant's normal dinner menu and pay as usual. The only catch: each adult in your party must order an entrée. When you get the check, your server will set you up with tickets for Fantasmic!'s reserved seating section.

Currently, two of the most vegetarian-friendly restaurants on property—Mama Melrose's Ristorante Italiano and the Hollywood Brown Derby—are participating in the package. When you make your Priority Seating, ask about your dining options; other restaurants on property may be participating as well.

that he immediately made it a regular menu item (the kitchen is still struggling to keep up with the demand). Thinly sliced oak-grilled eggplant, zucchini, yellow squash, Maui onion, and ripe tomatoes conspire with Boursin

# Veggie Kids at Disney-MGM Studios

*For the most part, vegetarian children's meals at Disney-MGM Studios consist of all the usual suspects, relying heavily on pasta and dairy. If you want your kids to eat a balanced meal, your best bet may be to skip the children's menu altogether and share two or three adult meals around the table.*

## Vegetarian Kids' Meals at Table Service Restaurants

**50's Prime Time Cafe (Echo Lake):**
   Peanut butter and jelly sandwiches; spaghettios

**Brown Derby (Sunset Blvd.):**
   Kid-sized salad; Mickey's macaroni and cheese

**Mama Melrose's (New York Street):**
   Spaghetti with tomato sauce; cheese pizza

**Sci-Fi Dine-In Theater (Commissary Lane):**
   Junior Red Planet pasta with meatless tomato sauce; The Galactic Grill—a triple-decker grilled cheese sandwich

## Kid-Friendly Vegetarian Offerings at Counter Service Restaurants

**Catalina Eddie's (Sunset Blvd.):**
   Individual cheese pizzas

**Rosie's All-American Cafe (Sunset Blvd.):**
   Vegan Boca burgers

**Sunset Market Ranch (Sunset Blvd.):**
   Baked potatoes

**Toy Story Pizza Planet (Commissary Lane):**
   Individual cheese pizzas

## Healthful Snacks

**Anaheim Produce (Sunset Blvd.):**
   Fruit; granola bars

**The Writer's Stop (Commissary Lane):**
   Frozen natural fruit drinks

**Echo Park Produce (Echo Lake):**
   Fruit; vegetables; pickles

**Starring Rolls Bakery (Sunset Blvd.):**
   Sugar-free pies & strudels; fruit cups; fresh fruit

**Studio Catering Co. Nut Wagon (NY Street):**
   Nuts

cheese and scrumptious ciabatta bread to make this by far the most satisfying meatless sandwich in the park (though it's price tag is also a whopper, weighing it at $10.95). Vegans can order the panino without cheese, the only dairy in the concoction.

A selection of pastas (all of which are vegan), bruschetta, and a savory oak grilled portobello mushroom—topped with creamy polenta, Gorgonzola, and a sweet, smoky Merlot reduction—secure Mama's position as one of the best bets for vegetarians on property.

---

 **Studio Catering Co. Nut Wagon**
   **Vegebility: Excellent**
   **Price: Moderate**
   Snacks
   New York Street
   Disney-MGM Studios

If you find yourself on New York Street, waiting for your table at

Mama Melrose's, grab a bag of nuts from the Studio Catering Co. Nut Wagon to tide you over. Some scientific studies have indicated that a daily serving of as little as one ounce of nuts high in monounsaturated fats can reduce the levels of LDL cholesterol in the blood, thereby reducing the risk of heart disease by as much as 10 percent. Two of the nuts highest in these "good" fats—almonds and pecans—are available in individual servings from the nut wagon, warmed just a bit to bring out their delicious flavor. Cashews, not quite as good for you but oh-so-sweet-and-buttery, are also available.

# Chapter 7

# Disney's Animal Kingdom

**Walt Disney World General Information:** *(407) 824-4321*
**Priority Seating Arrangements:** *(407) WDW-DINE (939-3463)*
**WDW Switchboard:** *(407) 824-2222*
*Call the switchboard to be transferred to
a chef at the restaurant where you'd like to dine.*

isney's Animal Kingdom, the company's fourth Florida park, opened to fanfare and controversy on Wednesday, April 22, 1998. Journalists, celebrities, and several thousand of the teeming masses came in droves to see whether Disney could pull it off: an animal park that would make zoos seem dated and confined, while still turning a profit and delivering the Disney magic. Animal advocates like Jane Goodall were there on opening day to laud the company's ambitious conservation efforts. But animal rights advocates outside the gates decried the recent deaths of four baby cheetahs and two rare cranes through carelessness while the park was being built.

Disney was eventually cleared of any wrong doing in the animal deaths, and by and large reports on the park are no less favorable than on the country's better zoos. What's more disturbing to vegetarians is the dearth of meatless meals at the Animal Kingdom's restaurants. The park is by far the least vegetarian-friendly of the four—especially for vegans, whose choices amount to one rice and vegetable dish, or an assortment of tossed salads or side dishes. This relative paucity of vegetarian options is puzzling in light of the park's ostensible mission: to inspire a sense of respect for our planet and its creatures.

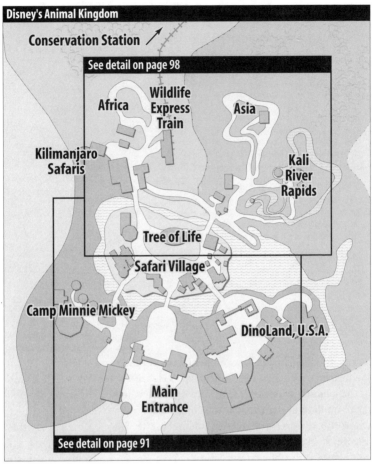

Disney's Animal Kingdom

Conservation Station

See detail on page 98

Africa

Wildlife Express Train

Asia

Kilimanjaro Safaris

Kali River Rapids

Tree of Life

Safari Village

Camp Minnie Mickey

DinoLand, U.S.A.

Main Entrance

See detail on page 91

To be fair, if we looked at just the fast food restaurants in Epcot or the Magic Kingdom, we'd probably be pretty discouraged by the vegetarian options there, too. What's missing from the Animal Kingdom are the in-park table service restaurants and nearby resort dining rooms that Magic Kingdom, Epcot, and Disney-MGM Studios guests enjoy. It's primarily in these full service restaurants that chefs are encouraged to explore innovative and healthful options, including vegan and vegetarian meals.

The good news is that sometime in 2001 the much-anticipated Animal Kingdom resort —the Safari Lodge—is slated to open. The fine dining restaurant in the Lodge will reportedly be the most

# Disney's Animal Kingdom: Best of the Best

**Key to Categories and Abbreviations**

**O/L, V: Ovo-lacto and vegan selections**

• - Always available    + - Available upon request    A - Request in advance

**Es: Type of establishment**

T - Table Service        C - Counter service        S - Snack stand or cart

**$: Average price for a single vegetarian entrée**

| | | |
|---|---|---|
| 1 - under $10 | 3 - $16 - $20 | 5 - $31 - $40 |
| 2 - $10 - $15 | 4 - $21 - $30 | 6 - over $40 |

**Meals:**

B - Breakfast        L - Lunch        D - Dinner        S - Snacks

| | O/L | V | Es | $ | Meals |
|---|---|---|---|---|---|
| **Entrance Plaza** | | | | | |
| ☆ Rainforest Cafe | • | + | T | 2 | B, L, D |
| **DinoLand U.S.A.** | | | | | |
| ☆ Donald's Prehistoric Breakfastosaurus | • | A | T | 2 | B |
| **Asia** | | | | | |
| ☆ Chakranadi Chicken Shop | • | • | S | 1 | L, D, S |
| **Africa** | | | | | |
| ☆ Harambe Fruit Market | • | • | S | 1 | S |

veg-friendly restaurant yet to occupy Disney soil. Grain- and legume-based cuisines, with a special focus on African foods, will take center stage (for more information see the sidebar on page 134).

# Entrance Plaza

## Best of the Best in the Entrance Plaza

☆ **Rainforest Cafe**
**Vegebility: Fair**
**Price: Moderate–Expensive**

Casual American
Table Service
B, L, D
Entrance Plaza
Disney's Animal Kingdom
(407) 939-3463
MC/V/AE

The Rainforest Cafe at the Animal Kingdom is the seventh in a chain of over twenty eco-themed restaurants founded by former ad salesman Steven Schussler in the early nineties. Much of the food at the Rainforest Cafe has a mass-

# What can you do to save the Rainforest?

*Go vegetarian!*

From a personal perspective, the myriad reasons to go veg are compelling; reduced cholesterol and a reduced risk of cancer are just a couple of the big rewards new vegetarians can expect to reap from a simple change in diet. But becoming a vegetarian has enormous ramifications for the well-being of the planet, too.

Livestock-based agribusinesses contaminate delicate ecosystems and deplete their resources, in addition to causing suffering among the animals they raise and slaughter. In Central and South America, the environmental cost of a quarter pound of beef is paid for with the loss of 55 square feet of irreplaceable rainforest. It's been estimated that 1,000 rainforest species are driven to extinction each year by the practice of clear cutting for farmland in tropical countries—and the rate of loss is accelerating.

Both in foreign countries and here at home, the raising of animals for meat is one of the leading causes of environmental degradation. To date, the U.S. has lost over 60 percent of its topsoil to grazing farm animals. Poorly monitored slaughterhouses and overcrowded factory farms leach vast quantities of animal waste into our water supply. And frequent outbreaks of bacterial contamination force consumers to question whether meat products are safe from deadly diseases.

It seems pretty clear to us: Being vegetarian is the best thing you can do for yourself—and for the world!

produced quality—almost as if the raw ingredients were manufactured rather than grown. But this spectacularly themed restaurant—with its animatronic elephants, gorillas, and leopards—offers more vegetarian options than any other place in the Animal Kingdom. Portions at the Rainforest, as at all modern chain restaurants, are huge. Even children's portions could feed two moderately hungry adults.

Most of the veggie menu selections involve pizza, pasta, or a portobello mushroom. The Plant Sandwich, for example, is a portobello cap smothered with sautéed vegetables and a side salad. It's quite flavorful, but vegans will need to substitute ketchup or mustard for the rich mayonnaise remoulade, and the side salad's Caesar dressing does contain anchovy. For a variation on this theme, try the Rainforest Natural Burger—a grain-and-bean burger with the same toppings and sides as The Plant.

At breakfast, vegans can tuck into the Paradise Plate, a huge platter of pineapple, kiwi, strawberries, and red seedless grapes. The lemon poppyseed mini muffins on the side do contain egg, however. If you want something sweet and sticky, try the Tonga Toast—thick white Italian bread soaked in egg and coated with a sinfully sweet cinnamon walnut topping. The "Pie of the Viper" is

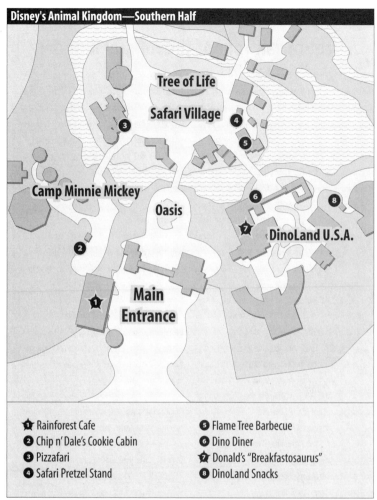

Disney's Animal Kingdom—Southern Half

Tree of Life

Safari Village

**3**

**4**

**5**

Camp Minnie Mickey

Oasis

**6**

**8**

**7**

DinoLand U.S.A.

**2**

**1** Main Entrance

**1** Rainforest Cafe
**2** Chip n' Dale's Cookie Cabin
**3** Pizzafari
**4** Safari Pretzel Stand

**5** Flame Tree Barbecue
**6** Dino Diner
**7** Donald's "Breakfastosaurus"
**8** DinoLand Snacks

a meatless Mexican-style breakfast pizza topped with roma tomatoes, cilantro, and red, green, and poblano peppers. Vegans can request the Viper without egg and cheese. Avoid the grilled breakfast potatoes; they're littered with diced bacon.

You could eat at worse places than the Rainforest Cafe, but beware: a number of Web sites featuring Disney restaurant reviews by ordinary diners are filled with horror stories about long waits, disappearing servers, and cold food. Furthermore, virtually none of the raw ingredients used in this eco-friendly restaurant's food is organic—and one chef told us

# A Vegetarian Tour of the Animal Kingdom

*There's not as much for vegetarians to eat at the Animal Kingdom as there is at the other parks, but you can still enjoy a full day of meatless meals in Walt Disney World's newest theme park by following one of our suggested itineraries. Be sure to make your Priority Seating reservation at least 24 hours in advance by calling (407) WDW-DINE. To order a special meal, call the WDW switchboard (407/824-2222) a few days ahead and ask to speak with a chef at the restaurant where you wish to dine. Don't forget to confirm the opening and closing times of the park before scheduling your meals.*

### Itinerary One

**7 AM:** Tuck into an early breakfast at the Rainforest Cafe, located on the left side of the Entrance Plaza as you approach the park.

**8 AM:** Enter the park and proceed directly to Africa. Spend the morning exploring DinoLand U.S.A., Camp Minnie-Mickey, and Safari Village.

**10 AM:** While waiting for the next showing of the "Festival of the Lion King" in Camp Minnie-Mickey, grab a quick snack of freshly baked cookies, or whole fresh fruit from the Harambe Fruit Market in Africa next door.

**12 PM:** Make your way to Africa and the ever-popular Kilimanjaro Safaris.

**1 PM:** Lunch on the Marinated Vegetable Sandwich or a light salad at Tusker House. Bring your meals outdoors to the Dawa Bar, a great place to enjoy a cool drink and live performances of contemporary and traditional African music and dance. After lunch, take the train to Conservation Station, and then head over to Kali River Rapids in Asia and DinoLand U.S.A.

**3 PM:** In Asia, stop for a sweet and creamy yogurt concoction at the Anandapur Ice Cream Truck or a frozen lemonade at the stand nearby. If you had a small salad at lunch, fortify yourself with the vegan rice bowl from Chakranadi Chicken Shop.

**6 PM:** Exit the park. Head back to your hotel for a shower and a nap, and then out to one of the more veg-friendly resort restaurants for dinner.

### Itinerary Two

**7 AM:** Before leaving your hotel, stock a small cooler with a vegetarian lunch.

**7:30 AM:** Enter the park. Stow your cooler in a locker at Guest Relations immediately after coming through the gate. Continue to DinoLand U.S.A.

**8 AM:** Breakfast at Donald's "Prehistoric Breakfastosaurus" in DinoLand U.SA. Be sure to tell the hostess that your party has made prior arrangements with the management for special vegan or vegetarian meals.

**12 PM:** After spending the morning exploring DinoLand and Asia, head back to Guest Relations to retrieve your cooler. Enjoy your gourmet vegetarian goodies in the cool of the Oasis, or alongside Discovery River, then head to Camp Minnie-Mickey.

**2 PM:** Take some time to explore Safari Village. If you're feeling a bit peckish, grab a soft pretzel (100% vegan) from the Safari Pretzel Stand, or a piece of fruit from Harambe Fruit Market on the way into Africa.

**6 PM:** After spending the rest of the day in Africa and at Conservation Station, exit the park. Head back to your hotel for a quick shower and a nap, and then out to one of the more veg-friendly resort restaurants for dinner.

that the company might begin using irradiated produce to minimize spoilage. With news like this, the Rainforest Cafe's veg-friendly menu comes off seeming like a mixed blessing.

## Safari Village

### Worth a Mention in Safari Village

Located near the bridge to Camp Minnie-Mickey, ❸ **Pizzafari** offers two quick meals for vegetarians who eat dairy, but nothing for vegans (unless you're counting the frozen lemonade). The Hot Vegetable Sandwich—a tasty mix of yellow

# A Vegan Survival Guide to the AK

*Here's an accident waiting to happen: You're vegan and, having decided to visit the Animal Kingdom with your family, you begin to plan your day's adventure by scanning through these reviews and listings. Suddenly you're struck by a harsh reality: there's practically nothing for you to eat, short of salads and fruit!*

*Uh-oh. What are you going to do? Here are a few suggestions to help make your day in Disney's newest park gastronomically feasible:*

**1. Breakfast offers the most appealing** possibilities for guests on strict vegetarian diets. Stop at the Rainforest Cafe on your way into the park for the Paradise Plate—a huge platter of pineapple, kiwi, strawberries, and red seedless grapes. Or, for a true Disney experience, book a table at Donald's Prehistoric Breakfastosaurus inside the park—and be sure to speak with a chef or manager a couple of weeks in advance to arrange a palatable meal.

**2. If you feel like salad once lunchtime** rolls around, you could do worse than heading to Restaurantosauraus for the Vegetarian Platter—an Asian-influenced salad featuring broccoli, chow mein noodles, and a sesame vinaigrette. A similar concoction is available at Flame Tree Barbecue, but be sure to ask for their version of the Asian salad without turkey and without the bread bowl.

**3. Make your way to Chakranadi Chicken** Shop in Asia for a simple but delicious bowl of Japanese sticky rice and seasonal vegetables—the only truly vegan meal in the park.

**4. Bring your own bread to Tusker House,** and ask the chefs on duty to make your Marinated Vegetable Sandwich with your bread in place of the foccacia, and without the Havarti cheese. Side orders of salad or sautéed vegetables (ask for these without butter) round out your vegan meal. When conferring with chefs and servers, be sure to use the "V" word as much as possible, so they understand what it is you're after.

**5. If all this fussing and negotiating seems** like a bit too much, your best bet is simply to pack your own food and port it into the Animal Kingdom with you. The practice of bringing coolers into the theme parks is frowned upon for most guests, but an exception is made for people with special diets. Lockers are located on both sides of the Entrance Plaza.

squash, zucchini, onion, and green and red peppers—is topped with provolone cheese, Caesar salad, and pesto-marinated tomatoes, and served on a muffuletta roll. The pesto contains Romano cheese, and the muffuletta contains egg; no other rolls are available for substitution. If you want an entirely meatless meal, be sure to order the salad without Caesar dressing—it's chock full of anchovy paste. Instead, ask the kitchen to toss your lettuce with the oil and balsamic vinegar kept in the back. And if you're willing to wait an extra five minutes, it's possible to score a cheeseless pizza, made with seasonal vegetables like zucchini and yellow squash. But strict vegetarians beware: the pizza shells contain nonfat dried milk.

If you don't mind the smell of meat on the grill, stop in at ❺ **Flame Tree Barbecue**, near the bridge to DinoLand U.S.A. Inside you'll find a pretty decent salad. Ask for Flame Tree's Bread Bowl Salad without turkey, and in its place you'll get copious amounts of broccoli, tomato, onion, carrot, red cabbage, and kidney beans, topped with an Asian garlic and soy dressing. The salad is served in a sourdough bread bowl, which, according to the kitchen, is not vegan. Enjoy your feast outdoors at the

seating area alongside Discovery River. If the bread bowl doesn't appeal, pick up a soft pretzel from ❹ **Safari Pretzel Stand** nearby. They're 100% vegan. Cold bottled water is also available.

# Camp Minnie-Mickey

## Worth a Mention in Camp Minnie-Mickey

For a quick pick-me-up on your way to the Lion King Theater, ❷ **Chip 'n' Dale's Cookie Cabin** offers three tongue tempting options, but vegans beware: the chocolate chip cookies contain egg, the macadamia nut cookies contain milk, and the butter and sugar cookies contain… well… butter and sugar.

# DinoLand U.S.A.

## Best of the Best in DinoLand U.S.A.

✪  **"Donald's Prehistoric Breakfastosaurus"**
**Vegebility: Fair**
**Price: Expensive**
Casual American
Buffet/Table Service
B
DinoLand U.S.A.
Disney's Animal Kingdom
(407) 938-2905
MC/V/AE

𝓕or a comprehensive guide to our ratings system, see page xviii.

In the heart of DinoLand sits the McDonald's-owned Restaurantosaurus, unabashed testimony to the Walt Disney Company's ability to attract prominent corporate partners. Character breakfasts are a special treat at Breakfastosaurus, though, for one very important reason: it's one of only two places on property where you're certain to see Donald Duck (Chef Mickey's in the Contemporary Resort is the other). Along with Mickey, Pluto, and Goofy, the cuddly canard makes an appearance—with much fanfare—each morning. Surprisingly, though, there's more for vegetarians at Restaurantosaurus than the odd glimpse of everybody's favorite drake. Donald's Prehistoric Breakfastosaurus, the restaurant's breakfast buffet, is one of the most veg-friendly spots in the park, thanks to the kitchen's willingness to make meals not offered on the menu. Vegans or vegetarians who call the Restaurantosaurus's direct number (listed above) and speak with any manager will be pleasantly astonished at what can—and will—be done.

Given plenty of advance notice—48 hours minimum—Breakfastosaurus chefs are happy to make any dish you request. Egg- and dairy-free pancakes and crêpes, vegetarian breakfast meats, meat free breakfast potatoes (potatoes on the buffet are not vegetarian), and large fruit plates are all possible. Got a favorite dish you'd like them to prepare? Send the chefs a recipe and they'll make sure it's on your plate. And, assures Manager Kristen Catalano (in typical bend-over-backwards Disney style), "If there isn't a chef in the restaurant who can make what you want, we'll bring one in who can! If the ingredients aren't in the kitchen already," Kristen continues "there are lots of great stores nearby, and our chefs will be happy to pop out and pick up anything that's needed." This kind of flexibility makes Breakfastosaurus the best place at the Animal Kingdom for anyone with special dietary concerns.

After breakfast, Restaurantosaurus becomes another Animal Kingdom fast food vendor with relatively few concessions for vegetarians. The one meatless item featured on the menu is a salad, but at least it's an interesting one: mixed greens, broccoli, corn, tomato, and Chinese chow mein noodles, tossed with an Asian sesame vinaigrette.

## Worth a Mention in DinoLand U.S.A.

In addition to the mammoth turkey legs that seem to have spread throughout the parks, ❻ **Dino Diner** offers an assortment of fresh fruit and large tubs of popcorn, all blessedly healthful. Other vegan treats include orange juice, iced tea, and soft drinks. Cokes and the like are on offer at ❽ **DinoLand Snacks**, as are McDonald's french fries, no longer pre-soaked in beef tallow.

# Asia

## Best of the Best in Asia

🏯 **Chakranadi Chicken Shop**
**Vegebility: Fair**
**Price: Moderate**
Asian Kiosk
L, D, Snacks
Asia
Disney's Animal Kingdom
MC/V/AE

The name may not sound promising, but there's better veg food to be had at Chakranadi Chicken Shop than anywhere else in Animal Kingdom's Asia. And three out of five menu items are vegetarian, a better ratio than any other theme park eatery.

The menu's vegetarian items are authentic Japanese... almost. The vegan rice bowl is a savory mix of traditional Japanese yellow sticky rice and seasonal vegetables served in (here's the twist) a corn tortilla bowl. Ask for the chicken and Asian slaw wrap without the foul (oops, that's fowl), and you'll find yourself biting into a delicious ovo-lacto sandwich, with just a hint of fresh pear. Corn on the cob, roasted in the husk, is available vegan or dipped in melted butter. And although there was only a meat-based noodle bowl available at press time, kiosk managers promise that a vegan version will be available sometime in the year 2000—if there's enough demand. Be sure to stop by and register your vote for meatless alternatives!

## Worth a Mention in Asia

The heart of the Animal Kingdom's Asia is Anandapur, patterned after the rural villages of India, Thailand, and Indonesia. The Sanskrit name of this make-believe town means "place of bliss," but vegetarians visiting Anandapur didn't have much to be blissful about before November, 1999, when Disney installed a rice and noodle kiosk (see Chakranadi Chicken Shop review, this page). Before then the only place to get a

*Phun Phacts*

Chakranadi Chicken Shop's food may not be totally authentic, but the structure itself is. Animal Kingdom Imagineers saw the kiosk's arched gateways on a trip to Japan and, after clearing things with customs, brought them back—lock, stock, and barrel—to Orlando, re-assembling them on-site.

## An Idea for the Imagineers...

Traveling through India and Thailand, it's not too difficult to find low fat, healthful vegetarian meals. Unfortunately, this is not always the case in the Animal Kingdom's version of the East.

One way to mitigate the paucity of vegetarian food in the park would be to open a truly Asian restaurant in Asia. Food and Beverage gurus Dieter Hannig and Franz Kranzfelder both spent time cooking, working, and eating in the East, and both are fans of simple, Asian food. So how about opening an Indian restaurant, featuring traditional and delicious South Asian breads, curries, and tandoori specialties? Or a more upscale *Indochine* concept, with French-influenced Southeast Asian cuisine at its core? Disney guests are more than ready for a challenge to their taste buds!

**dapur Ice Cream Truck,** tuck into frozen yogurt or soft serve ice cream in an assortment of delicious dairy-rich concoctions. A **lemonade stand** offers popcorn, caramel corn, cotton candy, and refreshing frozen lemonade.

**"Where do you find great fast food?**

Great street food? It's in Asia. You go to the floating market in Bangkok, or to Snake Alley in Taipei... street food is instant and fresh. It's very flavor intensive.

– Dieter Hannig
VP of Food and Beverage, Walt Disney World

full meal was Mr. Kamal's Burger Grill—a distinctly un-veg friendly spot (try not to spend too much time puzzling about the placement of a burger joint in an Indian village where, according to tradition, cows are sacred).

Of course, you needn't worry about expiring from hunger: Anandapur offers the peckish guest a wealth of snacking opportunities. At ❾ **Drinkwallah**, you'll find fruit, rice crackers, and yogurt crackers, in addition to a selection of cool beverages. Nearby, at the ❿ **Anan-**

## Africa

### Best of the Best in Africa

⭐ **Harambe Fruit Market**
**Vegebility: Excellent**
**Price: Inexpensive–Moderate**
Snacks
Harambe Village
Disney's Animal Kingdom

Near the entrance to Kilimanjaro Safaris, the Harambe fruit market boasts the largest concentration

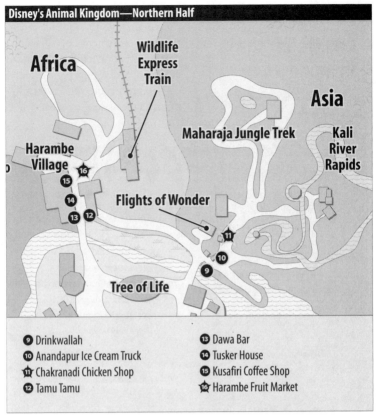

**Disney's Animal Kingdom—Northern Half**

Africa

Wildlife Express Train

Asia

Maharaja Jungle Trek

Kali River Rapids

Harambe Village

Flights of Wonder

Tree of Life

**9** Drinkwallah
**10** Anandapur Ice Cream Truck
**11** Chakranadi Chicken Shop
**12** Tamu Tamu

**13** Dawa Bar
**14** Tusker House
**15** Kusafiri Coffee Shop
**16** Harambe Fruit Market

of vegetarian items anywhere in the park. Bananas, oranges, apples, and pears are complemented by peanuts, raisins, and a selection of freshly squeezed juices. Chunks of juicy watermelon and grapes are also available. Keep your fingers crossed that something just as quick but more substantial—like a hummus and tabbouleh wrap or a black bean burrito or an Ethiopian flatbread topped with lentils—will be offered to vegan guests soon.

## Worth a Mention in Africa

In Disney's fictional East African village of Harambe, the main spot to grab a bite is **14** **Tusker House**. Outfitted like a safari orientation center, Tusker House offers its guests a delicious meatless entrée: the Marinated Vegetable Sandwich. Portobello mushrooms, yellow squash, and zucchini are roasted (separately from the meat served in the restaurant's other dishes), then topped with tomatoes, let-

# Veggie Kids in the Animal Kingdom

*Parents trying to raise their kids "off the grid" of meat, dairy, and egg products have a long row to hoe if they want to feed the family well in the Animal Kingdom. Your best bet is to bring your own food into the park or to share adult meals around the table.*

## Vegetarian Kids' Meals at Table Service Restaurants

### Rainforest Cafe (Entrance Plaza):
Breakfast: "Tonga Toast" french toast; cereal
Lunch and Dinner: Grilled cheese sandwich; cheese pizza; cheese ravioli

## Kid-Friendly Vegetarian Offerings at Counter Service Restaurants

### Chakranadi Chicken Shop (Asia):
Vegan rice bowl with seasonal vegetables; corn on the cob

### Pizzafari (Safari Village):
Cheese pizza; cheeseless pizza topped with grilled veggies (special order)

## Healthful Snacks

### Harambe Fruit Market (Africa):
Fresh whole fruit

### Tamu Tamu (Africa):
Low-fat vanilla and chocolate frozen yogurt

### Drinkwallah (Asia):
Fruit; rice crackers; yogurt crackers

### Dino Diner (DinoLand U.S.A.):
Fruit; popcorn

### Safari Pretzel Stand (Safari Village):
Soft pretzels

---

tuce, a tangy tabbouleh dressing, and Havarti cheese and served on foccaccia bread. Strict vegetarians should note that all Tusker House breads, including the foccaccia, contain egg or dairy products.

A makeshift meal for ovo-lacto vegetarians can be made from the restaurant's side dishes. Sautéed vegetables, mashed potatoes, and macaroni and cheese are all meatless; the house rice, however, is made with chicken stock. All sides contain dairy. The Tusker House Grilled Chicken Salad can be prepared without fowl, but the pretzel bread bowl is only suitable for diners who eat dairy and egg. A side salad is also available.

Just outside Tusker House, the ⓭ **Dawa Bar** is a great place to enjoy a cool drink and live, contemporary and traditional African music. Low-fat vanilla and chocolate frozen yogurts are on offer at ⓬ **Tamu Tamu**, and a selection of (high fat) pastries and coffees can be found at ⓯ **Kusafiri Coffee Shop**.

# Chapter 8

# Walt Disney World's Resorts

- - - - - - - - - - - - - - - - - - - - - - - - - - - - - - - - - - - - - - - - -

**Walt Disney World General Information:** *(407) 824-4321*
**Priority Seating Arrangements:** *(407) WDW-DINE (939-3463)*
**WDW Switchboard:** *(407) 824-2222*
*Call the switchboard to be transferred to
a chef at the restaurant where you'd like to dine.*

*I*n the past few years, the Walt
Disney Company has expanded Walt Disney World's lodging and dining
abilities enormously through the construction of themed resorts. It is
these vast resort complexes that people forget when they think of Walt
Disney World as just another Disneyland spread out over four theme
parks. It's much more than theme parks: it's a hospitality complex like
no other on the face of the earth.

More than 30,000 hotel rooms beckon to every demographic: business travelers attending conferences, newlyweds on their honeymoons,
cash-conscious families enjoying a total Disney vacation, single adults
looking for an educational experience at the Disney Institute. There
are nights during the year when every one of those 30,000 rooms is
booked—and all those people have to eat somewhere.

The best vegetarian food to be found on Disney property is served
in the resorts, give or a take a few standouts elsewhere. Restaurants
like Cinderella's Royal Table in the Magic Kingdom offer a dining
experience that can be very special. But the fundamental mission of
a theme park restaurant is to provide good value for money, while
still getting you out the door and on to the next attraction in a
reasonable time frame. On the other hand, just a few steps from
your room in the Grand Floridian or the Contemporary, you'll find
restaurants that give vaunted eateries in New York or Los Angeles a
run for their money.

## At-a-Glance Grid

# WDW Resorts: Best of the Best

**Key to Categories and Abbreviations**

**O/L, V: Ovo-lacto and vegan selections**

• - Always available    + - Available upon request    A - Request in advance

**Es: Type of establishment**

T - Table Service    C - Counter service    S - Snack stand or cart

**$: Average price for a single vegetarian entrée**

1 - under $10    3 - $16 - $20    5 - $31 - $40
2 - $10 - $15    4 - $21 - $30    6 - over $40

**Meals:**

B - Breakfast    L - Lunch    D - Dinner    S - Snacks

| Magic Kingdom Resorts | O/L | V | Es | $ | Meals |
|---|---|---|---|---|---|
| ❶ Artist Point | • | • | T | 3 | B, D |
| ❷ California Grill | • | • | T | 3 | D |
| ❸ Grand Floridian Cafe | • | + | T | 3 | B, L, D |
| ❸ Narcoossee's | • | A | T | 3 | L, D |
| ❸ Victoria & Albert's | • | A | T | 6 | D |
| ❹ Kona Cafe | • | • | T | 2 | B, L, D |
| **Epcot Resorts** | | | | | |
| ❺ Beaches & Cream Soda Shop | • | A | T | 1 | B, L, D, S |
| ❺ Yacht Club Galley | • | A | T | 2 | B, L, D |
| ❻ Coral Café | • | • | T | 2 | B |
| ❼ Garden Grove Café | • | A | T | 3 | B |
| ❽ Spoodles | • | + | T | 2 | B, L, D |
| **Downtown Disney Resorts** | | | | | |
| ❾ Seasons Dining Room | • | • | T | 2 | B, L, D |
| **Animal Kingdom Resorts** | | | | | |
| ❿ Pepper Market | + | + | C | 1 | B, L, D |

According to Walt Disney World Food and Beverage VP Dieter Hannig, the split between the two types of restaurant is no accident. "[An upscale restaurant concept] becomes a challenge if you have 45 minutes to dine, and you want to make it to another five attractions, and the kids want to ride the roller coaster," Hannig says. "You put the guest in a difficult situation there. Once you

## Magic Kingdom Resorts

The Magic Kingdom

World Drive

Monorail

Disney's Grand Floridian Resort and Spa ❸

❷ Disney's Contemporary Resort

■ River Country Water Park

❶ Disney's Wilderness Lodge

Disney's Polynesian Resort ❹

Seven Seas Dr

■

Fort Wilderness Trail

Shades of Green

Floridian Way

Monorail

Disney's Fort Wilderness Resort and Campground ■

Walt Disney World Speedway

Vista Boulevard

❶ Artist Point
❷ California Grill

❸ Grand Floridian Cafe, Narcoossee's, Victoria & Albert's
❹ Kona Cafe

take it out of the park environment, then it becomes more of a neutral ground. People come back to the resort—maybe they've had a shower and a little nap—then it's a little bit easier to have [a special] experience."

The restaurants included here are among the best of the best, chosen for their overall dining experience and their range of healthful possibilities—either on the menu, or hidden in the fertile brains of their magnificent master chefs. After a long, hot day of pounding the theme park pavement, head back to the room and relax—but

be sure you've made your Priority Seating arrangements at one of these resort restaurants for later in the evening. Even if you're staying off-property, the food is well worth the trip.

## Magic Kingdom Resorts

The resorts that border the Seven Seas Lagoon and Bay Lake are some of the finest that Walt Disney World has to offer. Disney's Contemporary and Polynesian Resorts, along with the Fort Wilderness Campground, were the only accommodations on prop-

# Where to Stay Veg at Walt Disney World

*On-property, off-property… What's a vegetarian to do? As is the case for any Walt Disney World visitor, there are pros and cons associated with both. If you do decide to stay in the Mouse's family compound, some venues are better than others in terms of nearby vegetarian options. Here are our recommendations to help you have the perfect vegetarian vacation.*

### Stay in an Epcot Resort

There are many reasons to stay near Epcot, but the most important one is the food: there are literally dozens of dining options within easy walking distance. **Disney's BoardWalk** boasts Spoodles, one of the best places to eat as a vegetarian, and the BoardWalk Bakery, featuring—hold on to your seats—vegan breakfast treats. There are even a few vegan beers on tap at Big River Brewing Company. The **Swan** and **Dolphin** Resorts offer a handful of outstanding restaurants: what can we say about a breakfast buffet that includes tofu? And there are at least four places to grab a vegetarian burger—the **Beach Club's** Beaches & Cream, the ESPN Club, the Dolphin's Cabana Bar, and the **Yacht Club** Galley. Best of all, the Epcot Resorts are less than a 15-minute walk from the restaurants of Epcot's World Showcase, some of which offer truly outstanding vegetarian meals, and are a short water launch to The Hollywood Brown Derby, Mama Melrose's and all the other restaurants at Disney-MGM Studios.

### Stay in a Magic Kingdom Resort

Another great option is to stay at the Magic Kingdom. Although some of the architecture may seem a bit tired—two of these, the **Contemporary** and the **Polynesian**, were the first hotels at

WDW—the restaurant scene is decidedly not, with some of the most innovative cuisine to be found on property. The leader of the pack is clearly the Contemporary's California Grill, with a West Coast menu sporting an array of options for even the most jaded vegetarian diner. Across the Seven Seas Lagoon at the **Grand Floridian** is Narcoossee's. Or, for a really special dining experience (planned many months in advance), you can indulge in Victoria & Albert's seven-course vegetarian and vegan "tasting menus," complete with selected wine pairings. Disney's newest culinary attraction is the Polynesian Resort's Kona Cafe, another excellent choice for meatless fare. If you're staying at the Contemporary, you're a brief, enjoyable boat ride from Artist Point at Disney's **Wilderness Lodge**, another standout for vegetarians thanks to Chef Anette Grecchi. And don't forget that the Contemporary, Polynesian, and Grand Floridian are direct monorail rides from the Magic Kingdom, expanding your dining options even more.

### Stay Elsewhere on Property—with a Car!

The Epcot and Magic Kingdom resorts offer some of the nicest accommodations at Walt Disney World, and are on direct boat or monorail routes to the most popular theme parks. They're great if you don't have a car. But there's a serious downside to staying at Epcot or the Magic Kingdom: it ain't cheap.

If you don't have upwards of $200 to spend on a room each night, your best bet is to do what lowly travel writers do: stay in a less expensive resort and rent the nicest car you can afford. This last part is critical for enjoying all the culinary delights the

*Continued on next page*

# Where to Stay...

*Continued from previous page*

World has to offer. Without a car, you're doomed to a torturous limbo of bus connections. Who wants to spend 4 hours just to get to and from dinner? Beleive it or not, it could easily happen to you...

With a car, the entire retinue of Disney dining options is yours to sample. You can buzz around Disney property from resort to resort, taking advantage of free self-parking or—for just a few bucks—valet curb-side service (the latter is especially handy if you're late for dinner). With a car, you might also head into Orlando to dine at one of the area's all-vegetarian restaurants, or at a fantastic Indian restaurant, something that's not available on property. In fact, with a car, you can even choose to stay somewhere other than on Disney property. Imagine the possibilities!

erty when the Vacation Kingdom opened in 1971. Today, they are still a major draw, along with Disney's Wilderness Lodge—a beautiful, arts-and-crafts structure inspired by the lodges of America's National Parks—and Walt Disney World's flagship retreat, the Grand Floridian Resort & Spa. All—with the exception of Fort Wilderness— offer top-notch vegetarian dining in convenient locations.

# Places to Eat

## Best of the Best in the Magic Kingdom Resorts

★ **Artist Point**
**Vegebility: Good**
**Price: Expensive**
Casual Pacific Northwest
Table Service
B, D
Disney's Wilderness Lodge
(407) 939-3463
MC/V/AE

The nicest way to arrive for dinner at Artist Point, the signature dining room in Walt Disney World's faux-rustic Wilderness Lodge, is by boat launch from the Ticket and Transportation Center. As you skim across the raw, untamed wavelets of man-made Bay Lake, the wind in your hair, your stomach dances in anticipation of the Northwest-inspired treats being cooked up in Chef Anette Grecchi's kitchen. The Lodge itself is a breathtaking amalgam of National Park Service lodges from the turn of the century, with rustic Arts and Crafts woodwork and cathedral ceilings that recall the primeval evergreen forests of the Pacific— but with unlimited dining options, of course.

*F* **or a comprehensive guide to our ratings system, see page xviii.**

# Anette Grecchi

*Grain Diva.*

Her nickname alone should clue you in to Anette Grecchi's passion for grains. Spelt, quinoa, couscous, and wheat berries sprout from plain old seeds into culinary art in her hands. When she isn't in the kitchen testing new recipes or giving symposiums at *Gourmet* magazine, Grecchi spends much of her free time surfing the web for nutritional information and global inspiration—or reading her latest copy of *Vegetarian Times*.

Chef at Artist Point since the Autumn of 1998, Grecchi started her career with the Walt Disney Company in Paris. After moving to the Vacation Kingdom, she did a stint with Clifford Pleau at the California Grill before snagging the top spot at Narcoossee's in the Grand Floridian. The move across the Seven Seas Lagoon to Disney's Wilderness Lodge has allowed Grecchi to come into her own, with mouth-watering menu temptations like sweet and succulent chilled Crenshaw melon soup, topped with crystallized ginger bits and sliced mint, or hearty, wild mushroom risotto—dishes that dovetail perfectly with Artist Point's Pacific Northwest motif. Grecchi has broadened the theme to include traditional Native People's cuisine, including the occasional native bread or vegetable dish.

Grecchi's philosophy of healthful eating is based upon a balanced vegetarian-inspired diet, and she rewards health-conscious diners with great flavors and new ideas about food. "We need to start educating our guests to think like vegetarians," she says. "We need to watch out for ourselves. Eating healthfully is proactive—it keeps the doctor away."

When you make your Priority Seating arrangements at Artist Point, mention this book and ask Grecchi to surprise you with a special vegetarian meal. And expect nothing short of nirvana.

Since trading her position at Narcoossee's with Robert Adams, Chef Grecchi has taken a vegetarian-friendly menu and expanded it, painting a true culinary portrait of the cuisines—both indigenous and imported—of North America's Pacific coastline.

Grecchi's interpretations of the continent's simplest and earliest comfort foods— earthy staples like whole grains, root vegetables, squash in autumn and melon in summer—mesh perfectly with the Craftsman-inspired woodwork of the Lodge's dining room. Look particularly for creative grain dishes, like the smooth and savory forest mushroom risotto.

To make the widest variety of food available to the largest audience, Grecchi builds many of her dishes, from the stocks right up to the seasonings, to be vegan-friendly, adding cream or meat only as a garnish. With a few minutes' notice, she and her team can whip up beautiful entrées that are a feast for the eyes as well as for the palate. "We can pretty much accommodate any special request with 48 hours' notice," she encourages. "If a guest calls us and lets us know that he or she is vegetarian, we'll let them know what is currently on the menu. We can find out right there and then if we need to make special arrangements for them and cook something special."

"Usually," Grecchi continues, "our vegetarian guests are amazed at what we can do." Amazed, and very pleased!

---

⭐ **California Grill**
**Vegebility: Good**
**Price: Expensive**
Casual/Upscale Californian
Table Service
D
Disney's Contemporary Resort
(407) 939-3463
MC/V/AE

High atop the Contemporary sits the California Grill, Walt Disney World's top candidate for the title of world-class dining destination. If the Contemporary looks a little dated—think 1979 techno-Maya, with a little Battlestar Galactica thrown in for good measure—the 15th-floor penthouse Grill is every bit a restaurant for the end of this Millennium. Servers in crisp black and white outfits bustle around the stunning "neo-deco" interior. The bar is packed with upscale Orlando natives and t-shirted vacationers waiting for their tables. The chefs in the open, "on stage" kitchen

are churning out the evening's 3,000-odd meals in a state of controlled hysteria. And that view… The restaurant's fifteenth-floor vista over the Magic Kingdom is breathtaking, to say the least.

The Grill's menu is comprised largely of, as one frustrated meat-and-potatoes man called it, "food I don't understand and whose names I cannot pronounce"—in other words, California cuisine: the market-driven foodie fuel pioneered by luminaries like

---

*"The California Grill was the first benchmark, the trend setter which everything else followed.*

*There is such a confidence level in the kitchen there. Sometimes I arrive late at night. I sit alone, on the corner of the pastry counter, and I watch it. And it's just beautiful. They have a mastery over there, of treating people with respect. There are certain things that you just cannot explain. It's my special place."*

*— Dieter Hannig*
VP of Food and Beverage, Walt Disney World

# Clifford Pleau

*Chef Clifford Pleau and his daughter Nicole*

Tired of "vegetarian plates?" Portobello mushroom everything? "Garden" *anything*? If you're looking for vegetarian fare that defies categories and breaks molds, Clifford Pleau, chef at the California Grill atop Disney's Contemporary Resort, would like to invite you to dinner.

Pleau has won national acclaim with his attention to the diner's experience. In 1998, USAToday said he serves the "Best Meal in America" and Wine Spectator tapped him as a "Rising Star of American Cuisine." His ability to delight even the most beaten-down portobello-burnout vegetarian is so complete, he scoffs at the half-hearted attempts of his less respectful colleagues in kitchens elsewhere.

"Other places say, 'We can serve vegetarian, too,' and they tack a plate down in the corner of the menu. What's up with that? Or they say, 'Oh, vegetarian? Sit over there.' Here you don't feel like an oddball when you order vegetarian. And you know it's going to be something special, not some blah side dish." Thanks to Pleau, many of the "new concept" restaurants at the Walt Disney World Resort—like Spoodles and the Flying Fish—are very vegetarian friendly.

And we mean very. Though he's not vegetarian himself, Pleau has created meat-free zones in the California Grill's on-stage kitchen where only vegetarian items are prepared. Why? Because he knows it's important to us.

"The other day I caught a guy using the wrong spatula, and I read him the riot act," says Pleau. "Meats never go where the fish is; tofu never touches either. Most cooks will say, 'A little residue won't hurt 'em.' But after working for a lot of people for many years, you learn what's important."

The proof of Pleau's passion is in the food he and his team deftly prepare—dishes like Mesquite Roasted Tofu, served on lemongrass skewers, or Grilled Salinas Asparagus drizzled with citrus butter, or smooth but tangy Sonoma Goat Cheese Ravioli, topped with shiitake mushrooms, basil, and sundried tomatoes. *Mmmm...* And now, along with a few other talented chefs, he's devising an equally tempting vegetarian menu for a new restaurant in the Safari Lodge. As long as Pleau is involved with the opening of a restaurant, we can almost guarantee it'll be a good bet for vegetarians.

Wolfgang Puck and Alice Waters. Chef Clifford Pleau paid his dues in many a West Coast kitchen, but he also brings classical French training to dishes like his savory Brick Oven Flatbread, smothered in grilled mushrooms, roasted garlic, caramelized red onions, and feta cheese. Not surprisingly, the California Grill's fertile mix of garden-derived cuisines makes the place a haven for vegetarians.

"How many times," asks Pleau, "do you go into a place, and they say, 'Well, we'll just reduce cream, throw all the veggies in it, throw it over some noodles, and call it a vegetarian dish.' We try to do the opposite, and *not* make pasta a vegetarian concept.

"Instead, we explore different unconventional cooking methods, like roasting on a grill. The flavor is incredible, on something as simple as tofu; just baste it in lemon and soy, roast it on an oak-burning grill, and you get a whole different experience out of it!"

For a few delicious embodiments of Pleau's philosophy, ask your server for "Vegetarian Unplugged," a tempting medley of vegetarian and vegan side dishes, such as soft, creamy polenta, zippy Asian slaw, or a garden fresh, hearty vegetable ratatouille doused in a tomato basil sauce and sprinkled with olive oil. An exemplary, all-California wine list rounds out the restaurant's offerings.

Dinner at the California Grill costs about what a fine meal would in any American city. But like most Walt Disney World restaurants (and unlike restaurants in most American cities), the guest experience is almighty, and service is first class. So feel free to ask for something special if the menu's vegetarian selections don't exactly float your boat. Two caveats, though: first, portions can be small, espe-

cially when compared with the gargantuan plates offered in most American eateries. And second, be sure to tell the chef what you don't like before giving him or her free reign to astonish and delight you. You may end up with something you can't pronounce, understand—or eat.

---

**Grand Floridian Cafe**
**Vegebility: Good**
**Price: Moderate**
Casual American
Table Service
B, L, D
Disney's Grand Floridian Resort & Spa
(407) 939-3463
MC/V/AE

A spacious, light-filled atrium overlooking the resort's pool and gardens, the Grand Floridian Cafe boasts a surprising complement of vegetarian and vegan meals. At lunchtime, no fewer than five veg-friendly entrées can be prepared. And, as an added bonus, the cafe gets high marks for service and ambience, too. Two vegan flatbread pizzas—including one topped with roasted red peppers, portobello mushrooms, asparagus, sweet onions, and optional Asiago cheese—are serious mid-day

temptations. Or how about the Mediterranean Vegetable Pasta (penne tossed with red pepper, zucchini, black olives, mushrooms, yellow squash, and sprinkled with Feta cheese) or a portobello mushroom lavosh "wrap" sandwich? Leave off the Feta on the former, or the cream cheese on the latter, for a completely dairy- and egg-free meal.

If you're in the mood for something different, ask Chef Marie Grimm for the (totally vegan) Cuban hot pressed sandwich to be made with roasted veggies instead of meat. *Muy bueno*!

---

☆ **Kona Cafe**
   **Vegebility: Fair**
   **Price: Expensive**
   Casual Pan-Asian
   Table Service
   B, L, D
   Disney's Polynesian Resort
   (407) 939-3463
   MC/V/AE

Formerly the Coral Isle Cafe, the Kona Cafe has been refurbished and restyled as a casual Pan-Asian restaurant and coffee bar. Since its opening in late 1998, Kona Cafe has become a gathering place for people seeking delicious meatless meals, thanks to the tireless and creative work of Chef John Guillemette and his talented team.

Although the menu doesn't look terribly veg-friendly, nearly

# A Bug's Lunch

Wanna commune with some cute creepy-crawlies and help yourself, Walt Disney World, and the environment, all at the same time? Participate in a ladybug "release party," held Thursday mornings at Disney's Polynesian and Wilderness Lodge Resorts. You don't need to be a resort guest to help with the release. Just call ahead to find out when and where it will occur, then show up ready to be crawled on!

The release of even a hundred ladybugs is a decidedly low-key "attraction." A cast member will give you a matchbox containing ladybugs and will tell you how best to place the little critters on the plants. Once deployed, the ladybugs then go to work, combating aphids and other pests as part of the resort's Integrated Pest Management program. A more environmentally-friendly way to rid the Vacation Kingdom of unwanted insects, the program has resulted in a 90% reduction in the use of insecticides throughout the theme parks, and more than 70% elsewhere on property. As a volunteer, you'll get a little something for your efforts, too. Cast members often give participants a Ladybug Release Certificate, Jiminy Cricket Environmentality stickers, or a pocket magnifying glass.

So, how do the ladybugs combat aphids and other pests? Well, let's just say that there are very few vegetarian ladybugs, if any. You won't find your new buddy chowing down on scrambled tofu at the Kona Cafe; she's more likely to be munching on Aphids Benedict on a leaf outside. Ladybugs, like many insects, are decidedly carnivorous. *Vive la difference!*

all stocks, soups, and many dishes are wholly meatless, providing a cornucopia of options for vegetarian diners. John's larder is stocked full of items like tofu and an array of interesting grains, and his brain is equally full of ideas for turning these raw ingredients into a great meatless meal.

A morning at Kona Cafe would not be complete without Tonga Toast: a thick and sticky breakfast creation similar to French toast, but with a luscious ripe banana tucked in between the layers of bread. With just a little notice, the kitchen is happy to prepare a vegan Tonga Toast, or a meal of scrambled tofu and vegetarian hash browns (the Cafe's standard breakfast potatoes contain lard).

One of the best things on the menu at lunch and dinner is the Asian noodle soup, a 44-ounce bowl of steaming broth made with miso and—unfortunately—flakes of bonito, a small Asian tuna. 24 hours' notice will get you a completely vegetarian bowl of aromatic, steaming soup made with fresh Asian vegetables and soba noodles, and topped with small squares of tofu. It's simple, and simply delicious.

Nowadays, more and more restaurants feature show kitchens. But the Kona Cafe has a show *dessert* kitchen—tribute to the genius of the Cafe's pastry chefs. All of them are adept at designing and implementing wondrous vegan desserts, using seasonal fruits and dark chocolate as a springboard to confectionery heaven. Be sure to give at least 24 hours' notice for vegan desserts. For vegetarians who don't mind eggs and dairy in their desserts, the sky's the limit.

And, yes, Kona Cafe does serve aromatic and intensely caffeinated Kona coffee from Hawaii. What a great way to end an extraordinary meal! —*Thanks to gardenia for her help with this review.*

---

**☆ Narcoossee's**
**Vegebility: Fair**
**Price: Expensive**
Casual Seafood/American
Table Service
L, D
Disney's Grand Floridian Resort & Spa
(407) 939-3463
MC/V/AE

Narcoossee's had long been a favorite of the steak-and-seafood set until 1997, when veg-friendly Chef Anette Grecchi took over the kitchen of this picturesque restaurant on the Seven Seas lagoon. Vegetarians breathed a sigh of relief upon seeing dishes like marinated grilled zucchini served with focaccia bread, or wild mushroom risotto, on the menu. But Narcoossee's regular customers, saddened by the transformation of their comfortable Surf n' Turf hideaway, stopped coming.

> " *You know what's unique about all the chefs that are here?*
>
> *We each have, number one: passion for food; number two: passion for people. We prepare everything from scratch ourselves. We have an undying pursuit of the freshest ingredients. We each have our own concept, but the same high standards.*"
>
> – Clifford Pleau
> *Chef, California Grill*

Since then, Grecchi has traded places with Artist Point Chef Robert Adams, whose way with comfort food won him many a fan—vegetarian and otherwise—at the Wilderness Lodge. In his new position, Adams is focusing less on veg-friendly innovations than on winning back Narcoossee's old clientele, but vegetarians who aren't afraid to do a little negotiating can still eat quite well here with advance notice. For a very special vegetarian meal, call to speak with the chef a week before your visit.

The menu is generally lean on veggie selections, but what's there bears the mark of Adams' genius

for rich, mellow flavors. A salad of mesclun greens and warm peaches is enlivened by rice wine-ginger dressing and sweet roasted pecans. For an Indonesian-inspired appetizer, try the portobello mushroom satays (usually accompanied by beef): the mushroom strips are marinated in coconut milk and served with a spicy vegetable relish and a peanutty dipping sauce. Ask for the relish without honey, and the morsels are entirely vegan. There's always at least one vegetarian entrée on the menu—like sweet corn risotto topped with grilled vegetables, served with a tomato coulis—but chefs like Adams encourage diners to work with them to create a unique and inspired entrée all their own.

For the guiltless gourmets among us, fresh fruit sorbets are available to cleanse the palate and delight the tastebuds. But for a total sensory overload, try a dessert that's fast becoming a Narcoossee's favorite, the tantalizing vegan "berry stack": seasonal fresh berries sautéed with Chambord liquer and sugar, served between two small pieces of white bread soaked in the berry juice and Chambord mixture. *Irresistible!*

⚑ **Victoria & Albert's**
**Vegebility: Good**
**Price: Very Expensive**
Elegant American/Continental
Table Service
D
Disney's Grand Floridian Resort & Spa
(407) 939-3463
MC/V/AE

The most elegant restaurant on Disney property is also one of the best places for vegetarians to enjoy a special meal. We owe it all to Chef Scott Hunnel and the talented staff at Victoria & Albert's— rated the number one restaurant in Orlando and among the top ten in the country by the Zagat Guide (for a profile of Hunnel, see page 129). At a little over $100 a person, guests are offered seven-course "tasting menus"—complete with selected wine pairings—in an intimate, beautifully appointed dining room. A harpist plays softly in the background as your personal maid and butler ("Victoria" and "Albert") see to your every need. And believe us, these people know what you need.

An ovo-lacto vegetarian tasting menu is always available, but given 24 hours' notice, Hunnel and crew can put together a vegan feast you'll not soon forget, or a special vegetarian menu to suit your personal tastes. They even offer a seven-course vegetarian truffle menu when the pungent fungi are in season (from late fall to midwinter).

Vegetarians used to being treated like second-class citizens in upscale restaurants will come away feeling downright pampered. In Hunnel's capable hands, diners are showered with delicacies like hand-gathered forest mushroom risotto with Piedmont white truffles, or a grilled eggplant roulade with quinoa, roasted barley, and 100-year-aged balsamic vinegar. The restaurant's serene ambience, the congenial professionalism of your servers, the soothing harp music, and the measured flow of textures and flavors cascading across your taste-buds transport you to a plane where all is as it should be, where your personal pleasure is the goal of every right-thinking individual.

If you aspire to culinary greatness—or at least competency—you can get some tips from the masters by watching the talented kitchen staff prepare your meal at the Chef's Table. This four-person table tucked into an alcove of the Victoria & Albert's kitchen is extremely popular, and with good reason—Chef's Table diners typically get the opportunity to sample what the other patrons have ordered, as well as their own meals. Chef's Table patrons are also free to wander about the kitchen, ask questions, take photos or have them taken with the ever-obliging

V & A kitchen staff. But beware: you may not want too many little tastes of your omnivorous fellow diners' meals... and even if you do, you should put in your reservation at least 180 days (yes, six months) in advance. Regular diners should make dining arrangements four months ahead.

## Worth a Mention at the Magic Kingdom Resorts

### Disney's Contemporary Resort

You can't get vegetarian vittles much better than those at the Contemporary's California Grill. (see review on page 107). But if you're staying in the resort and need a casual spot for breakfast, head over to the **Food and Fun Center**, located on the first floor of the Tower. The snack bar here is open from 6:00 AM until midnight, and at breakfast offers a variety of fruit, cereal, breakfast breads, and egg dishes.

**Chef Mickey's** serves a buffet character breakfast attended by Mickey, Minnie, Donald, Chip, Dale and Goofy. The usual ovo-lacto dishes are always on the buffet (including cheesy breakfast potatoes), but a number of alternatives—like vegan cheeses and soy milk—are kept in the back. With a little advance notice, chefs are happy to prepare an individual meal for guests with special dietary needs. Fax them your favorite recipe, and enjoy it as soon as the next day! Priority Seating arrangements are recommended.

### Disney's Grand Floridian Resort and Spa

Another character breakfast—this one featuring stars from Alice in Wonderland and Mary Poppins—can be found across the Seven Seas Lagoon at **1900 Park Fare**. Enjoy a large selection of lighter fare at the buffet, including fresh seasonal fruit, yogurt, oatmeal, and an assortment of breakfast breads. For a deliciously decadent afternoon tea—complete with crumpets, tea sandwiches, scones and Devonshire clotted cream—visit the **Garden View Lounge** between 3 and 6 PM.

### Disney's Polynesian Resort

**Captain Cook's Snack Company**, open around the clock, is a good spot to pick up a continental breakfast or a fresh fruit plate. **'Ohana**, the other dining venue at the resort, serves all-you-can-eat family-style meals with slim pickin's (salad, spring rolls and stir-fried vegetables) for vegetarians. Your best bet at dinnertime is to make your Priority Seating for the very veg-friendly Kona Cafe (review on page 110).

### Disney's Wilderness Lodge

For a quick breakfast at Wilderness Lodge, head downstairs to **Roaring Forks**, a small snack bar offering oatmeal, cold cereal, eggs, muffins, and vegan bagels. Cheese pizza,

# Veggie Kids at the MK Resorts

*There's no question that the California Grill's Rice Krispies sushi takes the cake when it comes to innovative children's fare. Children's meals at the other Magic Kingdom resorts rely somewhat more on noodles, cheese, and the ubiquitous PBJ, but there's some decent food to be had. Still, your best bet may be to eschew the kiddie menu and share two or three adult meals around the table.*

## Vegetarian Kids' Meals at Table Service Restaurants

**Artist Point (Wilderness Lodge):**
Macaroni and cheese; bowl of fresh strawberries

**California Grill (Contemporary):**
Peanut butter and jelly sandwich; macaroni and cheese; tomato and provolone cheese pizza; market fresh fruit cocktail; home-baked cookies; Rice Krispies sushi

**Grand Floridian Cafe (Grand Floridian):**
Breakfast: French toast; Mickey-shaped waffles; pancakes; fruit cup; oatmeal; cold cereals
Lunch and Dinner: Peanut butter and jelly sandwich; Mickey Mouse pasta with choice of cheese or marinara sauce; cheese pizza; grilled cheese sandwich

**Kona Café (Polynesian):**
Breakfast: Cold cereals; scrambled eggs; cinnamon toast; Mickey-shaped buttermilk pancakes; French toast; "Goofy Toast" (eggs in a basket)
Lunch and Dinner: Grilled cheese sandwich; peanut butter and jelly sandwich

**Whispering Canyon Cafe (Wilderness Lodge):**
Breakfast: Buttermilk pancakes; Belgian waffles
Lunch: Grilled cheese sandwich; peanut butter and jelly sandwich
Dinner: Macaroni and cheese; grilled cheese sandwich

## Kid-Friendly Vegetarian Offerings at Counter Service Restaurants

**Roaring Forks (Wilderness Lodge):**
Breakfast: Oatmeal; cold cereal; eggs; muffins; vegan bagels
Lunch and dinner: Cheese pizza; peanut butter and jelly sandwich

salad, and peanut butter and jelly sandwiches are available throughout the day. In a hurry? Grab some fruit or a low fat Quaker fruit bar from the **Wilderness Lodge Coffee Bar** in the lobby.

If you eat eggs and dairy, you can tuck into a bigger breakfast at the **Whispering Canyon Cafe**. The Miner is a three-egg frittata stuffed with red and green peppers, onion, and Tillamook cheddar, served with veg-friendly potatoes. French toast, waffles, and flap jacks are all available. If you need something without eggs or dairy, call Chef Richard Jennings a week in advance to plan your menu. And if you really want to start your day off with a bang, order "Craig's Creation": perfectly healthful oatmeal, deliciously corrupted with caramelized brown sugar, vanilla ice cream and a whiskey glaze.

Yee-HAW! At dinner, your best bet is to head over to Artist Point and put yourself in Chef Anette Grecchi's capable hands (see review on page 105). The only meatless option at Whispering Canyon is the "Vegetarian Skillet": sautéed veggies served with rice and corn on the cob.

**Miss Jenny's In-Room Dining** at the Lodge is good—if a bit pricey—for breakfast. Whole grain pancakes, a fresh fruit plate, oatmeal waffles, continental breakfasts, and yogurt are just a phone call (and a delivery charge) away.

### Disney's Fort Wilderness Resort and Campground

If you're staying at Fort Wilderness, there's nothing better than making your own fixin's on your private campfire—or in the kitchenette of your faux rustique Wilderness Home. Stop at the **Chuck Wagon**, not far from the campfire area, for an individual pizza, popcorn, or nachos. If you forgot to pack up marshmallows and your whittlin' knife, never fear: the Chuck Wagon sells marshmallows, complete with pre-whittled roasting sticks, for just $1.89, or an entire "S'mores Pack" for a few bucks

extra. Fruit juice and frozen fruit bars are also available. Pick up a late night cheese pizza from the **Trail's End Buffeteria** between 9:30 and 11 PM.

### Shades of Green

If you're among the lucky few able to bed down at Shades of Green—an upscale Disney resort with low, low prices, limited to U.S. military and their families—you'll be somewhat disappointed by the vegetarian selections at the restaurants. **Evergreens**, a sports bar serving lunch and dinner, used to offer vegetarian items, but removed them from the menu because they didn't sell. **The Garden Gallery** is a step up in food quality and selection. Appetizers include cheese ravioli, house salad, and a fruit plate, and pasta primavera is available as an entrée. Speak with chefs at the restaurant at least three days in advance for a more intriguing meal.

# Epcot Resorts

Staying at one of the resorts surrounding Epcot means being within easy walking distance of nearly two dozen restaurants, many of which offer outstanding vegetarian options. At Epcot's World Showcase, Disney's BoardWalk, or in one of the other Disney resorts, you'll have your pick of the cuisines of many nations—from

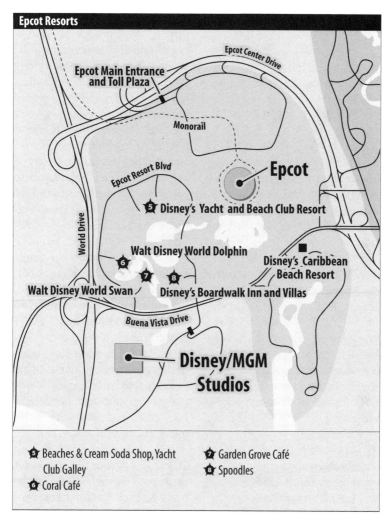

**Epcot Resorts**

- 5 Disney's Yacht and Beach Club Resort
- Epcot
- Walt Disney World Dolphin
- 6
- Walt Disney World Swan
- 7 8
- Disney's Boardwalk Inn and Villas
- Disney's Caribbean Beach Resort
- Disney/MGM Studios

Epcot Main Entrance and Toll Plaza

Monorail

Epcot Resort Blvd

World Drive

Buena Vista Drive

Epcot Center Drive

5 Beaches & Cream Soda Shop, Yacht Club Galley
6 Coral Café
7 Garden Grove Café
8 Spoodles

veggie sushi at Kimonos in the Swan to spicy Tunisian harissa at Spoodles to light but decadent millefeuille pastry at Les Chefs de France. And you'll be just a short boat launch to Disney-MGM Studios, where even more delicious decisions await!

## Places to Eat

### Best of the Best in the Epcot Resorts

5 **Beaches & Cream Soda Shop**
Vegebility: Fair

**Price: Inexpensive–Moderate**
Casual American
Table Service
B, L, D
Disney's Beach Club Resort
(407) 939-3463
MC/V/AE

A cozy ice cream parlor, the decor of Beaches & Cream is straight out of the turn of the century. Fortunately, at least one item on the menu is not! In addition to ice cream sodas, shakes, oversized sundaes, and decadent deserts, Beaches and Cream serves the "Flip Side": a grilled veggie burger on a toasted multi-grain bun, served with a side of seasonal fruit. Because seating is limited, the wait at the restaurant is often long. But if you've just left Epcot and are feeling a bit peckish, or if you've decided to stick around the pool for a lazy day, Beaches & Cream is a great place for a snack or a light lunch.

---

✪ **Coral Café**
**Vegebility: Good**
**Price: Moderate–Expensive**
Casual American/Japanese
Breakfast Buffet
B
Walt Disney World Dolphin Resort
(407) 934-4000
All major credit cards accepted

Looking for a breakfast buffet with something more than heat-lamped home fries and sausage gravy? Something like—tofu? Look no further than the Coral Café, a bright and airy restaurant on the ground floor of the Walt Disney World Dolphin. The Café offers one of the best value-for-money breakfasts for a vegetarian—if a big (and we mean BIG) breakfast is what you're after.

Both the Swan and the Dolphin are partly owned by a Japanese company, so both hotels see a lot of Japanese visitors. Thanks to them, the restaurant has a separate "Japanese buffet" featuring not only tofu, but other traditional Japanese breakfast foods, including steamed rice. Be warned, however, that the miso soup on the Japanese buffet (inexplicably) contains chicken stock.

At the larger American buffet, health-conscious western diners can tuck into more familiar morning goodies, including hot cereals, fresh fruit, and an assortment of juices and herbal teas. There are even a few vegan pastries and Danishes; ask your server to point them out (recipes are kept in the back for verification). For ovo-lacto vegetarians, delicious huevos rancheros, vegetable frittatas, made-to-order omelets, and eggs any way you like 'em are available at the hot bar. And if you have a sweet tooth, you're sure to be tempted by the never-ending supply of pancakes, French toast, waffles, and fruit-filled crêpes.

If filling up on lots of eggs and pancakes before heading over to Space Mountain doesn't sound wise, the Café offers a smaller version of the buffet. Stick to continental breakfast items—pastries, fruits and cereals—and receive a price reduction (about 2/3 the cost of the entire buffet).

---

**✪ Garden Grove Café**
**Vegebility: Fair**
**Price: Expensive**
Casual American
Breakfast Buffet
B
Walt Disney World Swan Resort
(407) 934-4000
All major credit cards accepted

The Garden Grove Café offers a bountiful all-you-can eat breakfast buffet that should satisfy any ovo-lacto vegetarian. An assortment of egg dishes, potatoes, waffles, and other breakfast breads are served in a beautiful garden atrium, which at night becomes Gulliver's Grill.

The Garden Grove's chefs are willing to bend over backward to accommodate vegans, as well, given 48 hours' advance notice. Scrambled tofu, vegan biscuits and "gravy," and an endless variety of potatoes can be specially made just for you. While chefs at the Café might not be as knowledgeable about special diets as others on property, they are eager to learn

and gracious in the final presentation. —*Thanks to gardenia for her help with this review.*

---

**✪ Spoodles**
**Vegebility: Good**
**Price: Expensive**
Casual Mediterranean
Table Service
B, L, D
Disney's BoardWalk
(407) 939-3463
MC/V/AE

Though it's located at the heart of Disney's increasingly popular BoardWalk resort, Spoodles is still-something of a best-kept secret among Disney diners. The restaurant's extremely veg-friendly menu, inspired by the cuisines of the Mediterranean, was inaugurated by former Chef David Reynoso and has been expanded by Chef Bart Hosmer to include regional American influences. Hosmer cut his Disney teeth next door at the sophisticated Flying Fish with Chef John State, and despite the cultural differences between the two restaurants—the urbane and adult Fish versus chaotic and family-oriented Spoodles—Hosmer's bold, freewheeling approach goes well with the vibrant "cuisines of the sun" concept at the center of Spoodles' menu.

Spoodles' Breakfast Buffet is extremely popular, and ovo-lacto vegetarians can choose from the

" *F*ood could be considered entertainment.

*But we're going back to the basics.
We're trying to provide
an environment where
the food and the service
are the key."*

*— Dieter Hannig*
VP of Food & Beverage, Walt Disney World

usual American fare, or more global dishes like frittatas, breakfast pizza, and an unusual breakfast "wrap" with hummus, eggplant, zucchini, and olive oil in phyllo dough.

But while other restaurants revert to the Vegetarian Plate mentality after the breakfast hour, Spoodles' veggie options multiply as the day goes on. At lunch, Hosmer complements Mediterranean classics—pizza margherita, an heirloom tomato salad—and the obligatory portobello mushroom sandwich with creative leaps like a roasted beet salad with roasted walnuts, pecorino romano cheese, and a citrus vinaigrette.

Dinnertime ushers in a whole vegetarian segment of the menu—almost unheard of at a Disney restaurant—in addition to plenty of oak-fired flatbreads, interesting salads, and the intriguing Chef's Vegetarian Tour: a selection of grains, veggies, and starches from elsewhere on the menu. There's also the option of adding oak roasted organic tofu to any item for just $3. Vegans will find cheese in almost everything, but it's usually used as a savory garnish. Most Spoodles dishes can be easily "veganized" with plenty of bold Mediterranean flavor to spare. If you enjoy fine wines, your server will invite you to try a few, free of charge, before you decide to order a glass or a bottle.

If you're staying at Disney's BoardWalk resort, don't miss Spoodles' walk-up pizza counter, providing a perfect meal to enjoy sitting outside by the water, or as a less hectic dinner in your room.

---

**☆ Yacht Club Galley**
**Vegebility: Fair**
**Price: Expensive**
Casual American
Table Service
B, L, D
Disney's Yacht Club Resort
(407) 939-3463
MC/V/AE

The traditional-looking gray and white clapboard exterior of Disney's Yacht Club is modeled after New England seaside resorts, with a nautical theme that carries through to the resort's sunny, bright interiors. The coastal resort motif is also seen in the décor of the casual Yacht Club Galley, with brightly tiled tables arranged amid model ships and pictures of people "simply messing about in boats," to quote Kenneth Grahame. Maybe it's the seafaring theme, but the Yacht Club Galley's menu, and its monthly vegetarian dinner specials, show the influence of virtually every global cuisine.

Chef Roger Hill, also the Chef at the Yachtsman Steakhouse, has designed a menu with the input of several vegan and vegetarian staffers, and their involvement has made a marked improvement in the restaurant's offerings in the past year or so. With two days' notice, Chef Hill and his staff will prepare an elaborate vegan meal for you or your party, whether for breakfast, lunch, or dinner. Little or no notice is necessary for most ovo-lacto diners or less exacting vegans.

For breakfast, the Galley provides an enormous buffet featuring pancakes, breakfast pastries, oatmeal, scrambled eggs, frittatas, fresh fruit, broiled tomatoes, cobblers, sushi, and rice (the miso soup, however, is made with a fish stock). À la carte table service is also available. Your pre-arranged vegan breakfast could include scrambled tofu, vegan pancakes, and a delicious mix of sweet and white potatoes.

Lunch offerings include a grilled vegetable Napoleon served with herbed ravioli, or a smoky-tasting black bean and vegetable burger—designed by one of the kitchen's prep chefs—served on a cracked whole wheat bun and accompanied by vegetable chips. For something fresher and more subtle, try an entrée-sized spinach salad, topped with an inspired apple-walnut dressing.

But it's at dinner that the Galley's globetrotting influences really come through, from a hearty onion soup made with Guiness stout and cheese to a deeply flavored vegan risotto topped with grilled vegetables. And then there's dessert: with a couple of days' advance notice, Chef Hill and his staff will have dairy- and egg-free—but still decadent—after dinner confections waiting especially for you.

—*Thanks to gardenia for her help with this review.*

## Worth a Mention at the Epcot Resorts

### Disney's BoardWalk Inn & Villas

A large shopping and evening entertainment complex, Disney's BoardWalk offers a cornucopia of options for vegetarian and vegan diners. Located next door to Spoodles (our favorite dinner destination; see review on page 119) is the **Flying Fish Cafe**, architect Marty

# Facts for Foodies

**H**ey, waiter! There's a fish in my beer! *Sound odd? A bit unappealing?*

*U*nfortunately, it's likely to be true! A majority of beers in this country and abroad are "fined" or clarified with a substance known as isinglass: a type of gelatin from the air bladders of fish, usually sturgeon. Other fining materials include animal-based gelatin, egg whites and shells, or diatomaceous earth—a sand-like "soil" made from the skeletons of diatoms: single-celled algæ.

*N*early all cask-conditioned ales are fined using isinglass. Many boutique or handcrafted beers—typically the darker porters and stouts—are not. No traditional German beers are fined with animal ingredients, nor are American beers from Rolling Rock, Pete's, or Anheuser-Busch. While you're at Disney's BoardWalk, be sure to stop in at Big River Grille and Brewing Works to sample a few all-veg beers for yourself.

*F*or more information on vegetarian beers, wines, and ciders, consult the Vegetarian Society of the United Kingdom's Website: http://www.vegsoc.org/Info/alcohol.html.

Dorf's masterful homage to Coney Island and its coasters. The Fish's seasonal dinner menu changes nightly and places an emphasis on seafood and healthful entrees, including one vegetarian selection —frequently a pasta dish. Give Chef John State some advance notice, however, and he'll happily apply his prodigious talent to something special just for you. Be sure to leave room for the Warm Chocolate Lava Cake with Liquid Chocolate Center and Tarragon Crème Anglaise.

In the morning, stroll over to the **BoardWalk Bakery**, one of the few places on property where you can find vegan breakfast goodies. Cherry and apple turnovers are 100% egg- and dairy-free, and fruit tarts and baguettes are darn close—the latter two are lightly sprayed with an egg white wash before baking. The Bakery opens daily at 6:30 AM, giving you plenty of time to grab a bite before heading to the parks.

Wondering where you can find a strictly vegetarian microbrew on property? Move clockwise around the BoardWalk until you hit the **Big River Grille and Brewing Works**. According to former Brew Master Ken Akins, Wowzer's Wheat and Tilt Ale are 100% vegetarian, and nine out of ten specialty beers brewed seasonally at Big River will be as well. Always ask a manager to be certain.

Down at the other end of the BoardWalk, the **ESPN Club**—a high-tech sports bar—offers no fewer than three vegetarian entrées. Cool off during a hot day with a lemonade and an "In the Pocket Pita:" pita bread loaded with chilled, marinated grilled vegetables, cucumbers, and sprouts, and served with chips or fresh fruit. Or stop your tummy from rumbling with an ovo-lacto Gardenburger®, or "Bull Penne Pasta"—grilled, sautéed vegetables, puréed tomatoes, garlic, and basil tossed with penne.

### Disney's Caribbean Beach Resort

The sit-down dining destination at the Caribbean Beach Resort is the **Captain's Tavern**, best known for its decidedly un-vegetarian prime rib, chicken, and pork loin. Meatless menu items include an appetizer-sized garden salad and "Paradise Pasta:" garden vegetables and pasta in your choice of an herbed cream sauce or a traditional marinara. The Tavern's chefs are happy to provide more options for guests who make their arrangements in advance. **Old Port Royale** is the Caribbean Beach's food court, offering typical fast food fare like pasta, pizza by the slice, and a salad bar.

### Disney's Yacht & Beach Club Resort

The Beach Blast breakfast at the **Cape May Cafe** is a character buffet stocked with the usual morning goodies, including omelets, home fries, oatmeal and fresh fruit. If you're on a strict diet but still want to dine with Goofy, Pluto, Chip, and Dale, be sure to call Cape May to make advance arrangements.

If members of your party are craving red meat, you could do worse than accompany them to the **Yachtsman Steakhouse**. Chef Roger Hill—also chef at the Yacht Club Galley (see review on page 120)—offers health conscious diners a weekly "vegetarian special," which may include dishes like rosemary-skewered mushrooms, vegetable ravioli, or grilled portobello mushrooms. Be sure to try the eggplant-smashed potatoes if they're on the menu—*yum*! Fabulous desserts are always available. And, although vegetarian entrées are noticeably missing from the menu, you can head into the Yacht Club's **Crew's Cup Lounge** for veg-friendly nachos and a tossed salad.

If you're staying at the Yacht and Beach Club, don't overlook the **In-Room Dining** menu. After a long day of theme parking, what could be nicer than relaxing in your room—especially with pasta primavera with roasted red peppers and artichoke hearts, tossed in a spicy white wine caper sauce, just a phone call away? Or how about a hot, chewy pizza—your choice of whole wheat or white vegan crusts—topped with onions, black olives, green peppers, and

# Veggie Kids at the Epcot Resorts

*For all the variety they offer adults, most Epcot resort restaurants don't exactly push the envelope when it comes to kids' fare. If your toddler has an adventurous palate, your best bet may be to forgo the kid's menu and share your adult meals around the table.*

## Vegetarian Kids' Meals at Table Service Restaurants

**ESPN Club (Boardwalk):**
Macaroni and cheese; peanut butter and jelly sandwich

**Flying Fish Cafe (BoardWalk):**
Romaine lettuce with little croutons and ranch dressing; bowl of Mickey pasta with real tomato sauce and parmesan cheese

**Gulliver's Grill (Swan):**
Cheese pizza; grilled cheese sandwich; peanut butter and jelly sandwich

**Spoodles (BoardWalk):**
Macaroni and cheese; pasta with tomato sauce; peanut butter and jelly sandwich; cheese pizza; side of fresh vegetables

**Yacht Club Galley (Yacht Club):**
Breakfast: Plain or blueberry pancakes; fresh fruit cup; cold or hot cereals; French toast
Lunch and Dinner: Mickey pasta with marinara or cheese sauce; grilled cheese sandwich; peanut butter and jelly sandwich

**Yachtsman Steakhouse (Yacht Club):**
Linguini with marinara sauce; Mickey noodles with cheese sauce

## Kid-Friendly Vegetarian Offerings at Counter Service Restaurants

**Beaches and Cream (Beach Club):**
Veggie burgers, served on toasted multi-grain buns

**Cabana Bar (Dolphin):**
Veggie burgers; fresh fruit bowls; cheese pizza

**Kimonos Sushi Bar (Swan):**
Vegetarian maki rolls

**Old Port Royale (Caribbean Beach):**
Pasta; pizza by the slice

---

mushrooms, with or without cheese? Healthful munchies like vegetable and fruit platters, mixed nuts, pretzels, and popcorn are also available.

### Walt Disney World Dolphin Resort

When its menu focus changed from Mexican to Southwestern cuisine, **Juan and Only's** lost its only vegetarian entrée. Until recently, guests absolutely raved about the portobello mushroom fajitas, often making a separate trip to the Dolphin just for them. Today, chefs are happy to whip up a special order for vegetarian diners, or another meatless meal—vegetable enchiladas, pasta primavera, or a vegetarian platter of goodies like grilled asparagus, portobello mushrooms and cilantro scalloped potatoes—even without advance notice. Juan and Only's house salad—topped with julienned jicama, kalamata olives, and poblano pepper croutons, and dressed with a smoked pepper-cilantro vinaigrette—and spinach and shiitake mushroom flautas are featured on the appetizer menu year-round.

At lunch, the poolside **Cabana Bar** offers the "Very Veggie Burger"—a meatless patty with all the fixin's on a 7-Grain Roll, served with tortilla chips, coleslaw, and a crisp dill pickle. Add a house salad for just a dollar more. Fresh fruit bowls and cheese pizzas are also available.

### Walt Disney World Swan Resort

A beautiful interior and strolling Italian musicians give **Palio** a romantic ambience that is hard to equal elsewhere on property. But with a menu emphasizing seafood and veal, Palio offers precious few entrées to tempt even an ovo-lacto vegetarian. Fortunately, the most reasonably priced items—the Fettuccine Alfredo and the selection of wood-fired pizzas—are the meatless ones as well. Our favorite pies include the Pizza Con Funghi—topped with mozzarella, wild mushrooms, sun-dried tomatoes, and sweet roasted garlic—and the Rustica, a combination of grilled asparagus, zucchini, yellow squash, carrots, and shiitake mushrooms, available (if requested) in a cheeseless form. Priority Seating arrangements are recommended.

At **Kimonos Sushi Bar,** try kappa maki—a yummy vegetarian hand roll stuffed with cucumber and sticky rice—or an ichiban roll, filled with rice and assorted vegetables. Although miso soup is also available, strict vegetarians should note that it does contain flakes made from bonito, a small tuna native to the Pacific.

## Downtown Diz Resorts

Although the hotels in the Downtown Disney area are more scattered than those around Epcot and the Magic Kingdom—requiring guests to use their own transportation or rely on Disney's bus and monorail service—they offer some of the best values on property. Mid-priced options include Disney's Port Orleans and Dixie Landings. Unoccupied suites and villas at Old Key West, a resort complex designed for Disney Vacation Club members, are available to be rented on a nightly basis, perfect if you want to cook in your own kitchen. Another self-catering option is the Disney Institute. Just north of Downtown Disney, the Institute is our favorite place to get away from the theme park crowds— and to cook our own meals. Also in the Downtown Disney area are the seven hotels of the Disney Village Hotel Plaza, clustered on and around Hotel Plaza Boulevard. Prices can be cheaper here than at some WDW hotels, depending upon the room and the season. With the exception of the

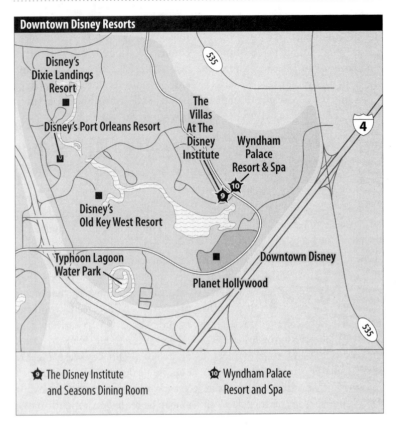

**Downtown Disney Resorts**

Disney's Dixie Landings Resort

Disney's Port Orleans Resort

The Villas At The Disney Institute

Wyndham Palace Resort & Spa

Disney's Old Key West Resort

Typhoon Lagoon Water Park

Downtown Disney

Planet Hollywood

🅖 The Disney Institute and Seasons Dining Room

🅙 Wyndham Palace Resort and Spa

Disney Institute, however, none of these lodgings offers an outstanding vegetarian restaurant.

## Places to Eat

### Best of the Best in the Downtown Disney Resorts

🅖 **Seasons Dining Room**
   **Vegebility: Good**
   **Price: Expensive**
   Casual American
   Table Service

B, L, D
The Disney Institute
(407) 939-3463
MC/V/AE

Seasons Dining Room, located inside the Disney Institute Welcome Center, is a mecca for health-conscious diners. Seasons' menu emphasizes American cuisine and seasonal market fresh produce at the peak of its flavor, complemented year-round by Florida citrus, tropical fruits, and native spices. For vegetarians, the combination is superb.

In February, 1999, Marianne Hunnel (see the profile of Hunnel on page 129) came to Seasons from a stint in the parks—the 50's Prime Time Cafe at the Disney-MGM Studios—to replace long-time Chef Christine Weissman. Because the restaurant's emphasis on fresh market-driven cuisine showcases Hunnel's own vegetarian tendencies, the fit couldn't be more appropriate.

Under Hunnel's guidance, Autumn dinner menus feature a seitan "parmesan," layered with sundried tomato sauce, a drizzling of olive oil, and soy cheese. A Seasons signature dish, the smoked tomato and basil soup is low-fat, vegan, and downright beguiling, garnished with Himalayan Red Rice. For dessert, try the deliciously light dairy- and egg-free Banana Chocolate Mousse which contains (*shhh—don't tell anyone*) tofu. Speaking of which, Hunnel always has vanilla tofutti in the back, a tradition she instituted at 50's Prime Time Cafe.

For lunch, Seasons' menu offers vegans at least two choices. In the summer, a popular option is Hunnel's "summer on a plate": fresh raw corn, tomato, onion, fava beans, zucchini, cucumbers, and gently steamed asparagus, all tossed in a very light white balsamic vinegar.

Call 24 hours ahead to sample Seasons' house made seitan sausage for breakfast, flavored with sage, rosemary, onion, and just a hint of pure maple syrup. If you're in the mood for a sweet breakfast, the kitchen always has egg substitute on hand, and can whip up delicious whole wheat crepes filled with seasonal fresh fruit in a moment's notice.

Other vegetarian menu items—like tempura vegetables with chili yogurt dip, or a refreshing mesclun salad with whole fresh cherries dressed in a cherry vinaigrette, or an exquisite portobello mushroom and vegetable strudel—make this one of the best places for healthful dining at this, or any, resort.

## Worth a Mention at the Downtown Disney Resorts

### Disney's Port Orleans Resort

Dine by candle light at **Bonfamille's Cafe**, Port Orleans' table service restaurant named for a character in The Aristocats. Although the menu looks abysmal for vegetarians—not a single appetizer or main course on the menu is meatless—chefs are happy to work with you to create a special meal, especially with advance notice. If you haven't had a chance to speak with a chef, ask for the Chicken Primavera without chicken, or ask your server to find out what can be done "on the fly."

At breakfast, this beautiful French Quarter-esque courtyard is transformed into a light, sunny space with plenty of options for a health-conscious diner. Try the Jackson Square breakfast: seasonal fruit paired with a freshly baked bran muffin. Or tuck into a *beignet*, a traditional New Orleans pastry that is deep fried and coated with confectioner's sugar. It may not be totally healthful, but it is 100% vegan!

Food court fare with a Creole twist is available at **Sassagoula Floatworks & Food Factory**. The red beans and rice contains andouille sausage, but with 24 hours' advance notice chefs are happy to make a vegan version, ready for your arrival. Fresh breakfast beignets are available here, too, along with an assortment of pan-American food court eats. The **Sassagoula Pizza Express** delivers fresh 16" cheese or deluxe veggie pizzas to Port Orleans, Dixie Landings, and Old Key West Resorts from 4 PM to midnight. A cheeseless or soy cheese version is available with advance notice, but vegans beware: the pizza dough does contain dried milk.

### Disney's Dixie Landings Resort

If you're stuck in your hotel all evening, your best bet may be to order in from The Sassagoula Pizza Express. In addition to large cheese and veggie pizzas, small

and large salads and a selection of beers and wines are also available. At **Boatwright's Dining Hall**, order the Shrimp Primavera sans shrimp, and you'll get fresh garden vegetables tossed with pasta and a sun-dried tomato basil cream sauce, topped with sharp, nutty Asiago cheese. If you're an animal lover, think twice about heading to Boatwright's for breakfast, where "cute" menu items like Oink! Cluck! Moo! ("The barnyard's aflutter with this meat lover's treat!") are a bit tough to take. **Colonel's Cotton Mill** is Dixie Landing's food court, offering prototypical fast food fare, including pasta with marinara, mac-n-cheese, pizza, and salads.

### The Villas at the Disney Institute

In addition to the very veg-friendly Seasons Dining Room (see review on page 126), the Disney Institute provides a number of health-conscious dining venues, all under the watchful eye of Chef Marianne Hunnel. **The Gathering Place** offers dessert samplers and sophisticated finger foods, like a smoked portobello mushroom tart on whole grain wheat bread, topped with melted Brie cheese. A vegan or low-fat version of this yummy treat can be easily assembled. The Institute's **Spa Menu** presents a wealth of healthful options, including a tropical fruit platter served with a sesame scone, a vegetarian burger, or

# Marianne and Scott Hunnel

At home, the only thing that Disney Chefs Scott and Marianne Hunnel don't like to do in their kitchen is the dishes. "It's always fun to cook!" says Marianne. True enough. But it's even more fun to eat when the kitchen is manned by two exceptional chefs.

Marianne is one of Disney's "Divas," an elite group of women chefs changing the culinary face of the resort. In addition to overseeing the meals at Seasons—the signature dining room at the Disney Institute—Marianne is in charge of the menus at two D.I. lounges, a snack shop, and custom meals for the Institute's huge convention business. She's recently garnered national attention, hosting a dinner at the James Beard House in New York City.

Scott was the very first Disney chef to give a dinner at the Beard House. His restaurant, Victoria & Albert's in Disney's Grand Floridian Resort & Spa, has been awarded three stars from Mobil, and was named the number one restaurant in Orlando by the Zagat Guides. Zagat's readers also picked Scott's restaurant as one of the ten best in the nation—quite a journey from his humble beginnings as a dishwasher in a Chicago-area Lums.

But what's it like to share their kitchen at home?

"Our rule," says Scott, "is whoever starts the dish gets to finish it without the other's influence."

Considering the size of the Hunnels' kitchen, that's probably a good idea. Scott and Marianne chose their home more for its location—a beautiful piece of land on a canal leading to the local lake, with lots of distance (physical and psychological) from work—than its culinary amenities. Built in 1966, the house has only a small galley kitchen, with most original appliances still intact, and with barely enough room for one world-class chef, let alone two.

"If you looked at our kitchen," says Scott, "you'd think, 'No chefs live here!'"

Still, those humble surroundings have produced their share of culinary masterpieces, like Scott's wild mushroom risotto, which Marianne describes as "out of this world," or Marianne's favorite dish to prepare: a whole pot of artichokes, drizzled with extra virgin olive oil and topped with freshly cracked pepper. *Mmmm mmm good!*

It's also the place where the two put their heads together over morning coffee.

"It's great," Marianne elaborates. "We try things out on each other—new menu items, new recipes."

"We'll change each other's menus so they're better," Scott continues, "and we can talk together about problems we're experiencing, because we understand exactly what the other is going through. It's such a major advantage."

The two recently began teaching cooking classes together, too, something they're both enjoying a great deal.

But what's their favorite over-coffee activity these days?

Putting their wish list together for—you guessed it—a new dream kitchen.

# Veggie Kids at the Downtown Diz Resorts

*A kid could go almost an entire week at Downtown Disney's resorts without eating anything but pancakes and grilled cheese sandwiches. If healthful dining and variety are your goals, your best bet may be to eschew the kiddie menus and share a few adult meals around the table.*

## Vegetarian Kids' Meals at Table Service Restaurants

**Boatwrights (Dixie Landings):**

Breakfast: French toast sticks; Mickey-shaped pancakes; cold cereals

Lunch and Dinner: Macaroni and cheese; cheese pizza; pasta with tomato sauce; grilled cheese sandwiches

**Bonfamille's Cafe (Port Orleans):**

Breakfast: Mickey-shaped pancakes with strawberries and whipped cream; French toast; assorted cereals

Dinner: Grilled cheese sandwich

**Olivia's Cafe (Old Key West):**

Breakfast: Waffles; buttermilk pancakes; cold cereal

Lunch and Dinner: Grilled cheese sandwiches; peanut butter and jelly sandwiches

**Seasons (Disney Institute):**

Breakfast: Pancakes; French toast; oatmeal; cold cereal

Lunch and Dinner: Kid-sized tossed salad; Mickey pasta with marinara or cheese sauce; peanut butter and jelly sandwich; grilled cheese sandwich

## Kid-Friendly Vegetarian Offerings at Counter Service Restaurants

**Colonel's Cotton Mill (Dixie Landings):**

Pasta with marinara sauce; macaroni and cheese; pizza

**Reflections Gourmet Coffee & Pastries (Disney Institute):**

Fruit salad; vegetarian wrap sandwich

**The Sassagoula Pizza Express (Dixie Landings, Old Key West, Port Orleans):**

Cheese or vegetable pizza (available cheeseless—or with soy cheese—with prior notice)

---

grilled fresh vegetables on focaccia bread—all of which contain 0 grams of cholesterol. On the shores of Willow Lake, **Reflections Gourmet Coffee & Pastries** serves breakfast and all-day snacks, including fruit salads, pastries, Greek salads, and an assortment of coffees and black, green, and herbal teas. Don't miss the Vegetarian Hovan, a wrap sandwich made with lowfat yogurt cheese, vegetables, and spices, rolled in pita bread.

**In-room grocery delivery** is also available at the Disney Institute, helping guests with special diets (and busy schedules) prepare their own meals. You can purchase items at the Gourmet Pantry in the Downtown Disney Marketplace or at Dabblers in the Disney Institute Welcome Center and have them delivered directly to your villa. If you're not available to receive your purchases, arrangements can be made for the groceries to be left in your kitchen, with perishables safely stowed in the suite's mini-fridge. If you don't like the selection (or the high prices) at Dabblers or the Gourmet Pantry, you'll find natural and organic ingredients at Chamberlin's Market and Café on Dr. Phillips Boulevard, or conventional groceries at the 24-hour Goodings supermarket, located in nearby Crossroads of Lake Buena Vista Shopping Center (see reviews on page 210).

### Disney's Old Key West Resort

The full-service restaurant at Disney's Old Key West Resort—the flagship Disney Vacation Club property—is **Olivia's Cafe**, a casual eatery serving up a decent amount of veggie fare, especially at lunchtime. Vegetarians who eat dairy should try the Vegetable Sandwich: grilled vegetables and goat cheese, served on a ciabatta roll and accompanied by fresh fruit. If you don't eat dairy, ask for the penne pasta without Asiago cheese, but with sundried tomatoes, baby spinach, olive oil, and garlic. Both the pasta and the ciabatta roll contain egg, but if you want something vegan, Olivia's kitchen boasts a fully trained staff of professionals who are happy to make dishes to your specs. At dinnertime, take the

boat launch to Downtown Disney and your options increase myriad-fold, or cook out on one of the grills around the resort. And don't forget **The Sassagoula Pizza Express** (reviewed on page 128) during an attack of the late-night munchies!

# Places to Stay

## Our Favorite Veg-Friendly Lodgings near Downtown Disney

⚑ **The Disney Institute**
**Vegebility: Good**
**Price: Expensive**
Bungalows, Townhouses, Villas, Vacation Homes
Lake Buena Vista, FL 32830
(800) 282-9282
MC/V/AE

The most relaxing place to stay on Disney property is unquestionably the Disney Institute, Michael Eisner's self-improvement resort at the edge of the Disney World/Reality interface. Prices are reasonable (by Disney standards), the sylvan campus includes five pools, suites and villas feature kitchenettes, and the nearest restaurant—Seasons—boasts a fantastic selection for veggies (see review on page 126).

Even if you don't stay on campus, consider expanding your knowledge of things culinary, horticultural, or artistic by taking a Disney Institute class. An educational highlight is "The Art of Healthy Cooking," the Institute's most popular cooking class. The class menu changes seasonally and three out of four are completely vegetarian (call in advance to be sure your class won't be preparing chicken or fish). As the class's concoctions bake, Institute chefs like Missy Graf instruct participants in knife safety, introduce potentially unfamiliar ingredients such as quinoa and wheat berries, and impart a number of useful strategies for healthful eating.

At the end of class, participants tuck into their scrumptious creations—like a delicious mango-quinoa studel, paired with red bean ice cream—and discover that

it's not too hard to cook healthfully, after all. A packet of informational materials, including recipes, a copy of the vegetarian diet pyramid, and a list of mail-order ingredient sources ensures that students can take home what they've learned, along with their leftovers.

If you just want to relax and shed some theme park stress, book a treatment at the Disney Institute's Spa. Five different kinds of massage, facials, other beauty treatments, and aromatherapy sessions—all using cruelty-free, natural beauty products—are offered to guests and day visitors. A state-of-the-art fitness room, gymnasium, indoor exercise pool, saunas, steam rooms, and whirlpools are available to guests who've booked a Spa treatment.

" *Healthful eating, nutritionally-balanced eating, today's lifestyle*—

these were all big factors in the new vision for dining at Walt Disney World. We constantly look not just at what people eat today, but what they will eat tomorrow. We take risks, and take a step forward."

— *Franz Kranzfelder*
Walt Disney World Food & Beverage

---

🔟 **Wyndham Palace Resort & Spa**
**Vegebility: Fair**
**Price: Moderate–Expensive**
Suites, Rooms, EverGreen™ Rooms
1900 Buena Vista Drive
Lake Buena Vista, FL 32830
(800) 327-2990
(407) 827-2727
All major credit cards accepted

For pampering on Disney property, but not in a Disney-themed hotel, consider the Wyndham Palace Resort & Spa. The resort's megalithic tower presides over its 27-acre complex across from Downtown Disney, offering 90,000 square feet of meeting space and a full-service spa and fitness center. Like many non-Disney institutions around Orlando, the Palace provides excellent value for money. For as little as $130 a night in the off season, rooms at the Palace feature private balconies or patios, speaker phones with computer and fax hook-up, and personalized voice mail. Suites can be had with as many as five bedrooms, living and dining rooms, and fully-equipped kitchens—perfect for cooking up a mess of greens (and, if you're a real meany, leaving the mess of dishes for housekeeping!).

Wyndham Palace sets itself apart from the competition with 65 EverGreen™ Rooms: nonsmoking guest rooms guaranteed to be free of allergens through independent, EPA-recommended air cleaning systems. In addition, each individual EverGreen™ Room is equipped with an independently filtered drinking system, making tap water delicious for drinking and luxurious for bathing (a critical amenity, as all who've experienced Orlando tap water know). Bathroom tissues, towels, and linens in the rooms are undyed, and non-allergenic.

The first European-style spa in a Central Florida resort, The Spa at Wyndham Palace is also the largest, at 10,200 square feet. More than 60 rejuvenating treatments and services are offered to Palace guests and day visitors, including a number of special treatments perfect for tourists from the frigid north. Has your delicate, winterized skin been out in the strong Florida sun a bit too long? Head down to the Spa for a "Sun-Lovers Facial." Another big seller at the Palace (which owes much of its business to conventions) is the "Meeting Relief Neck & Shoulder Massage," a great way to loosen up during a 25-minute break between sessions. But our favorite restorative is the "Theme Park Leg Relief Wrap": a leg and foot wrap of cool mud "applied to relieve pain and reduce water retention... leaving legs and feet feeling refreshed and light." Aaaahhhh.... And most importantly, all health and beauty products used in the spa and provided in rooms are specially formulated for the Palace from natural, cruelty-free ingredients.

# Animal Kingdom Resorts

At press time there were only two resorts in the Animal Kingdom area, neither of which is especially vegetarian friendly. The Animal Kingdom should become decidedly more attractive to vegetarians with the opening of Disney's Safari Lodge, which will reputedly feature an extremely veg-friendly African-themed restaurant. But for now, there are the Coronado Springs and the All Star resorts, both of which cater to guests seeking

# Dining at the Safari Lodge

In January, 2001 Walt Disney World plans to open the Safari Lodge. Overlooking an "African" savanna, balconies on each of the 1300 premium rooms will provide guests with unparalleled wildlife viewing, Animal Kingdom-style.

As with all Walt Disney World resorts, the Safari Lodge will feature an upscale "signature" restaurant, but this one will be as close to meatless as Disney is likely to get. "The menu will be largely vegetarian," promises Franz Kranzfelder, Walt Disney World Manager of Menu Development and Culinary Standards, and will focus on light, lean, simple cooking of "foods from the land." A large open kitchen located in the center of the restaurant will give guests the opportunity to interact with chefs from different regions of Africa, and sample ethnic vegetarian dishes they might otherwise not try.

"The specialty restaurant is really gonna give you a warm feel of Africa," continues Kranzfelder. With two wood-burning ovens, the restaurant features a unique kitchen plan, reminiscent of a kosher establishment—with one side reserved for preparing meat and seafood dishes and the other for vegetarian meals. "We'll separate the operation totally," says Vice President of Food and Beverage Dieter Hannig, "using different operating equipment, different chinaware, and with a wait staff trained to keep everything apart."

Why not an all-veg restaurant, as was once the buzz around property? According to Hannig, there simply isn't enough customer demand to support a fully vegetarian restaurant. Many Disney guests aren't too sure about eating at the bottom of the food chain, and still crave that piece of chicken to go with their greens and grains. In a place like Walt Disney World, where guest experience is paramount, chefs have to give the people what they want—whether it's a vegan dessert or a hunk of meat. And in a streamlined, separable operation like the one in Safari Lodge, that will be possible, without undermining the commitment to maintaining a meat-free kitchen.

The restaurant—which has yet to be given an official name—will begin testing menu items sometime during the summer of 2000.

Another great idea from the febrile brains of Disney food and beverage planners is the "African Market," the Safari Lodge's family restaurant. Guests will dine in the traditional open-air market of an African village, with multiple fireplaces, grills, wok stations, open kitchens, and a bakery located within the dining area itself. Watching vegetables cook on the grill and smelling freshly baked flatbreads as they come from the ovens will inspire guests to try interesting new foods, making for a lively and informative dining experience. Menus will be seasonal in both restaurants, but a number of meatless items, incorporating vegetarian curries and exotic African fruits, will always be available.

reasonably priced lodgings, and inexpensive, family-friendly food. Disney's Coronado Springs, a mid-priced Southwest-themed resort, offers few concessions to vegetarians, with the exception of the Pepper Market, an interesting "open air market" take on the ubiquitous American food court. The All-Star Music, Sports, and

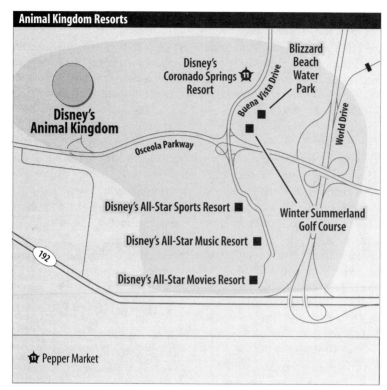

**Animal Kingdom Resorts**

Disney's Animal Kingdom

Disney's Coronado Springs Resort

Blizzard Beach Water Park

Buena Vista Drive

World Drive

Osceola Parkway

Disney's All-Star Sports Resort ■

Winter Summerland Golf Course

Disney's All-Star Music Resort ■

192

Disney's All-Star Movies Resort ■

🏛 Pepper Market

---

Movies resorts are Disney's least costly resorts. All three have food courts which are, sadly, all-American and quite ho-hum.

## Places to Eat

### Best of the Best in the Animal Kingdom Resorts

🏛 **Pepper Market**
**Vegebility: Good**
**Price: Moderate–Expensive**
Casual Mexican/Asian/Italian/American
Counter Service

B, L, D
Disney's Coronado Springs Resort
(407) 939-3463
MC/V/AE

As one of the least expensive resorts on Walt Disney World property, Coronado Springs is inundated with guests from all cultures and walks of life, and the Mexican-style resort boasts an equally diverse and popular food court. The Pepper Market is modeled after an ethnic farmer's market *cum* multicultural cafeteria, where diners travel from booth to booth inspecting the wares—except at the Pepper Market, you're selecting prepared foods and salad bar fixin' instead of produce. When you're done, the cost of your meal is tallied, including a 10% gratuity.

This spells good news for vegetarians, who return again and again to ethnic cuisines for variety and inspiration. At the Pepper Market, one can enjoy huge burritos made with black beans and smothered in a vegan sauce, vegetables stir fried to order in their own pans, or eggless pastas and pizzas with vegan crust made fresh to order by attendant cooks. The made-to-order preparation stations are complemented by cafeteria-style fare: grilled veggies, baked potatoes, prepared salads, and all you need to assemble the salad of your dreams.

—*Thanks to gardenia for her help with this review.*

## Worth a Mention at the Animal Kingdom Resorts

### Disney's All-Star Resorts

Food courts rule the day at Walt Disney World's value-priced All-Star resorts: **World Premier** at All-Star Movies; **Intermission** at All-Star Music; and **End Zone** at All-Star Sports. Garden lasagna, pizza, pasta, and salads are available in all three, as are large and small fruit cups, whole fruit, large tossed salads, and a tabbouleh wrap sandwich. Pizzas, pasta, and lasagna are served from 11 AM to midnight. You can also get pizza (with an ovo-lacto crust) in your room from the **All-Star Pizza Express** between 6 PM and midnight. BUT—and this is a big but—the food courts' marinara sauce and the sauce used to dress the All-Star Resorts' pizzas contain chicken stock. To get any of these items in a truly vegetarian form, you must ask as far in advance as possible—even if it's only an hour—for a meatless tomato sauce to be prepared.

# Veggie Kids at the AK Resorts

*Disney's most reasonably priced resorts offer kids cheese, cheese, and more cheese. For more variety (and a little fiber), avoid the kiddie menu altogether and share two or three adult meals around the table.*

### Vegetarian Kids' Meals at Table Service Restaurants

**Maya Grill (Coronado Springs):**
Mickey pasta with cheddar cheese sauce; cheese pizza; cheese nuggets

### Kid-Friendly Veggie Offerings at Counter Service Restaurants

**All Star Food Courts (All Star Resorts):**
Garden lasagna; fruit cups; fresh fruit; tabbouleh wrap sandwiches

**Pepper Market (Coronado Springs):**
Black bean burritos; baked potatoes; pasta

# Chapter 9

# Other Disney Venues

**Walt Disney World General Information:** *(407) 824-4321*
**Priority Seating Arrangements:** *(407) WDW-DINE (939-3463)*
**WDW Switchboard:** *(407) 824-2222*
*Call the switchboard to be transferred to
a chef at the restaurant where you'd like to dine.*

hen the Disney Company purchased land south of Orlando, they purchased a lot of it: 43 square miles, roughly twice the size of Manhattan and larger than ten countries around the globe. Even with a sizeable chunk of that property declared off limits as a nature preserve (an environmental commitment Walt Disney himself made in the early stages of planning), there's still been plenty of room for expansion. And, of course, there's plenty of cash to bankroll growth in all directions.

Disney's Imagineers have taken full advantage of this abundance, creating just about every kind of fun-filled venue that can be imagined. There are shopping districts, adult entertainment complexes, golf courses, water parks, a sports complex, a nature preserve… Heck, there's even Goofy Golf! There's a lot of splashing, shopping, dancing, hiking, laughing, and—best of all—dining to be done all around Disney property. The reviews here, separated by venue, will help point you toward the most healthful and delicious culinary alternatives in this vast sea of opportunities.

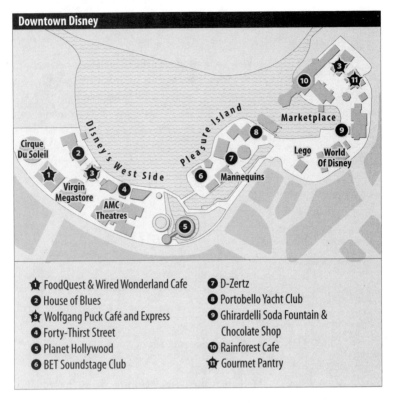

**Downtown Disney**

**1** FoodQuest & Wired Wonderland Cafe
**2** House of Blues
**3** Wolfgang Puck Café and Express
**4** Forty-Thirst Street
**5** Planet Hollywood
**6** BET Soundstage Club
**7** D-Zertz
**8** Portobello Yacht Club
**9** Ghirardelli Soda Fountain & Chocolate Shop
**10** Rainforest Cafe
**11** Gourmet Pantry

## Downtown Disney

Apart from being a congested shopping and dining area, Downtown Disney is unlike any downtown we've ever seen. Wide, pedestrian-only avenues, upscale theme restaurants, and huge plazas featuring Lego sea monsters aren't part of your average American city center. But regardless of the name, this sprawling entertainment complex east of the theme parks offers guests a plethora of dining, shopping, and entertainment options, owned and run—for the most part—by third parties in partnership with Disney.

The district is divided into three distinct areas: Pleasure Island, Disney Marketplace, and Downtown Disney West Side.

### Pleasure Island

The first portion of Downtown Disney to open to the public, Pleasure Island was Disney's initial effort to expand Walt Disney World into a playground for adults as well as children—and the pleasures to be found at PI are decidedly adult-oriented. After 7 PM, no one under the age of 18 (unless accompanied by a parent or legal guardian) may enter the six-acre property: an amalgam of music and comedy clubs, elaborately themed lounges, and casual clothing stores, and the scene of a nightly "New Year's Eve" celebration complete with fireworks. Dining options are largely comprised of foods designed to appeal to revelers—expect plenty of fried things, with chunks of Andouille sausage thrown in for good measure.

### Downtown Disney Marketplace

The Marketplace is a family-friendly fun zone, with plenty of opportunities to buy your favorite Mickey apparel or grab a chocolate-dipped banana at the Ghirardelli Soda Fountain and Chocolate Shop. Parents will welcome the opportunity to relax by the shores of the Mouse-made Buena Vista Lagoon while their kids have a blast at the enormous LEGO Imagination Center. A good selection of veggie eats awaits at the Wolfgang Puck Express—featuring Puck's legendary pizzas, as well as sushi and sandwiches—and the deli at the Gourmet Pantry, which offers vegan and vegetarian salads, as well as snacks and sweets.

### Disney's West Side

The West Side is where you'll find many of Downtown Disney's high-profile dining, shopping, and entertainment venues. You can buy a CD at the Virgin Megastore, take in a show by The Wallflowers at the House of Blues, or grab a bite to eat at one of Wolfgang Puck's three restaurants, with stunning interiors by Puck's wife, Barbara Lazaroff. You can also see nightly performances by Cirque du Soleil (a circus without performing animals). But don't leave the West Side without playing a virtual reality arcade game—and sampling some unexpectedly good veggie snacks—at DisneyQuest.

## Places to Eat

### Best of the Best in Downtown Disney

🏆 **FoodQuest and Wired Wonderland Cafe**
**Vegebility: Fair**
**Price: Moderate-Expensive**
Casual American
Counter Service
L, D
DisneyQuest
Downtown Disney West Side
(407) 938-6290
MC/V/AE

𝓕 **or a comprehensive guide to our ratings system, see page xviii.**

The Walt Disney Company has seen the future of its theme park business, and it is DisneyQuest: a series of virtual reality arcades deployed around the country. The flagship Orlando location is a five-story funhouse, featuring amazing VR games and other high-tech diversions like CyberSpace Mountain, a virtual roller coaster the riders design themselves.

Of course, an arcade is the last place you're gonna find decent veggie food, right? Wrong! The Cheesecake Factory, legendary purveyor of decadent sweets, owns and operates DisneyQuest's two cafés, and they're surprisingly veg-friendly. The company has gone out of its way to make sure its offerings can be easily adapted for vegetarian gamers who've worked up an appetite snatching virtual thunderbolts out of the "sky."

FoodQuest, located on the 5th floor next to the CyberSpace Mountain ride, offers a huge menu with a lot of veggie options, including that rarest of treats: truly vegetarian vegetable soup. None of FoodQuest's breads and rolls contain dairy, either, so vegans can enjoy a hearty lunch of soup, salad, and garlic rolls with marinara sauce, or get a freshly made, ethnically-inspired wrap sandwich without the meat, or try the portobello mushroom sandwich without Jack cheese. Ovo-lacto veggies should try the warm spinach and artichoke dip with chips and salsa, or dig into a freshly baked pizza—hardly a low-fat repast, but tasty.

The Wired Wonderland Cafe on the 4th floor offers a few sandwiches as well as Internet access, but neither the sandwiches nor the Web is the main attraction here. This is really the place to be if you're in the mood to completely blow your diet on a brownie, a slice of fabulous cheesecake, or a hunk of mud pie. The Cafe also offers a multiplicity of caffeinated beverages and another refreshing surprise: herbal tea.

---

### ✪ Wolfgang Puck Cafe and Express
**Vegebility: Good**
**Price: Moderate–Expensive**
Casual American
Table and Counter Service
L, D
Cafe: Downtown Disney West Side;
Express: Downtown Dis. Marketplace
(407) 938-WOLF
MC/V/AE

---

Culinary icon Wolfgang Puck is best known for introducing Hollywood—and subsequently mainstream America—to the concept of the gourmet pizza at LA's Spago in the 1970s. Since then, Puck and his flamboyant partner and wife, interior designer Barbara Lazaroff, have built up a small empire of Puck restaurants, frozen foods, and cookware. Puck's presence at Disney World began with the small Express at the Downtown Disney Marketplace, which continues to serve food-courty versions of Puck's casual fare priced to gouge. Vegetarians can put together a decent meal here, but not inexpensively. A prepackaged tomato, basil, and garlic linguine will set you back $8.95. A freshly baked spinach, mushroom, and Gorgonzola pizza is a better deal at $7.95. But the best bargain at the Express is the $3.95 gourmet macaroni and cheese.

If you're not in a rush, you can put your dollars to better use at one of the three distinct restaurants squeezed into the Wolfgang Puck Cafe in the heart of Disney's West Side. You'll get a better meal and a much wider range of options.

If you just want to walk in off the street and get a nice meal in a casual environment, the regular old Cafe in the ground floor seating area is for you. The chopped vegetable salad and one of the Cafe's fabulous pizzas—with a flavorful thin crust that holds up on its own as a delicious flatbread—can easily satisfy two people. The signature pad thai is also very popular, but make sure you use the V-word when you order: pad thai normally contains shrimp, at Puck's and elsewhere.

The cafe's ultracool sushi bar, tucked into an intimate space by the building's entrance, is a great place for vegetarians to get an education in Japanese appetizers, with constantly changing daily offerings. A sushi chef is always on hand to provide diners with custom-made fresh sushi according to their likes and dislikes, or to suggest a sampler for the uninitiated.

The upstairs Dining Room offers a more upscale culinary experience, a more attentive wait staff, and scrumptious Puck-ish vegetarian offerings. Highlights include a seasonal heirloom tomato salad, an out-of-this-world watercress salad, and a mellow, flavorful wild mushroom spaghettini dish drizzled with aromatic truffle oil. The Dining Room is the only Puck location where all the food is made to order, guaranteeing a wonderful—if expensive—dining experience.

## Worth a Mention at Downtown Disney

### Pleasure Island

The ❺ **BET Soundstage Club** is definitely one of the coolest looking clubs in Pleasure Island, and it's a great place to dance the night away—if you're 21 or older. You'll need to dance off some calories, too, after you try one of their veg appetizers. Jamaican Patties—pastries filled with sautéed vegetables—are joined on the gleefully unhealthful menu by twisted fries and onion rings, both accompanied by a spicy remoulade sauce.

# Veggie Kids at Downtown Disney

*If you want something more than pasta with mari-nara sauce, cheese pizza, or a cheese sandwich, your best bet is to share the adult's meals with the kids at the table. If not, here's what to expect:*

## Vegetarian Kids' Meals at Table Service Restaurants

**House of Blues (West Side):**
Grilled cheese sandwich; cheese pizza; rotini with marinara sauce

**Wolfgang Puck's (West Side):**
Cheese pizza; macaroni and cheese; buttered noodles

**Rainforest Cafe (Marketplace):**
Grilled cheese sandwich; cheese pizza; pasta with tomato sauce

**Planet Hollywood (Pleasure Island):**
Cheese pizza; penne pasta with tomato or butter sauce; cheese quesadilla

**Portobello Yacht Club (Pleasure Island):**
Cheese pizza; macaroni and cheese ravioli

## Kid-Friendly Vegetarian Offerings at Counter Service Restaurants

**Gourmet Pantry (Marketplace)**
Cheese tortellini salad; vegetable sandwich; fresh whole fruit

**FoodQuest, DisneyQuest (West Side):**
Cheese or veggie pizza; rolls with marinara sauce; wrap sandwiches

## Healthful Snacks

**Forty-Thirst Street (West Side):**
Fruit smoothies

**Ghirardelli Soda Fountain and Chocolate Shop (Marketplace):**
Strawberries and bananas dipped in dark chocolate

❺ **Planet Hollywood's** vegetarian offerings are pretty humdrum in comparison with the glitzy, movie-themed surroundings. The celebrity-owned chain serves wood-fired pizzas, pasta, and an ovo-lacto Gardenburger® with all the trimmings. Warm, creamy spinach dip—blended with sautéed portobello mushrooms and served with dipping crackers—is on the appetizer menu.

Choosing an Italian restaurant over, say, a steakhouse is a no-brainer for a vegetarian. But the ❻ **Portobello Yacht Club** is better than most for ovo-lacto vegetarians. Funghi Arrostiti con Polenta—slices of mushroom served with warm, soft polenta and gorgonzola cheese—is yummy enough to make us lift our self-imposed ban on portobello mushroom anything. Vegans have a tougher time of it, thanks to the restaurant's policy of using egg pasta, though 24 hours' notice will get you any type of noodle you wish.

If you're in need of a boost, grabba cuppa joe, an ice cream cone, or a vegan Raspberry slushie at ❼ **D-Zertz**.

## The Marketplace

The ❷ **Ghirardelli Soda Fountain and Chocolate Shop** is an ovo-lacto vegetarian's dessert heaven, but even vegans can get in on the action when strawberries are in season. From November through June, the Fountain keeps vats of vegan dark chocolate on hand for dipping strawberries. While the dark stuff is on hand, you can also enjoy a chocolate-dipped frozen banana.

The first ❿ **Rainforest Cafe** on Disney property serves the same big, vegetarian-friendly menu as its Animal Kingdom counterpart but this time in a better setting, with outdoor seating overlooking Lake Buena Vista. And don't miss the ✪ **Wolfgang Puck Express** across the way (reviewed on page 140).

## West Side

The ❷ **House of Blues** is the place to go if you're jonesin' for slightly yuppified southern food in an irresistibly funky environment. The ubiquitous portobello mushroom sandwich puts in an appearance on HOB's menu, but with a couple of interesting twists: the meaty fungus is roasted and served on whole grain bread with tomatoes, smoked gouda, and spicy radish sprouts. A watercress and jicama salad is served on the side. A classic southern Poor Man's Dinner could almost be assembled from the club's side dishes: corn bread, mashed potatoes, sweet potatoes, sautéed vegetables, fries, and coleslaw. All you need is beans n' greens, but unfortunately—and this is a tragedy—the menu's turnip greens are braised with ham in great big vats, and the restaurant's chefs will *not* whip up a meatless mess (at least not for us).

If you feel like a fat-free smoothie or a freshly roasted coffee drink, stop in at ❹ **Forty-Thirst Street**, right before you get to (vegetarian-unfriendly) Bongos Cuban Cafe.

# Places to Shop

🏪 **Gourmet Pantry**
**Deli/To Go: Good**
**Produce: N/A**
**Prepackaged Natural Foods: Fair**
**Non-Food Items: Fair**
Downtown Disney Marketplace
(407) 828-3886

Staying in one of the Disney Institute's self-catering suites? Stock your shelves with snack foods and baked goods, and your mini-fridge with an array of vegetarian—and some vegan—prepared salads and sandwiches from the Gourmet Pantry, located near the West Side bus stop. The deli features a dairy- and egg-free mushroom salad: three kinds of mushrooms drizzled with a light vinaigrette. Cheese tortellini pasta, tossed with roasted red, green, and yellow peppers and black olives in basil pesto, is also on offer, as is a selection of totally vegan mixed fruit and tossed green salads. Ovo-lacto vegetarians can tuck into a yummy sandwich of three different cheeses, herbs, lettuce, tomato, cucumber, and tabbouleh rolled up in lavosh bread, either on its own, or as a platter. The platter gives you a choice of two sides: hummus, tabbouleh, or potato salad.

At the in-store bakery, stock up on vegan applesauce raisin squares. If you're a strict vegetarian, you'll have no problems with the Jelly Belly gourmet jelly beans, which don't contain gelatin, but look out for the rice crispy treats, which do. There's no produce to speak of—other than the occasional apple or orange—and, although beauty products are limited to travel-sized shampoos and soaps, there is a selection of non-animal tested products from St. Ives. Kitchen gadgets and culinary supplies, cookbooks, and a selection of wines are also available.

If you're serious about cooking in your suite, there are some non-perishables on offer—including vegan Mickey Mouse-shaped pasta! Of course, we're not saying it's the cheapest place to shop, or that it has the best selection, but it does offer delivery right to your Disney Institute villa. Now that's convenience!

*"Picture the average tourist coming to Orlando. The first things he eats are cotton candy, ice cream and hot dogs—already the tongue is covered with fat.*

*You come to the California Grill, we strip your tongue—with vinegars, reductions—and then we put black pepper on it, and red wine on it. In a three-day visit, you get two parts oil. You come here and you get the vinegar."*

— Clifford Pleau
*Chef, California Grill*

## Disney's Water Parks

In summer, the average high temperature in Orlando is 92 degrees. On some days, it's beastly hot before you're even awake and so humid that—after a sticky morning of battling the theme park crowds—your clothing is practically plastered to your skin.

Now's the time to head to one of Disney's three water parks. If you're vegetarian, you'd be wise to bring along a cooler packed with goodies: the pickin's are slim at these all-fast food venues. However, rumor has it that if you give the head chefs at Typhoon Lagoon or Blizzard Beach a few day's notice, the kitchen will have vegetarian burgers awaiting your arrival. Call the Walt Disney World switchboard at (407) 824-2222 to be transferred to the correct extension, and keep your fingers crossed that your burgers will be at the park when you are.

# Places to Eat

## Worth a Mention at Disney's Water Parks

### Typhoon Lagoon

According to Disney legend, Typhoon Lagoon was once a bustling little resort town. Hit by a massive typhoon (then an earthquake… and then a volcano), the village was in ruins, leaving the villagers to rebuild as best they could. The resulting "shambles" is Typhoon Lagoon.

Unfortunately, the series of catastrophes also seems to have wiped out the majority of healthful dining selections. Vegetarian choices at **Leaning Palms** are limited to pizza (cheese or veggie), a side pasta salad, and a side garden salad. The pizza shells are vegan, however, and can be made without cheese. An assortment of fruit concoctions is available at **Typhoon Tilly's**, including fruited yogurt and tropical fruit boats. Hot soft pretzels are sold at stands throughout the park.

### Blizzard Beach

A snow storm in Orlando? Sounds crazy, but that—apparently—is what happened here at Blizzard Beach, resulting in a fabulous winter sports-themed water park.

The vegetarian food at Blizzard Beach is a definite improvement over the other water parks. At **Lottawotta Lodge**, right as you enter Blizzard Beach, you can order a totally vegan linguine with marinara sauce (be sure to ask for no meatballs). The dressing on the Lodge's Caesar salad contains egg but no anchovy paste, and Italian dressing can be substituted by request. Cheese pizza, potato salad, fruit cups, and fresh whole fruit are also available. Near **Frostbite Freddie's** (a great place to get frozen fruit drinks—with or without alcohol), a small beverage cart sells 100% natural strawberry bars as a cool and delicious treat. You can pick up fruit cups at **Avalunch** or at the **Warming Hut**. Both concession stands also serve "Nordic Nachos"—tortilla chips with your choice of salsa or cheese.

### River Country

Built on a corner of Bay Lake near Fort Wilderness Campground, River Country was the first water park on Disney property. Today, it is the smallest—and least crowded—of the three. Modeled on the "Ol' Swimmin' Hole" theme, River Country is also the most natural feeling of Disney's water parks. It's a great place to relax after a hectic morning at the Magic Kingdom.

Unfortunately, River Country offers the fewest choices for vegetarian guests. Lettuce and tomato sandwiches (with or without cheese), side salads, and french fries are all you're likely to find at **Pop's Place**, a fast food restaurant located near the changing rooms. Your best bet is to bring your own picnic meal. Drop your cooler in one of the large lockers available near the changing rooms, and tuck into your meatless munchies whenever the urge hits. And remember, no swimming for at least 30 minutes after eating!

# Disney's Wide World of Sports

*Take me out to the ball game.*
*Take me out with the crowd.*
*Buy me some peanuts and Cracker Jack...*

If you like peanuts and Cracker Jack, you'll be in heaven at Disney's Wide World of Sports: a 200-acre complex that hosts professional and amateur sporting events of all kinds, and serves as an off-season training ground for the Atlanta Braves and the Harlem Globetrotters. With more than 30 concession stands scattered across property, there's plenty of peanuts to go around.

# Places to Eat

## Worth a Mention at Disney's Wide World of Sports

The only sit-down restaurant in the complex is the **Official All Star Cafe**. This sports-themed eatery is part of a chain owned by professional athletes, including André Agassi, Tiger Woods, Wayne Gretzky, and Monica Seles. Vegetarians who eat eggs and dairy will find plenty of options on the menu, including a mushroom and barley Gardenburger®—dubbed the "Victory Garden Grille"—served with all the trimmings and a side of french fries. A baked potato can be substituted for an additional charge. "André's Ace Pomodoro" is a mix of tomato, garlic, basil, and olive oil, tossed with linguine and parmesan; the linguine—like every other All Star pasta—contains egg.

Vegans are cheerily accommodated by Chef Tom Hughes, who dished out lots of vegetarian fare during his stint as chef to the bands at Woodstock, 1999. With a day's notice, Tom will be happy to stir fry some veggies over rice, and can be sure to have egg-less pasta on hand. If you come in off the street looking for a dairy-free meal, ask for the Southwest-inspired Rodeo Salad—smokey black beans, roasted corn, and pico de gallo tossed with fresh seasonal greens—without the chicken. A selection of ovo-lacto appetizers and a house salad are also available, as is a grilled cheese sandwich or pasta with butter sauce for the kids.

*Facts for foodies*

*panish for "rooster's beak,"* **pico de gallo** *[pronounced PEE-koh day GUY-yoh] is a spicy relish made from finely chopped ingredients, including tomatoes, jícama (a Mexican root vegetable), onions, bell peppers, jalapeño peppers, oranges, and cucumber. Used as a condiment with Mexican food, the relish got its peculiar name from the practice of eating it with the thumb and fore finger: an action resembling the pecking of a rooster. Pico de gallo is originally from northern Mexico, and in the U.S. is practically indistinguishable from salsa.*

## WDW Dinner Shows

It should come as no surprise that the creative folks at Walt Disney World—masters of entertainment in all its forms—might put on a dinner show or two. In fact, there are several dinner shows nightly on property, the most popular and long-running being the Hoop-Dee-Doo Musical Revue and the Polynesian Luau. You'll have a great time, and enjoy some good food, at either. But don't wait until the last minute to decide whether you really want to go: cancellations for all dinner shows must be made at least 48 hours before showtime to avoid paying full price.

### Hoop-Dee-Doo Revue
**Vegebility: Fair**
**Price: Very Expensive**
*Shows nightly at 5, 7:15 and 9:30 PM*
Casual All-American
Pioneer Hall
Fort Wilderness Campground
(407) 939-3463
MC/V/AE

Make your reservations far in advance for this corny, Wild West-style show staged nightly in the Fort Wilderness Pioneer Hall. Wildly popular, the show consists mostly of bad puns, slapstick, and a whole lot of hootin' and hollerin'. It's a lot of fun if you like that sort of thing, and the all-you-can-eat food and drink helps to make up for the $46 adults/$24 children entry ticket.

Unless, of course, you're that rarest of cowpokes who doesn't eat cows. Vegetarian vittles are scarce.

Barbecued ribs and fried chicken are the obvious draws for most folks, so the fact that the baked beans are really pork and beans should come as no surprise. Your best bet for a good meal is to call the reservationist at Fort Wilderness and ask to speak with Chef Ray Talley directly. With at least 48 hours' notice, Talley and crew are happy to do just about anything you like, including a grilled veggie plate with foccacia on the side. If that doesn't appeal, feel free to suggest something that does: tofu, tempeh, or other specialty products can easily be bought and prepared on your behalf. If you forget to speak with a chef in advance, you can expect little more than steamed veggies, pasta with a marinara sauce, and baked potatoes.

Chef Talley is also in charge of the **All-American Backyard BBQ**, another Fort Wilderness dinner show (this one featuring country music and line dancing), offered seasonally from April through October, and on a more limited basis during the November-December holiday season. Buffet selections are similar to those on offer at Hoop-Dee-Doo, and vegetarians are accommodated in similar style with advance notice.

**Polynesian Luau**
**Vegebility: Good**
**Price: Very Expensive**
*Shows nightly at 5:15 and 8:00 PM*
Casual
Eclectic/Asian
Disney's Polynesian Resort
(407) 939-3463
MC/V/AE

Call no sooner than seven days and no later than 48 hours in advance to select your special meal for the Polynesian's nightly food fest on the shores of the Seven Seas Lagoon. Chef Eugene Schlienger offers five vegetarian dishes to choose from, four of which are vegan. Enjoy traditional Hawaiian music and dancing while munching on roasted vegetables served atop lentils and pearled barley. Or sink your teeth into an Asian/Middle Eastern fusion of couscous and sautéed vegetables, topped with marinated grilled tofu.

A chef's choice platter of grilled or steamed vegetables and rice is available, as is a veggie lasagna. If you choose the latter, try to take part in the hula lessons offered to audience members later in the program. You'll need to do something if you want to say "aloha" to the calories in all that cheese!

# Chapter 10

# The Disney Cruise Line

**General Information:** *(407) 939-3727*
210 Celebration Place, Suite 400
Celebration, FL 34747
http://www.disneycruise.com
FAX: *(407) 939-3750*

ot content with providing more entertainment than your average landlubber can handle, the Walt Disney Company has now set its sights on the remaining three-quarters of the earth's surface. With the christening of the Disney Magic in the summer of 1998, and the addition of its sister ship, the Disney Wonder, one year later, Disney entered the Cruise world with a massive splash. And right from the start, Disney Cruise Line was different. Original Broadway-style musical productions (one for each night of the cruise), a section of each boat reserved for adults, and more children's activities than any other cruise line at sea (including nearly an entire deck just for kids) are among the features that set Disney ships apart.

And then there's the private island. On the last day of each cruise, Disney boats dock at Castaway Cay, a 1,000-acre tropical oasis in the Bahamas, directly east of Ft. Lauderdale. Activities include snorkeling, biking, hiking, and sand volleyball. There are two large beaches, one meant for kids and families, and another—more secluded and romantic (complete with "massage cabanas")—for adults only.

# Strategies for Cruising with Mickey

### If you eat eggs and dairy...

*You shouldn't have a problem eating on a Disney Cruise Line ship. Menu planners have assured us that—regardless of the season—there will always be at least one ovo-lacto appetizer and one entrée on every restaurant's menu. However, you may want to take the following steps just to be safe.*

**Ask the cruise line specialists to fax or** mail copies of the menus to you. Be sure to get menus that will be in place at the time of your cruise. If you don't see anything suitable on one or more of the menus, follow the advice given for vegans below.

**If you don't like what you see on just** one of the restaurant's menus, book a dinner at Palo for the evening you're scheduled to eat at the offending restaurant. But be warned: Reservations cannot be made at Palo until the day of embarkation. For this reason, we recommend that you board the ship as early as possible. Restaurant changes and bookings for Palo are taken at the restaurant's own reservation desk shortly after boarding, so try to get there as soon as it opens—usually at 2 PM.

**If your heart is set on eating at a Disney** Cruise Line restaurant where you can't find anything vegetarian on the menu, you have two options: **(1)** if you like a dish that you see on the menu, but it needs a simple modification (substituting marinara sauce for bolognese, for example), Cruise

Line chefs do not require more than a half day's notice. Simply visit the restaurant that morning, make your request, and you'll be served the new, improved version later that night; **(2)** for anything requiring special ingredients—tofu, soy milk, or gluten free pasta, for example—chefs will need a minimum of two weeks notice to obtain the products you've asked for.

### If you're vegan...

*You'll have to do a little telephone calling and legwork to guarantee delicious, strictly vegetarian meals during your cruise. Follow these tips to ensure a pleasant time at sea:*

**Call the Cruise Line at least two weeks** in advance to discuss your special dietary needs. Be sure that the person taking your request understands exactly what you can—and cannot—eat. It can't hurt to give them an idea of the sorts of dishes you'd like to eat, too! In fact, Disney Cruise Line specialists assure us that the kitchens on board will cook anything your heart desires, and that chefs frequently receive faxed recipes from cruise ship guests with special dietary needs.

**Once you're on board, speak with the** restaurant chefs directly about your meals.

**Bring your own food! Every cabin on board** has its own mini fridge (but no freezer).

---

Dining aboard Disney's ships is refreshingly different, too, thanks in part to the input of Walt Disney World's Food and Beverage team. Disney Cruise Line vacations fea- ture "rotation dining," allowing guests to sample a new themed dining experience each night of their journey. It's just like eating out at a different restaurant each night—except that the wait staff and your table companions travel right along with you. For a quiet meal *without* Mickey's favorite crewmembers, adults can opt out of the rotation and enjoy a quiet meal at Palo.

In typical Disney style, people with special diets are accommodated on the cruise, although you won't find a plethora of offerings the way you would at many Walt Disney World eateries. Ovo-lacto vegetarians will always see at least one entrée on each restaurant's menu, but vegans and those on stricter diets must take care to order their meals in advance— once the ship sails, there's no "popping out to the grocery store" to pick up special ingredients!

## Worth a Mention on the Disney Cruise Line

*PLEASE NOTE that all Disney Cruise Line menus change twice each year. The entrées listed are meant only to give an idea of what was available at press time, and will not necessarily be offered when you, fair reader, hit the deck.*

### Animator's Palate
Disney Magic and Disney Wonder

Disney Imagineers must have herniated their creative muscles designing Animator's Palate, which offers a dining experience unlike any other in the world. A tribute to the art of animation, the dining room itself transforms from a stark black and white "sketch" into a full color work of art. Later in the meal, diners join in the fun, creating their own edible masterpiece for dessert.

The creativity of the vegetarian food—when it's available—is equal to that of its surroundings. For starters, vegetarians can tuck into delicacies like grilled California goat cheese and roasted red peppers, served atop crisp greens and drizzled with a balsamic vinaigrette. Disappointingly, though, no vegetarian entrées were listed on the late fall menu. But with a few hours' warning, chefs can make a vegetarian version of the Penne Pasta dish (which normally contains pancetta). The result is tender penne bathed in a delicious, simple sauce of sautéed garlic, crushed plum tomatoes, leeks, and olives in basil cream. A vegan version is available with a few hours' notice as well.

### Lumière's/Triton's
Disney Magic/Disney Wonder

On both Disney cruise ships, guests are treated to at least one evening of elegant dining. Lumière's— Disney Magic's casual upscale venue—is named for the candelabra character in Disney's Beauty and the Beast, and is appropriately candle-lit, with sparkling chandeliers and a large mural depicting scenes from the movie. On the

Wonder, Triton's is an elegant nautical-themed restaurant inspired by Disney's Little Mermaid. Both serve lunch and dinner, and feature an identical menu.

At lunch, vegetarian starters might include grilled Mediterranean vegetables, marinated in balsamic vinegar, olive oil, and fresh herbs, or a refreshing grapefruit and orange salad, topped with roasted walnuts, and served with low-fat cottage cheese. A lunchtime main course frequently offered is penne pasta with marinara sauce; at dinner, expect a more elaborate entrée, like a stack of grilled portobello mushrooms, spinach, and tomato, drizzled with roasted red pepper-basil oil. Delectables like Crème Brûlée, Chocolate Truffle Delight, and Frozen Grand Marnier Soufflé are featured on the dessert menu. For vegans, true sorbets are always available.

### Parrot Cay
Disney Magic and Disney Wonder

At Parrot Cay, cruise ship guests dine in a Bahamian room, Disney style, with vibrant colors and palm-leaf ceiling fans under a gingerbread-trimmed verandah. At press time (Winter, 2000) vegans were especially well-cared for at Parrot Cay. Two appetizers—a tropical fruit cocktail drizzled with sweet guava nectar, and a house salad including jicama and a delicious cilantro dressing—were featured on the menu, along with the Linguini Pasta Martinique entrée: linguini sautéed with seasonal vegetables, roasted garlic, and fresh basil. Be sure to check on the availability of vegan options at Parrot Cay before your boat sails, however, as menus change every six months.

### Palo
Disney Magic and Disney Wonder

The designers of the Disney Cruise Line must have children, because they clearly know how important it is—*occasionally*—for parents to abandon their wee charges for an evening out. An entire entertainment zone, including three nightclubs, has been constructed for adults only on each Disney ship. At dinnertime, too, adults have a kid-free option that's perfect for quiet conversation or a romantic meal. Palo was designed by Marty Dorf (the same genius behind the California Grill, Flying Fish and Citricos at Walt Disney World), and is the most sophisticated room on either ship. Warmly toned woods, muted venetian glass, and an exhibition kitchen quietly complement the sweeping 270-degree ocean view.

Named for the multicolored poles used by the gondoliers of Venice, Palo serves traditional Northern Italian cuisine, giving it

## Rotation Dining

If you have a special diet, you're probably sick of having to explain to servers everywhere you go, on every night of your vacation, what you can and cannot eat. Aboard a Disney cruise ship, that problem is eliminated by the rotation dining system, where servers are assigned to the same rotating schedule of restaurants you follow. Tell your servers about your special diet the first day of your trip, and they'll be sure to look out for your needs the whole time you're on board. Ask nicely, and you may even get them to finagle special meals for you ahead of time! Just be sure they know exactly what your diet entails, and it can't hurt to mention the ingredients you especially like. It's the next best thing to having a butler!

by far the most vegetarian-friendly menu onboard. Prepared in the kitchen's wood-fired oven, Pizza del Levante Funghi Seliaggo e Pesto is a vegan masterpiece, topped with roasted peppers, wild mushrooms, and that rarest of rare: a cheeseless pesto. And, of course, Palo chefs are more than happy to leave the cheese off the pizza—no advance notice needed. For antipasti, vegetarians have four options, two of which are vegan. Melanze alla Griglia translates as grilled eggplant (for those of you who don't speak Italian), topped with a tomato-balsamic relish and goat cheese. Portobello della Veltellina features grilled portobello mushrooms atop polenta, bathed with a shallot sauce and sprinkled with shaved parmesan cheese. Ask the kitchen to leave off the parmesan for a deliciously dairy- and egg-free starter.

For a first course, vegans can tuck into the Orecchiette alle Verdure: small, ear-shaped pasta tossed with fire-roasted vegetables, garlic, and basil (vegans can ask that the shaved parmesan be omitted). For less strict vegetarians there's Ravioli delli Alpi: housemade raviolis filled with artichokes, ricotta cheese, and oven dried tomatoes. Most of the risottos at Palo are made with a chicken stock, but with advance notice, chefs will make a version using vegetables, mushrooms, and other meatless ingredients. And, when you make your reservation, be sure to ask for a vegetarian *Secondi Piatti*, or second course, as well. You won't find one on the menu.

At dessert, don't miss the Soufflé Romantico: a warm chocolate and hazelnut soufflé topped with a vanilla bean sauce. And although they aren't always listed on the menu, Italian sorbetto and fresh fruit are always available for guests who choose not to eat eggs or dairy.

---

### Beach Blanket Buffet/Topsiders
Disney Magic /Disney Wonder

On the eighth floor of each vessel you'll find the massive buffet

# The Last Repast Before Mickey's Mast

Back in the Dark Ages of the Disney Cruise Line (we're talking 1998 here), guests on a four-night cruise were presented with two choices for the last meal of the journey. They could either stick with their pre-selected dining rotation and repeat a night in one of the ship's three family restaurants, or opt out of the system on the last night and eat at adults-only Palo. But that was before the Cruise Line enlisted the help of the capable folks at Walt Disney World Food & Beverage. In a single, masterful stroke—and without any new construction—the WDW and Cruise Line team together created a program that transformed the last meal on the cruise into an evening to remember.

*Those smarty pantses!*

The team instituted a constantly changing "Master Chef Menu," presented on the fourth evening in each restaurant on the ship (except Palo) and showcasing signature dishes from the best chefs on the ships and on Walt Disney World property. In addition, one of the Walt Disney World master chefs will be on board the cruise and—earlier that day—will demonstrate a cooking technique from their own signature dish. That dish (which, according to Disney Food & Beverage cognoscenti, will often be vegetarian) will be served that evening as a special, along with the rest of the master chef menu.

The results of this culinary collusion can be sublime, as one menu suggests. Robin Stotter (chef at the Wolfgang Puck Cafe) contributes his Butternut Squash Soup, made with cream and topped with a delicious red pepper coulis. Chef Robert Adams from Narcoosssee's lends his coveted recipe for raspberry vinaigrette and roasted walnuts to the menu's tossed mixed greens. Tender orrechiette pasta—tossed with roasted vegetables, garlic, basil, and shaved parmeggiano regiano—is bestowed by Antonio Sambasile, chef of Palo on the Disney Wonder. And Kona Cafe Pastry Chef Tracy Carew gives diners a taste of her Chantily Koko Puffs with Chocolate Sauce.

*To die for?* After this last meal, we'd happily walk the plank.

---

spreads travelers have come to associate with cruise ship dining. Vegetarians can expect an extensive salad bar, a number of vegetarian appetizers, and a few vegetarian sides and main dishes, including stir-fried vegetables. A dessert buffet is also available. Outside on the pool deck there's an outstanding tropical fruit buffet—perfect, in our not-so-humble opinions, for a delicious breakfast or lunch all on its own!

## Pluto's Dog House, Pinnochio's Pizzeria, and Scoops
Disney Magic and Disney Wonder

For a quick (but healthful) bite during the day, point your hungry crew toward the pool deck. At Pluto's Dog House you'll find veggie burgers and at Pinocchio's Pizzeria, the pizza shells are 100% vegan, ready to be topped with veggies of your choosing. After lunch—or as a mid-day snack—

satisfy your craving for ice cream treats at Scoops.

## Room Service
Disney Magic and Disney Wonder

Feel like sleeping in and having breakfast delivered to your room? Worried that, as a vegan, you'll be stuck ordering dry cereal? Not on a Disney cruise ship. Fresh fruit is always available, and all Danishes served (excluding the cheese Danish) are vegan. Vegan pizzas and roasted vegetable focaccia sandwiches can also be delivered directly to your cabin. Oh, and about that cereal: rice or soy milk will be available if you ask for it two weeks ahead of your departure date.

# Bigger, Better, Faster:
# Universal Orlando

**Universal Orlando Main Number:** *(407) 363-8000*
**Dining Requests:** *(407) 224-6339*
**Universal Orlando Food Service Office:** *(407) 363-8340*
*foodserviceCUF@uescape.com*
*Call the food service office to arrange special meals.*

# Chapter 11

# Universal Orlando

**Universal Orlando Main Number:** *(407) 363-8000*
**Dining Requests:** *(407) 224-6339*
**Universal Orlando Food Service Office:** *(407) 363-8340*
*foodserviceCUF@uescape.com*
*Call the food service office to arrange special meals.*

*F*or years, theme park lovers anxiously awaited the day when Universal Studios' $2 million expansion would open its gates. In 1999, Universal finally delivered, opening a fun, state-of-the-art theme park, a 30-acre entertainment and shopping complex, and the first of five world-class resorts: an audacious triple salvo aimed at the grand-daddy of all theme parks just a few miles to the south.

And so was born Universal Orlando, and the inevitable comparisons began. Indeed, the similarities are striking: on-property themed hotels; "early opening" mornings for resort guests; audio animatronics galore; character dining experiences. And long time park watchers have noted uncanny similarities between the Magic Kingdom and Islands of Adventure, like the separation of the parks into themed "lands" and the inclusion of two rollercoasters, one flume ride, and a cartoon-based kids' character area.

There's no question that Universal has learned at the feet of Mouse. Some say they've even done 'em one better.

Have they? Well, that all depends on you.

If it's thrill rides and multimillion-dollar media productions, stunt shows, special effects, and robotics you're after, then Universal Orlando is for you. And that's what an amusement park is traditionally all about:

# Strategies for Great Veggie Dining at UO

**1) Book early...**

At the UO theme parks, lunch and dinner reservations aren't necessary, except at Lombard's Landing, Mythos, and possibly Confisco Grill (once the word about the character lunch gets out). If you want to be absolutely certain your party of 20 will have a table at 7pm, reservations are accepted for all table service restaurants up to 48 hours in advance.

**2) But not too early!**

If you call to request a special meal at a theme park or a CityWalk restaurant, do so just a few days before you plan to dine there. Otherwise your request may be lost.

**3) Go to the source**

Be sure to speak directly with a chef about your special meal. Phone operators and theme park information specialists are not always able to pass your request along. And even if they do, there's no guarantee some aspect of your needs and preferences won't get muddled or misconstrued. Your best bet is to call or e-mail the food service office directly.

**4) Stay on message**

Mention your special meal request—and the name of the chef with whom you've arranged it—upon your arrival at the restaurant, and again to your server after being seated.

**5) Special advice for Emeril's!**

If you want to eat at Emeril's in CityWalk, make your reservation as early as possible. Weeknight tables are currently booked from three days to three weeks out, and getting a table on the weekend could take as long as three months. Above all, don't forget to call the day before your reservation to confirm your arrangements. *Reservations which are not confirmed before 3 PM on the day of seating will be cancelled!* Again, if you've ordered a special meal, make sure to mention it each time you call, and at the restaurant upon being seated.

---

Great rides, end of story. In our opinion, Disney still has the edge in other areas. Universal doesn't have a lot of space (certainly not as much as Disney) in which to build a zillion themed resorts and doesn't seem interested in competing with the likes of Epcot for the edutainment experience. And let's not forget the animated characters: Mickey holds a special place in the hearts of parents and children the world over. But Universal has partnered with some big guns—Curious George, the Cat in the Hat, and Barney, to name just a few—to bring kids, both little and big, some outstanding character experiences.

Another big difference—but one that's not immediately apparent—is the way in which the two companies think about dining. Much of the food at Universal is prepared in a central commissary kitchen: a 10,000 square foot state-of-the-art food production area where all soups, sauces, and prepared salads are made, all cheese is shredded, and all vegetables are cut. By contrast, one  of the first things that Dieter Hannig did upon arriving at Walt Disney World was dismantle the commissaries, and send Food and Beverage managers outside the parks to find their own suppliers and their own unique ingredients. The latter approach introduces a level of individuality and freshness which is often missing at large institutions.

Unfortunately, Universal's more streamlined approach sometimes undermines the company's sincere efforts to provide plenty of options for vegetarian and vegan guests. When food is brought in from a central commissary kitchen and reheated for patrons, restaurant workers who would love to adapt a dish for vegetarians are often unable to do so. If the potato salad made in the commissary contains bacon (which, in the case of Universal Orlando, it does) then all the potato salad, at every counter service location, contains bacon. And even plain old steamed vegetables, an ace in the hole for every vegetarian diner, can be effectively ruined—robbed of their precious nutrients, crunchy texture, and natural flavors—by steam tables and heat lamps.

The notable exceptions to this rule are the full service restaurants in Universal's parks and resort hotels, and in a few standouts at CityWalk. It is here that Universal Executive Chef Steve Jayson's team can really cater to the guest's experience, and where on-site chefs have the flexibility, the ingredients, and the ingenuity to create exciting meatless meals.

"We need to do more for the guests," Jayson elaborates. "We can't do it only with great rides. The food has to equal the experience of the rides. If you're vegetarian, your best bet is to steer toward a full service restaurant, where a chef will come right out to the table and work with you to create a memorable meal."

If you're vegan or have other strict dietary needs, Jayson recommends calling the UO food service office 48 hours in advance to alert restaurant chefs to your impending visit. This gives chefs a chance to stock up on fresh ingredients that you can enjoy, and an opportunity to brainstorm with you about your meal. At a counter service restaurant, don't be shy about asking to see the "plating guidebook": a ring binder containing ingredient lists for every dish on the menu. You might not get exactly what you're looking for, but you can steer clear of problem dishes.

"We've made a strong commitment to quality, and it's paid off," Jayson says. Time will tell if this commitment will pay off for vegetarians visiting the park, too.

# Chapter 12

# Universal Studios

- - - - - - - - - - - - - - - - - - - - - - - - - - - - - - - - - - - - - - - - - - - - - - - -

**Universal Orlando Main Number:** *(407) 363-8000*
**Dining Requests:** *(407) 224-6339*
**Universal Orlando Food Service Office:** *(407) 363-8340*
*foodserviceCUF@uescape.com*
*Call the food service office to arrange special meals.*

*T*he lure of Hollywood is strong. If there's anything people love, it's movies—in the theater, on cable, or curled up in front of a favorite video on Friday night. We love amusement parks, too. From classic roller coaster emporiums like Coney Island to annual hometown fairs, rides are a blast, the faster, more dazzling, and more thrilling the better. It took very little time for the smart folks at Universal to figure out that the two would go together nicely.

The attractions at Universal Studios are based on the biggest blockbuster films of the last 25 years: Terminator 2, Twister, Jaws, ET. Audience members become part of the action, embracing Universal's invitation to "live the movies." Universal attractions are state-of-the-art, leaving many Disney rides in the dust. Twister...Ride it Out, for instance, places guests within 20 feet of a live, five-story indoor tornado, where they encounter pounding rain, deafening noise, and intense winds. The ride exchanges enough air to fill four blimps per minute.

The first park in the new Universal Orlando complex, Universal Studios opened in 1990, and immediately began siphoning off guests from the human wave surging toward Disney World. In conjunction with the 1999 opening of the rest of Escape, the old park got a bit of a facelift, and a few nips and tucks here and there, too. For the kiddies, an entire area was added and reconfigured: Woody Woodpecker's KidZone

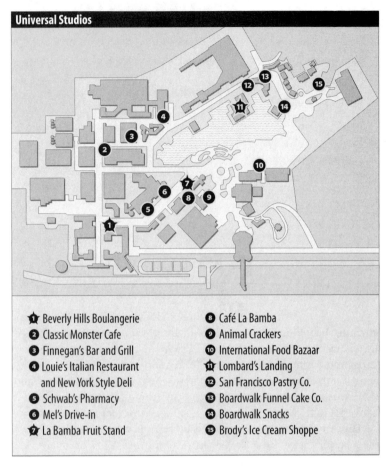

**Universal Studios**

- 🏠 Beverly Hills Boulangerie
- ❷ Classic Monster Cafe
- ❸ Finnegan's Bar and Grill
- ❹ Louie's Italian Restaurant and New York Style Deli
- ❺ Schwab's Pharmacy
- ❻ Mel's Drive-in
- 🍌 La Bamba Fruit Stand
- ❽ Café La Bamba
- ❾ Animal Crackers
- ❿ International Food Bazaar
- 🏠 Lombard's Landing
- ⓬ San Francisco Pastry Co.
- ⓭ Boardwalk Funnel Cake Co.
- ⓮ Boardwalk Snacks
- ⓯ Brody's Ice Cream Shoppe

includes a kid-sized roller coaster and a Curious George play area, complete with tire swings, climbing ladders, a fountain, and even a miniature city. Combine this with the already popular FUNtastic World of Hanna-Barbera (featuring Scooby Doo, the Flintstones, and other crowd pleasers), A Day in the Park with Barney, and Fieval's Playland, and it's hard to imagine a more kid-friendly park. Who says Universal is just for teens and adults?

Even better news: vegetarians and vegans will find a great deal more to eat in Universal Studios than they used to. Prepared salads and fruit are available practically everywhere, guaranteeing that you won't starve. The best place to eat in the park is Lombard's Landing,

# Universal Studios: Best of the Best

**Key to Categories and Abbreviations**

**O/L, V: Ovo-lacto and vegan selections**

· - Always available    + - Available upon request    A - Request in advance

**Es: Type of establishment**

T - Table Service    C - Counter service    S - Snack stand or cart

**$: Average price for a single vegetarian entrée**

| | | |
|---|---|---|
| 1 - under $10 | 3 - $16 - $20 | 5 - $31 - $40 |
| 2 - $10 - $15 | 4 - $21 - $30 | 6 - over $40 |

**Meals:**

B - Breakfast    L - Lunch    D - Dinner    S - Snacks

| Hollywood | O/L | V | Es | $ | Meals |
|---|---|---|---|---|---|
| 🏛 Beverly Hills Boulangerie | · | · | C | 1 | B, L, D, S |
| 🏛 La Bamba Fruit Stand | · | · | S | 1 | S |
| **San Francisco/Amity** | | | | | |
| 🏛 Lombard's Landing | · | + | T | 2 | B, L, D |

a full service restaurant where you can request special meals to your heart's content. For fast food, Beverly Hills Boulangerie and The Monster Café both provide adequate meatless meals with a very short wait. The Boulangerie even offers vegans something they can rarely indulge in at a counter service venue: dessert.

## Best of the Best at Universal Studios

🏛 **Beverly Hills Boulangerie**
**Vegebility: Good**
**Price: Moderate**
Casual French/American

Counter Service
B, L, D
Hollywood
Universal Studios
(407) 363-8340
MC/V/AE/Discover

Delicious and nutritious options are in abundance at Beverly Hills Boulangerie, a small counter service sandwich and pastry shop on the corner of Rodeo Drive and Plaza of the Stars. The aptly named Health Sandwich is packed full of sprouts, cucumber, avocado, tomato, and lettuce, served on a whole oat bun. Vegans can ask for the sandwich without cheese, and on a dairy- and egg-free hoagie (the whole oat bun contains butter). A large fruit platter and fresh garden salad are also available, as is a selection of sugar free cookies. Conscientious servers at the Boulangerie are quick to point out that the potato salad here—and, in fact, everywhere on property—includes plenty of bacon.

Sad news about the potato salad, but this might cheer you up: the Boulangerie is the only Universal theme park where you'll find vegan pastry. Grab a 100% egg- and dairy-free cherry turnover for breakfast on your way into the park, and stop by for two or three more on your way out. It can't hurt to have a supply of these guiltless goodies on hand when the rest of your party stops for ice cream later in the day.

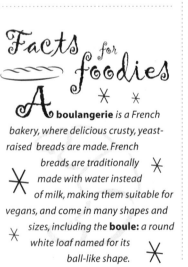

## Facts for foodies

**A** boulangerie *is a French bakery, where delicious crusty, yeast-raised breads are made. French breads are traditionally made with water instead of milk, making them suitable for vegans, and come in many shapes and sizes, including the* **boule:** *a round white loaf named for its ball-like shape.*

### ☆ Lombard's Landing
**Vegebility: Good**
**Price: Moderate**
Casual American
Table Service
L, D
San Francisco/Amity
Universal Studios
(407) 224-6400
MC/V/AE/Discover

On its own "wharf" in a quiet corner of the lagoon, Lombard's Landing takes its name and look from Lombardi's restaurant, one of the few waterfront structures in San Francisco left standing after the legendary 1906 earthquake. Arched ceilings, dark wood moldings, and warm-hued walls and tables add a *fin de siècle* (that's the 19th siècle, not this past one) quality to Lombard's, making it hands down the most relaxing place to eat in the park. Even the tropical fish in the restaurant's large quarium seem half asleep.

Lombard's is one of only two restaurants in the park that takes reservations, and for good reason: the restaurant gets consistently outstanding reviews. It's also the best place in the park to find vegetarian and vegan meals. The menu features a special section called "Health Conscious Cuisine," including an Original Gardenburger® served with all the trimmings on a seven grain bun. Both the patty and the bun contain eggs and dairy.

# A Vegetarian Tour of Universal Studios

*You won't find the same variety of veg-friendly food at Universal Studios as you will in Orlando's other movie park, Disney-MGM Studios. But you can still enjoy a full day of meatless meals in Universal Orlando's oldest theme park by following one of our sample itineraries. Make a reservation for Lombard's Landing—and inform their chefs of your special dietary needs—at least 48 hours in advance by calling (407) 224-6400. And be sure to confirm the opening and closing times of the park before scheduling your meals.*

### Itinerary One

**9 AM:** Enter the park. Proceed directly to the Beverly Hills Boulangerie for a vegan cherry turnover and coffee. Spend the morning exploring Hollywood Boulevard (try to see Terminator 2: 3D and the E.T. Adventure first thing).

**11 AM:** Hobnob with Hanna-Barbera animated characters—fresh fruit cup or frozen yogurt bar in hand—outside Animal Crackers. Spend the rest of the morning exploring KidZone, Expo Center, and Amity Avenue.

**1:30 PM:** Lunch at Lombard's Landing. Spend the rest of the day in San Francisco or New York, or (if you have toddlers in tow) head back to A Day in the Park with Barney and Fievel's Playland.

**3:30 PM:** In New York, stop for an Italian ice at Louie's Italian Restaurant (or for a pint of Guiness and some live music at Finnegan's Bar & Grill).

**6 PM:** After Twister—Ride it Out, grab a quick dinner of made-to-order veggie pizza at Universal Studios' Classic Monsters Cafe (request no cheese if your party is vegan). Exit the park, ready for a relaxing evening poolside—but watch out for those mosquitoes!

**Or:**

**6 PM:** Exit the park. Head back to your room in Portofino Bay for a quick shower and a nap before dinner.

**8 PM:** Enjoy a Universal fine dining experience at the resort's premier restaurant, Delfino Riviera, or at Emeril's Orlando in CityWalk.

### Itinerary Two

**7 AM:** Before leaving your hotel, tuck into an early breakfast of your own devising. If you're staying at Portofino Bay—Universal's only on-site hotel at press time—that means heading over to Sal's Market Deli for continental breakfast.

**9 AM:** Enter the park. Make your way to Hollywood Boulevard and Terminator 2: 3D.

**12 PM:** After spending the morning exploring Hollywood Boulevard, KidZone, and the Expo Center, head back to the Plaza of the Stars for a deliciously healthful lunch at Beverly Hills Boulangerie. Enjoy your gourmet veggie sandwich, then head over to the Production Studios and Twister—Ride it Out.

**3 PM:** Take some time to explore New York and San Francisco/Amity. If you're feeling a bit peckish, grab a frozen fruit slush (100% vegan) at Boardwalk Snacks, or a funnel cake at Boardwalk Funnel Cake Co. on the way into Amity.

**6 PM:** Dinner at Lombard's Landing. Be sure to ask for a seat on the terrace, in view of the Dynamite Nights Stuntacular.

**Or:**

**6 PM:** Make your way to Pastamoré Ristorante Italiano to begin a fun evening of dinner and dancing at CityWalk.

If you're vegan, or in the mood for something light, tuck into the Apple a Day Fruit Plate: a colorful variety of fresh fruits and berries, accompanied by a true raspberry-lemon sorbet.

On Lombard Landing's regular (Health Unconscious?) menu, ovo-lacto standouts include Ravioli with Five Cheeses, sautéed in extra virgin olive oil with fresh roma tomatoes, garlic, and Italian parsley. Ask for the dinner sized Spinach Salad without prosciutto and chicken, and you're left with a delicious vegan feast of fried pepperoncini peppers, grilled tomatoes, radish sprouts, and baby spinach, slightly wilted by a warm balsamic vinaigrette dressing. Another vegan meal can be had by ordering the linguini with marinara sauce from the Children's Menu. We've been assured that there's more than enough pasta for an adult and, at $5.95, you're certain to have enough cash left over for a fresh fruit cup dessert, also from the Kid's section.

The last dinner seating is a half hour before Universal shuts its doors for the night. Ask for a table outside on the verandah and, if your timing is right, you'll have a great view of the Dynamite Nights Stuntacular: a 15-minute live action boat show that starts just before the park closes. Now that oughta wake those fish up!

---

✿ **La Bamba Fruit Stand**
**Vegebility: Excellent**
**Price: Moderate**
Snacks
Hollywood
Universal Studios

---

This excellent little snack cart sits right outside the meat-heavy Café La Bamba, flaunting its ripe, delicious fruit at hot, tired theme parkers. Green and red apples, pears, oranges, watermelon, grapes, and mixed fruit cups are all available, perfect for a quick pick-me-up between rides. A never-ending supply of ice keeps drinks like Gatorade, Arizona Iced Tea, Tropicana juices, and bottle water cold and ready to revitalize the weariest guest.

---

## Worth a Mention at Universal Studios

---

### Production Sound Stages

For a frightfully good pizza that's 100% vegan, stop by ❷ **Universal Studios' Classic Monsters Cafe**. It might take a few minutes more than the cheesy pies on the menu, but the wait will seem more than worth while once your fresh, hot pizza—topped with onions, red and green

---

𝓕or a comprehensive guide to our ratings system, see page xviii.

peppers, mushrooms, carrots, zucchini, and yellow squash—emerges from the wood burning oven. Regular menu items at the Cafe include four cheese ravioli, egg linguine primavera, and a wood-fired cheese pizza. Fruit cups and a selection of ovo-lacto desserts are also available.

### New York

If you eat dairy, you can sink your teeth into the Original Gardenburger® at ❸ **Finnegan's Bar & Grill**, a table service restaurant with Irish-American pub ambience, live entertainment, and a daily happy hour. The Potato Onion Web—a deep fried mass of shredded potato, onion, and cheese dipped in an egg and beer batter—is available for a bit o' the ol' artery cloggin'. Fruit salad and steamed vegetable platters are easier on the body, if not too terribly inspired.

With the exception of salads and fresh whole fruit, all of the vegetarian menu items at ❹ **Louie's Italian Restaurant** contain dairy or egg. Upon special request, however, it is possible to get vegan spaghetti with marinara sauce. Other lacto Italian specialties include fettuccine Alfredo, cheese ravioli, and cheese pizza. A vegetarian panino sandwich can be prepared at ❺ **Louie's New York Style Deli**, a small counter inside the restaurant. Hidden ingredients at Louie's

include chicken stock in the minestrone, meat in the lasagna and in the pasta salad, and (as everywhere on property) bacon in the potato salad. For dessert, look for Louie's Italian ices, 100% vegan and delicious.

### San Francisco/Amity

If it's lunch hour when you reach the Embarcadero, your best bet is to head to Lombard's Landing. If you're still a bit peckish after your meal at Lombard's, pick up a delicious fruit plate next door at the ⓬ **San Francisco Pastry Co.** A small salad plate is also available.

For a more decadent treat, top your ovo-lacto funnel cakes from the ⓭ **Boardwalk Funnel Cake Co.** with strawberries, chocolate, Dutch apples, or fresh whipped cream. In the mood for something lighter, but just as sweet? Get a frozen fruit slush from ⓮ **Boardwalk Snacks**. Soft serve ice cream is also available. Old-fashioned hard-packed ice cream—in cones, sundaes, and floats—is just around the corner at ⓯ **Brody's Ice Cream Shoppe**, next to the Wild Wild Wild West Stunt Show. If all this sugar makes your lips stick together, wash it down with spring water, available in large bottles back on the main drag at Boardwalk Snacks.

# Veggie Kids at Universal Studios

*The pickin's are pretty slim for veggie kids at Universal's original Orlando theme park. For more variety, share your adult-sized meals around the table.*

**Universal Studios' Classic Monsters Cafe (Production Sound Stages):**
   Cheese or veggie pizza slice

### Vegetarian Kids' Meals at Table Service Restaurants

**Lombard's Landing (San Francisco/Amity):**
   Linguine with marinara sauce; kid's fruit cups

### Healthful Snacks

**La Bamba Fruit Stand (Hollywood):**
   Fresh whole fruit

**Animal Crackers (Expo Center):**
   Haagen Dazs yogurt bars; fresh fruit cups

### Kid-Friendly Vegetarian Offerings at Counter Service Restaurants

**Beverly Hills Boulangerie (Hollywood):**
   Health Sandwich; fruit; sugar-free cookies

**San Francisco Pastry Co. (San Francisco/Amity):**
   Fruit plate

**Boardwalk Snacks (San Francisco/Amity):**
   Frozen fruit slush

## Expo Center

Thanks in large part to the religious precepts of Buddhism, Hinduism, Judaism, and Islam, vegetarians can often eat very well at Asian and Middle Eastern restaurants. Sadly, this is not the case at the ❿ **International Food Bazaar**. The stir-fried vegetables, fried rice, spicy rice, and minestrone soup—perfectly vegan otherwise—are all cooked in chicken stock. But, we've been assured, steamed vegetable fajitas can be prepared upon request (we're not vouching for taste, mind you). And there are some side dishes—like an oriental salad and a fruit cup—that pass meatless muster.

Although Universal Studios doesn't have a character dining experience, a character bus stops by ❾ **Animal Crackers** at 11 AM and 4 PM daily. Snack on fresh fruit cups and Haagen Dazs yogurt bars as you pose for pictures with Yogi Bear, Boo Boo, Fred Flintstone, Barney Rubble, Scooby Doo, and others.

## Hollywood

More Texan than Mexican, ❽ **Café La Bamba** features BBQ ribs, burgers, and rotisserie chicken, and—unlike authentic Mexican cooking—offers relatively little for vegetarians. Most of the dishes contain meat and—because the baked beans are made with salt pork and bacon—there's precious little to substitute for it. Request either tacos or the tostada salad without cheese and meat for a makeshift, lettuce-heavy vegan meal, or get by on a combination of meatless sides like baked potatoes, fruit salads, tossed green salads, or corn on the cob. Be sure to ask for the latter without butter.

There's more lettuce to be had at ❻ **Mel's Drive In** where a garden salad, onion rings (dipped in egg), french fries, and orange juice are available. A few doors further along Hollywood Boulevard, dip into regular and sugar-free ice cream treats of all kinds at ❺ **Schwab's Pharmacy**.

# Chapter 13

# Islands of Adventure

**Universal Orlando Main Number:** *(407) 363-8000*
**Dining Requests:** *(407) 224-6339*
**Universal Orlando Food Service Office:** *(407) 363-8340*
*foodserviceCUF@uescape.com*
*Call the food service office to arrange special meals.*

When it opened in May, 1999, Universal's Islands of Adventure took its place in the record books as the most technologically advanced entertainment park in the world. Here, the worlds of Hollywood, children's books, comic strips, and mythology are recreated in astonishing detail on individual "islands" devoted entirely to their themes. On Marvel Super Hero Island, coaster lovers can have their guts turned inside out on a green monster of a coaster that hurls them upward with the G-force of a US Air Force F-16 fighter jet, flips them over into a state of complete weightlessness, then plunges them into two underground trenches. Hollywood's Jurassic Park features dinosaurs that hatch before your eyes, that blink and breathe, and that flinch when touched. And Seuss Landing is arguably the most whimsical park for kiddies ever created.

It's undeniable: Spiderman, the Cat in the Hat, Merlin the Magician, and a bunch of rowdy Velociraptors have combined to produce a kick-butt theme park, with more state-of-the-art thrill rides than any other park in the world.

Really, the only thing not state-of-the art at Islands of Adventure is the vegetarian food. Universal's head of food and beverage Steve Jayson promises food that equals the experience of the rides, but the trend toward healthful yet delicious dining is not informing the menus at IOA's counter service eateries. It's very difficult to

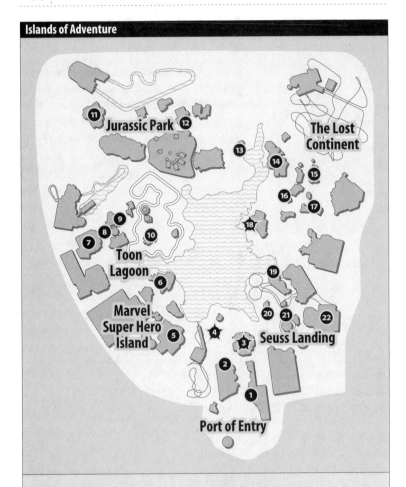

**Islands of Adventure**

Jurassic Park
The Lost Continent
Toon Lagoon
Marvel Super Hero Island
Seuss Landing
Port of Entry

1. Croissant Moon Bakery
2. Arctic Express
3. Confisco Grille
4. Port of Entry Fruit Stand
5. Café 4
6. Captain America Diner
7. Comic Strip Café
8. Cathy's Ice Cream
9. Blondie's
10. Wimpy's
11. Thunder Falls Terrace
12. Pizza Predatoria
13. The Watering Hole
14. Enchanted Oak Tavern
15. The Frozen Desert
16. Fire-Eater's Grill
17. Oasis Coolers
18. Mythos
19. Moose Juice Goose Juice
20. Green Eggs and Ham Café
21. Hop on Pop Ice Cream Shop
22. Circus McGurkus Café Stoopendous

# Islands of Adventure: Best of the Best

**Key to Categories and Abbreviations**

**O/L, V: Ovo-lacto and vegan selections**

• - Always available    + - Available upon request    A - Request in advance

**Es: Type of establishment**

T - Table Service        C - Counter service        S - Snack stand or cart

**$: Average price for a single vegetarian entrée**

| | | |
|---|---|---|
| 1 - under $10 | 3 - $16 - $20 | 5 - $31 - $40 |
| 2 - $10 - $15 | 4 - $21 - $30 | 6 - over $40 |

**Meals:**

B - Breakfast      L - Lunch        D - Dinner          S - Snacks

| Port of Entry | O/L | V | Es | $ | Meals |
|---|---|---|---|---|---|
| ⭐ Confisco Grille | • | + | T | 2 | L, D |
| ⭐ Port of Entry Fruit Stand | • | • | S | 1 | S |
| **The Lost Continent** | | | | | |
| ⭐ Mythos | A | A | T | 2 | L, D* |

*Dinner during high season only*

locate fast food that's good and good for you, especially if you require something more healthful—and enjoyable—than cheese pizzas, cheese ravioli, french fries, and onion rings. Okay, okay—there are side salads everywhere, and fresh fruit cups, and a few notable exceptions (a veggie deli sandwich at Blondie's in Toon Lagoon and an ovo-lacto falafel pita at the Lost Continent's Fire-Eater's Grill), and you can usually substitute this and remove that to make other meals possible. But in our not-so-humble opinions, Islands of Adventure has far to go to catch up with Epcot, Disney-

MGM Studios—or its own sister park, Universal Studios.

The meatless diner's best bet is to head to one of the park's two table service restaurants, Confisco Grille and Mythos. Here, Jayson's team can take the time to prepare more elaborate vegan and vegetarian feasts. Of course, this won't get you to the next ride quickly, but at least you'll feel happy and satisfied when you get there.

## Best of the Best in Islands of Adventure

⭐ **Confisco Grille**
**Vegebility: Fair**

**Price: Moderate**
Casual American
Table Service
L, D
Port of Entry
Islands of Adventure
(407) 224-9255
MC/V/AE/Discover

The first—and some say the most fun—restaurant you'll encounter at Islands of Adventure is Confisco Grille. Decorated with objects from the corners of the earth, Confisco's is a perfect point of departure for your theme park adventure, and a favorite dining spot for the Port of Entry's bustling "autocratic bureaucrats" (who often demand to see diners' passports before allowing further travel).

Open for lunch and dinner, Confisco's is known for its specialty burgers and grilled meats. But there's plenty for world travelers who prefer to eat lower on the food chain, too. For starters, tuck into the Spanakopizza, a savory flatbread topped with spinach, Greek feta cheese, and kalamata olives. Ask for it without feta for an entirely dairy- and egg-free pie. Another ovo-lacto appetizer is the Mediterranean Sampler, a platter loaded with hummus, baba ghanoush, tabouleh, Greek olives, marinated feta, and flatbread chips.

All but the last two of these Middle Eastern tastebud treats are vegan.

For a light but satisfying meal, try the dinner-sized Grilled Fruit Salad: fresh seasonal fruit grilled over an open fire, then chilled and served on a refreshing watercress salad. Be sure to ask for it without the complimentary side of chicken or tuna salad. The Grilled Vegetable Muffuletta—marinated grilled vegetables packed into a sesame roll and topped with smoked gouda—scores big points with vegetarians who eat dairy. Even more good news: both are less than $10. A full bar and a large selection of desserts are also available.

If you haven't had a glimpse of the Cat in the Hat, Spiderman, or Woody Woodpecker all morning, time your meal to correspond with Confisco's character lunch. Held each weekday between noon and 2 PM, the lunch features personalities from each of Universal's "islands," like Marvel Super Hero's Spiderman, the Grinch from Seuss Landing or, from the Lost Continent, Merlin the Magician. The characters do an excellent job covering the room, and you don't pay any extra to see them. Your best bet is to schedule your meal for 12:30 or 1 PM as the characters tend to skedaddle back to their own islands around 2.

*F*or a comprehensive guide to our ratings system, see page xviii.

# A Vegetarian Tour of Islands of Adventure

*The pickin's are slim for vegans, but if you follow one of our tried-and-true itineraries, you won't go hungry in Universal's newest theme park extravaganza. Make reservations for Mythos and Confisco Grille—and inform their chefs of your special dietary needs—at least 48 hours in advance by calling the Universal Food Service office directly at (407) 363-8340. And, as always, be sure to confirm the opening and closing times of the park before scheduling your meals.*

## Itinerary One

**7 AM:** Before leaving your hotel, tuck into an early breakfast. If you're staying at Portofino Bay—Universal's only on-site hotel at press time—that means heading over to Sal's Market Deli for vegan continental breakfast pastries.

**9 AM:** Enter the park. Stop at the Port of Entry fruit stand and stock your fanny pack, then make your way to Marvel Super Hero Island and three of the park's biggest attractions.

**10:30 AM:** On to Toon Lagoon. Now's the time to tuck into that fruit pack.

**12:30 PM:** Head back to the Port of Entry in time for your character lunch reservation at Confisco Grille. Spend some time schmoozing with Dr. Doom and Spidey before starting counter-clockwise around the park to Seuss Landing.

**3:30 PM:** Spend the rest of the day exploring the final two IOA lands: Lost Continent and Jurassic Park. Stop at Frozen Desert in the former for a refreshing icy lemonade.

**6 PM:** Exit the park. Head to CityWalk for a theme dining experience at Pastamoré. Spend the next couple of hours dancing off that fresh mozzarella at some of the venue's hottest clubs.

**Or:**

**6 PM:** Exit the park. Head back to your room for a quick shower and a nap before dinner.

**8 PM:** Thoroughly refreshed, you're ready to enjoy a fine dining experience at Portofino Bay Resort's premier restaurant, Delfino Riviera, or at CityWalk's top restaurant, Emeril's Orlando.

## Itinerary Two

**9 AM:** Enter the park. Stop at the Port of Entry fruit stand for a delicious, entirely natural breakfast. Start your tour of the Islands counter-clockwise, spending the morning with the kids in Seuss Landing.

**10:30 AM:** Grab a sweet and sour Frozen Goose Juice at Moose Juice Goose Juice, and continue your counter-clockwise tour to the Lost Continent. Don't miss Dueling Dragons!

**12:30 PM:** Tuck into your classically-inspired lunch at Mythos. Thoroughly sated, spend the early hours of the afternoon exploring the "wild life" in Jurassic Park.

**3 PM:** If you find yourself a bit peckish, split a vegan sandwich with someone at Blondie's in Toon Lagoon, then prepare to get wet on the Island's outrageously fun water rides.

**6 PM:** After drying out in the Incredible Hulk Coaster's G-force winds, head back to the Port of Entry in time for your dinner reservation at Confisco Grille. Exit the park.

**Or:**

**6 PM:** Exit the park. Head back to your digs at Portofino Bay for a vegan wood-fired pizza and grilled vegetable salad by the pool, courtesy of Splendido Pizzeria.

✿ **Port of Entry Fruit Stand**
   **Vegebility: Excellent**
   **Price: Moderate**
   Snacks
   Port of Entry
   Islands of Adventure

If you forget to bring snacks to the park with you, you can always hit this little gem in the Port of Entry. Ripe and delicious fruit is trucked in from Universal's produce suppliers daily, and this fruit cart brings the best of the best directly to you. Florida citrus, red and green apples, pears, grapes, watermelon, and mixed fruit cups are available for healthful one-stop shopping. Liquid refreshments include Tropicana juices, Arizona Iced Tea, Gatorade, and ice cold bottled water. Stick a bottle in your fanny pack, and you're ready to hit the rides!

---

⑱ **Mythos**
   **Vegebility: Fair**
   **Price: Moderate**
   Casual American
   Table Service
   L, D *(dinner during high season only)*
   The Lost Continent
   Islands of Adventure
   (407) 224-4534
   MC/V/AE/Discover

A masterpiece of restaurant staging, Mythos is one of the most popular places to eat in the Islands of Adventure. Set in a dormant volcanic "rock outcropping" (also known as poured concrete) overlooking the Inland Sea, the restaurant is a tribute to characters of classical myth and legend. Not to be outdone by Disney's Tree of Life in the Animal Kingdom, Universal craftspeople carved the images of Greek gods like Zeus and Poseidon, heroes such as Hercules, and mythic beasts—the Sirens from Homer's Odyssey and others—into the rock. The result is an indoor/outdoor bas relief guaranteed to make a fantasy lover's ears wiggle.

One might expect to find a dark, cavernous space awaiting diners inside. Far from it! Walls of windows, sky lights, and glass verandah doors help transform the space into the most upscale dining room in the park, with plenty of light and crystal chandeliers, to boot. The open kitchen features a state-of-the-art wood-fired oven and, in good weather, diners can sip wine on the verandah overlooking the inland sea.

*Some volcano, eh?*

Before being seated, diners are led on a brief tour of the restaurant, past the kitchen and over to the dessert table to check out the day's sweet offerings. A glance at Mythos' seasonal menu suggests a dearth of meatless entrees: a Thai-influenced pesto linguini is made with a chicken stock, as is the penne pasta (which also includes duck sausage) and all house risottos. But a single phone call in the morning ensures that special items will be awaiting your arrival that afternoon.

For vegans, Mythos' chefs are happy to toss the eggless penne with diced tomatoes, basil, and garlic, or to make a cheeseless wood oven pizza with gourmet toppings like asparagus, broccoli

## Facts for Foodies

As you munch on vegetarian delicacies at Mythos, you're following in the footsteps of the classical Greek gods. Perched atop Mount Olympus, Zeus, Athena, and their mythic cohorts feasted on ambrosia and nectar. Ambrosia, the food of the gods, was a vegetarian porridge made from fruit, cheese, olive oil, honey, water, and barley. Nectar is believed to have been a drink much like mead, a fermented honey-based "wine" consumed in ancient Greece before the advent of viticulture. According to legend, the gods and goddesses were rendered bloodless—and therefore immortal—by these heavenly delicacies.

Will a vegetarian diet make meatless diners live forever? We'll keep you posted...

rabe, red and yellow tomatoes, or even plantains. For less strict vegetarians, there's that delicious linguine with "minted Thai cilantro pesto" (made without the chicken stock, but with pecorino romano). Start with a mixed baby green salad topped with Maytag bleu cheese and a tart cherry vinaigrette, and you've got a terrific meal. Other tempting appetizers include a tomato and buffalo mozzarella plate, or grilled Salinas asparagus, drizzled with citrus butter and topped with crispy lemon rings. For those of us who don't do dairy, the butter is easily omitted.

During low season, Mythos is open for lunch only, re-opening for dinner between April and September and during the winter holidays. For either meal, reservations are strongly recommended.

## Worth a Mention at Islands of Adventure

### Port of Entry

At ❶ **Croissant Moon Bakery**, pint sized explorers can tuck into the Little Traveler's Meal: a peanut butter and jelly sandwich with potato sticks, fruit, and a small soda. Ask for it on peasant bread, and your little shaver will enjoy a totally vegan lunch. Coffee, a selection of cakes, Danishes, fruit tarts, tossed salads, and a fruit cup are available for travelers little and big.

Funnel cakes, Belgian waffles, and ice cream await adventurers willing to travel on the ❷ **Arctic Express**—and, of course, lots of delicious strawberries, cinnamon apples, and whipped cream can be heaped on top (just in case your calorie count is low for the day).

## Marvel Super Hero Island

Super vegans can save the universe on a full stomach, thanks to ❺ **Café 4's** Very Veggie pizza, made with a traditional dairy- and egg-free shell. Ask for it without cheese. Less than marvel-ous soups on the menu all contain chicken stock. And at ❻ **Captain America Diner**, you'll wage a mighty battle with the evil forces of thoughtless menu planning: side orders of garden salad, fries, and onion rings are the only meatless offerings.

## Toon Lagoon

❾ **Blondie's: Home of the Dagwood** offers deli sandwiches made to order. Ask for an all-veggie filling on one of two vegan breads—the pullman loaf and the peasant bread—for a portable dairy- and egg-free meal. Chef's salads, deep dish apple pies, sodas, beer, and wine are also on tap in this real-life rendition of the ditzy blonde's cartoon kitchen.

Jumping into the funnies at the ❼ **Comic Strip Café** is akin to walking into a minefield for vegetarians. This large multi-ethnic "food court" features dishes from three continents, most of which contain chicken or beef stock. In China, both the fried rice and the vegetable stir fry contain chicken stock; in Mexico, the Mexican rice and charra beans contain bacon, chicken, and beef stock; in Italy, the pasta salad is made with hard salami. What does that leave us? A few salads for vegans, and cheese pizza, cheese ravioli, and fettucini Alfredo for those of us who can handle a massive dairy hit.

At ❿ **Wimpy's**, a deceptively appealing spinach salad is on offer, but beware: the salad contains bacon, egg, and a hot bacon dressing. Ask for it with oil and vinegar, and sans pork. If you're not on a strict diet, you'll love the hot fudge sundaes and waffle cones at ❽ **Cathy's Ice Cream**.

## Jurassic Park

The restaurants in Jurassic Park are true to the Island's theme: they're right out of the Stone Age, at least for those of us who eschew flesh. For vegans, the only thing available at any eating establishment on this island are fruit cups, side garden salads, and sides of roasted corn and potatoes. Be sure to order the latter two sans butter. Oh, well. At least you can drown your sorrows with a frozen tropical drink at ⓭ **The Watering Hole**.

Vegetarians who eat dairy can scarf down a "Cheese Overload"

# Veggie Kids at Islands of Adventure

Starches and the ubiquitous PBJ play the starring roles in the kid's selections at Universal's Islands of Adventure. If your kids have small appetites but discerning tastebuds, your best bet may be to eschew the kiddie menu and share two or three adult meals around the table.

## Vegetarian Kids' Meals at Table Service Restaurants

**Croissant Moon Bakery (Port of Entry):**
The Little Traveler's Meal (Peanut better and jelly sandwich, potato sticks, fruit, and small soda)

**Circus McGurkus Café Stoo-pendous (Seuss Landing):**
Kid-sized cheese ravioli

**Comic Strip Café (Toon Lagoon):**
Child sized cheese ravioli; spaghetti with marinara sauce (special order)

**Café 4 (Marvel Super-Hero Island):**
Café 4 Kids Pizza Slice

## Healthful Snacks

**Port of Entry Fruit Stand (Port of Entry):**
Fresh whole fruits

**Moose Juice Goose Juice (Seuss Landing):**
Tangerine and green apple juices, fresh or frozen

**The Frozen Dessert (The Lost Continent):**
Frozen lemonade; fruit cup

---

personal pizza at ❷ **Pizza Predattoria**. And that side order garden salad we mentioned above is found here, too. ❶ **Thunder Falls Terrace** offers little more than sides: roasted corn, roasted potatoes, and rosemary flatbread all contain dairy. The Terrace's black beans and Thunder Falls rice are both made with a chicken base.

Another word of warning: all pudding cups found on menus in Jurassic Park—as elsewhere in the park—contain gelatin. Welcome back to the land that time forgot!

### The Lost Continent

The Vegetarian Falafel Sandwich at the ❻ **Fire-Eater's Grill** is a refreshing alternative to the meat-based fast food served elsewhere in Islands of Adventure. Made from the classic recipe combining chickpeas and parsley, the falafel is stuffed into pita bread and topped with tahini. The sandwich contains egg, but it might as well be vegan when compared with the dairy-rich Red Pepper Poppers: deep fried cream cheese and red pepper balls, served with a side of french fries. (Hey, who says vegetarians have to be healthy?) A small tossed green salad is also on the menu, as are double fudge brownies and home made cookies.

If you're hankerin' for a baked potato, head over to the ❹ **Enchanted Oak Tavern**, one of the only places on property to get a piping hot spud. And if you don't do dairy, be sure to ask for the potato—and the roasted corn on the cob—without butter.

If you've got a sweet tooth, stop by ⓯ **The Frozen Desert** after lunch. Swirled soft serve cups and sundaes, "Lost Cargo" fruit cups, cookies, and candy are all available. Fresh lemonade, pretzels, and more fruit cups can be had at ⓱ **Oasis Coolers**.

### Seuss Landing

*Would you, could you , Sam I am*
*Serve it up without the ham?*

At the ⓴ **Green Eggs and Ham Cafe,** all entrées are typically served with meat. But friends of Sam can request the signature dish—a Green Eggs, Grilled Ham, and Cheese sandwich—without the ham. Parsley adds the requisite color to this dish in the park's most Seussian dining experience. A side garden salad and fresh fruit cup are also on the menu.

Dine under the big top watching jugglers and trapeze artists at ㉒ **Circus McGurkus Café Stoo-pendous**. At lunch and dinner, vegans can special order spaghetti with marinara sauce (usually available only on the lasagna entrée and kids' ravioli), accompanied by the ubiquitous fresh garden salad. Less strict vegetarians have a choice of cheese pizza, lasagna, cheese ravioli with garlic cream sauce, and an assortment of sides. Chocolate cake, homemade cookies, and fudge brownies are highlights on the dessert menu.

At ㉑ **Hop on Pop Ice Cream Shop**, tuck into sundaes, banana splits, and other ice cream concoctions. But for something equally delicious—and a tad more healthful—head over to ⓳ **Moose Juice Goose Juice** for fresh or frozen Moose (i.e., tangerine) or Goose (i.e., sour green apple) juice. Fruit cups are available here, too.

# Chapter 14

# CityWalk

**Universal Orlando Main Number:** *(407) 363-8000*
**Dining Requests:** *(407) 224-6339*
**Universal Orlando Food Service Office:** *(407) 363-8340*
*foodserviceCUF@uescape.com*
*Call the food service office to arrange special meals.*

*T*he first portion of Universal's expansion plans to be realized, CityWalk opened in February, 1999. An unabashed challenge to Disney's Pleasure Island, CityWalk is a nighttime entertainment complex spread across 30 acres and home to a dozen themed restaurants and nightclubs. Unlike Pleasure Island, each establishment charges its own admission price.

Restaurants at CityWalk take the "eatertainment" concept to its ultimate conclusion. There's a restaurant devoted to the NASCAR auto racing league, where waitstaff don pit crew uniforms and utensils look like mechanic's tools. There's also the Motown Café, where diners sit beneath the largest vinyl record in existence, and the house bands are "tribute" combos who evoke the Temptations and the Supremes. And then there's Bob Marley—A Tribute to Freedom: a chain owned by Marley's family. No student of late-1900s pop culture can afford not to visit this eatery, which features selections like "No Woman, No Cry": a tasty salad named for a song meant to console a woman whose son has been shot dead in the street. We're not sure how those two were paired, but we do wish Bob were here to enjoy it with us.

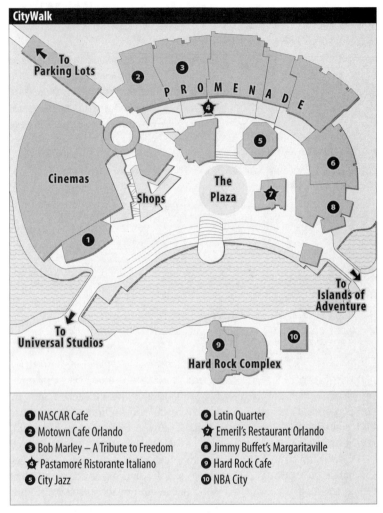

**CityWalk**

To Parking Lots

PROMENADE

❷ ❸ ❹ ❺ ❻ ❼ ❽

Cinemas

Shops

The Plaza

❶

To Islands of Adventure

To Universal Studios

❾ ❿

Hard Rock Complex

❶ NASCAR Cafe
❷ Motown Cafe Orlando
❸ Bob Marley – A Tribute to Freedom
❹ Pastamoré Ristorante Italiano
❺ City Jazz

❻ Latin Quarter
❼ Emeril's Restaurant Orlando
❽ Jimmy Buffet's Margaritaville
❾ Hard Rock Cafe
❿ NBA City

Of course, the concept restaurant that started the theming craze is the universally-known Hard Rock Cafe, which happens to have its world headquarters in Orlando. Not to be outdone by Motown, Nascar, and the other upstarts, the Cafe moved from its already large location adjoining Universal Studios into its new, even more monumental CityWalk digs. Appropriately patterned after Rome's Colosseum, the new Hard Rock Orlando is housed in a 140,000-square-foot building, with more eating space than any other

Hard Rock and an adjoining 2,000-seat live music venue.

According to experts on the ground, Great American Concept Eateries like Planet Hollywood and the Fashion Café are losing money right and left. But trends in the Real World don't necessarily hold true in the augmented reality of a theme park. That being said, CityWalk offers at least one restaurant that gives America's finest dining rooms a run for their money. Emeril's Orlando, owned and overseen by New Orleans celebrity chef Emeril Lagasse, kicks up the spice—and the standards—more than a notch, leaving its neighboring Universal eateries in the dust.

## Best of the Best at CityWalk

⭐ **Emeril's Restaurant Orlando**
**Vegebility: Fair**
**Price: Expensive**
Casual/Upscale New Creole-Acadian
Table Service
L, D
CityWalk
(407) 224-2424
All major credit cards accepted

Emeril Lagasse, one of the best-known chefs in America today, has been credited with revitalizing Creole-Acadian (Cajun) cooking. He is the chef and proprietor of three award-winning restaurants in New Orleans, a fourth in Las Vegas' MGM Grand Hotel, and now a fifth at Universal Orlando CityWalk. He sells cookbooks by the millions. He is the host of the Food Network's two highest rated programs, Essence of Emeril and Emeril Live. He's the weekly food correspondent for ABC's Good Morning America. In short, he is a megastar—a culinary supernova—in the galaxy of American tastemakers.

He's also an amazingly talented chef. One taste of an Emeril meal will leave no doubt in your mind why he's been a James Beard Foundation nominee for the nation's Outstanding Chef, or why two of his restaurants—Emeril's and NOLA—have been dubbed Restaurant of the Year by Esquire magazine's John Mariani.

The food at Emeril's Restaurant Orlando is, by every account, exquisite. Lagasse prides himself on pampering his guests, including vegetarians. "We try to take care of guests in any way we can," he says, "like vegetarian tastings. Which reminds me of our truffles... we're known for our truffles." If Lagasse gives you a hint like that, you'd be smart make a reservation for when the rare fungi are in season.

*F*or a comprehensive guide to our ratings system, see page xviii.

## At-a-Glance Grid

# CityWalk: Best of the Best

**Key to Categories and Abbreviations**

**O/L, V: Ovo-lacto and vegan selections**

• - Always available    + - Available upon request    A - Request in advance

**Es: Type of establishment**

T - Table Service    C - Counter service    S - Snack stand or cart

**$: Average price for a single vegetarian entrée**

| | | |
|---|---|---|
| 1 - under $10 | 3 - $16 - $20 | 5 - $31 - $40 |
| 2 - $10 - $15 | 4 - $21 - $30 | 6 - over $40 |

**Meals:**

B - Breakfast    L - Lunch    D - Dinner    S - Snacks

| CityWalk | O/L | V | Es | $ | Meals |
|---|---|---|---|---|---|
| ⭐ Pastamoré Ristorante Italiano | • | + | T | 2 | D |
| ⭐ Emeril's Restaurant Orlando | • | + | T | 3 | L, D |

In the meantime, you'll just have to make do with everyday treasures like smashed organic new potatoes, served with confit of wild and exotic mushrooms and flavored with essence of white truffle oil and shaved parmesan cheese. Or an open faced assortment of vegetable ravioli with a sweet onion crust, topped with a carrot emulsion. Or a deceptively plain-sounding "grilled and roasted vegetable plate." Simple. Elegant. Delicious.

And, of course, the chefs at Emerils can do anything your heart desires (and diet requires) with advance notice.

If you plan to dine on the weekend, we recommend booking ninety days (yes, that's three months)

in advance. For weekdays, booking anywhere from two to three weeks out should be sufficient. And be sure to confirm your reservation the day before dining, or risk being turned away at the door.

---

⭐ **Pastamoré Ristorante Italiano**
**Vegebility: Good**
**Price: Moderate**
Casual Italian
Table Service
D
CityWalk
(407) 224-9255
MC/V/AE/Discover

It's hard to walk past an Italian restaurant and not feel the urge to enter. The aromas of robust tomato sauces, baked cheeses, and garlic-infused breads waft enticingly nose-ward, and the hearts of those who love fruity olive oil skip a beat. Vegetarians routinely count their blessings that traditional Italian cooking is unabashedly pasta- and vegetable-based, and people who abstain from eating meat are nearly always well-served at a ristorante. Pastamoré—CityWalk's home-style Italian eatery—is no exception.

Diners enter the restaurant through a make-believe Italian marketplace which offers a variety of vegetarian and vegan delicacies. A selection of olives, fresh mozzarella, eggplant caponata, marinated artichoke hearts, and more can be ordered to go, or enjoyed alfresco on Pastamoré's outdoor patio, the Marketplace Cafe. Open from 7:30 AM to 2:00 AM, the cafe is a great place to stop for lunch, or after a night of club hopping. The café also offers Italian sandwiches (including a veggie version), pastries, ice cream, and a variety of coffees and cold beverages.

But the real treat for vegan and vegetarian diners waits inside Pastamoré's full service restaurant, open for dinner only. No fewer than five meatless appetizers grace the menu. A vegan antipasto plate—featuring such yummies as grilled portobello mushrooms, plum tomatoes, eggplant caponata, and marinated artichokes—can

be made to order, with no advance notice. One warning: the Italian Wedding Soup is made with chicken broth.

Vegetarians who eat dairy will have no problem finding a meal among the entrées, where eight selections are meatless, including delicious choices like a wild mushroom and asparagus risotto and freshly-made pizza margherita. Vegans can get in on the pizza action, too. On request, thin-crusted flatbreads are made without egg or dairy, topped with roasted veggies, and baked to perfection in the oak-fired oven. Advance notice? Not necessary. Another strictly vegetarian meal can be had by asking for the penne with roasted garlic and broccoli, but without cheese. The latter, along with three ovo-lacto pasta dishes, can be ordered "family style" and

*Facts for foodies*

*The word **alfresco** is derived from the Italian phrase al fresco, meaning "in the fresh air," and refers to the healthful Mediterranean practice of eating meals outdoors. In central Florida, eating under sunny blue skies is possible—and highly recommended—all year round.*

shared around the table for less than $15—a terrific deal.

If you have any room left, don't miss the large selection of Italian pastries and other *dolci*, including traditional cassata, tiramisu, gelati, and spumoni. Vegans will also be glad to note that the occasional sorbetto can be found in the back—but be sure to order in advance of your arrival if you have your heart set on one.

## Worth a Mention at CityWalk

Looking for a Gardenburger in paradise? Join the flock of parrotheads at ❽ **Jimmy Buffett's Margaritaville**, a Key West-themed restaurant that pays homage to the tequila-laced concoction and the song that made Buffett's career. Key West specialties, including Key Lime pie and various dishes involving conch, are featured on the menu. But sadly, the two vegan dishes that once joined them "didn't make the menu cut" and have been removed. With 24 hours' notice, however, the chefs are more than happy to resurrect one of them: a spinach tortilla wrap filled with an assortment of grilled vegetables. A word of warning: avoid

any seemingly vegetarian dish here that's made with black beans. The sweet little legumes are cooked with meat.

Original Gardenburgers® are also on the menu at the ❶ **NASCAR Cafe**. Tuck into your ovo-lacto burger—courtesy of Wholesome and Hearty and the restaurant's freezer—seated in your own gleaming racing machine, using utensils that look like mechanic's tools, and watching Richard Petty go round and round on the massive video wall. The only other meatless fuel on the menu comes in appetizer form: onion rings, fried mozzarella sticks, and cheese dip. If you're in the mood for salad, order the Mexican without the beef chili—and, if you're vegan, without the sour cream and cheese—and expect a mix of lettuce, black olives, green onion, diced tomato ,and jalapeño peppers, served with warm tortilla chips. And for all you race fans, here's a character dining experience with a twist: NASCAR legends stop in to sign autographs whenever a big race is in town at the Walt Disney World Speedway.

Unlike most other eateries, ❾ **Hard Rock Cafe** makes its own veggie burger—a delightfully nutty, spicy product that's now being marketed as direct competition to Gardenburgers in supermarkets across America. Happily, the Hard Rock burger, unlike the original Gardenburger, is vegan. Sadly, the

# Veggie Kids at CityWalk

*In general, vegetarian children's meals at CityWalk are heavy on cheese and starches. If you and your tots are vegan, or if you'd like them to have something green in their diets, your best bet may be to eschew the kiddie menu and share two or three adult meals or sandwiches around the table.*

## Vegetarian Kids' Meals at Table Service Restaurants

**Emeril's:**
  Kid's wood-fired pizza (request vegetarian)

**NBA City:**
  Grilled cheese sandwich; veggie pizza (request without cheese)

**Hard Rock Cafe:**
  Cheese pizza; grilled cheese sandwich; macaroni and cheese

**Pastamoré:**
  Five cheese ravioli; cheese pizza; peanut butter and jelly sandwich; spaghetti with tomato sauce

**The Latin Quarter:**
  Grilled flour tortilla, filled with cheese; veggie pizza

**Margaritaville:**
  Macaroni and cheese

**Nascar Cafe:**
  Cheese pizza; spaghetti with tomato sauce (substitute for meat sauce)

## Kid-Friendly Vegetarian Offerings at Counter Service Restaurants

**Marketplace Cafe (at entrance to Pastamoré):**
  Italian veggie sandwich

---

bun on which it's served here in Orlando is not. Another perfectly vegetarian meal—the HRC Grilled Vegetable Sandwich, with zucchini, yellow squash, roasted red peppers, and avocado—is delicious, but is also ovo-lacto due only to the bread. The solution for vegans? Bring your own bun! ;-) Grilled veggie fajitas, a massive nacho plate, and a green house salad round out the vegetarian entrées.

You'll find side dishes only at the ❷ **Motown Cafe Orlando**, where "slow-cooked" soul food, Motor City memorabilia, and house bands that bring back memories of the Temptations and the Supremes take center stage. Sweet potato and shoestring fries, baked macaroni and cheese, and a house salad aren't quite "All I Need," but they are the only meatless items available on the menu.

Next door to Motown is ❸ **Bob Marley—A Tribute to Freedom**, a replica of the reggae artist's home in Kingston, Jamaica. Since Marley himself was a member of the Rastafari religion—a faith in which eating a vegetarian diet and avoiding alcohol play a major role—you'd think the menu here would be extremely veg-friendly, if not entirely *ital* (salt-free, vegetarian Rasta cooking).

Far from it. The only meatless entrée on the menu is "Natty Dread:" vegan Jamaican vegetable patties served with smoky ketchup and yucca fries. Seems that the "Freedom" being saluted here is the freedom to drink Red Stripe beer and eat meat, two things which Marley himself did not do. That being said, the music and the overall vibe of the Marley family's club is laid-back and enjoyable, with fantastic live roots rock reggae bands and a large open air dance floor. Three other vegetarian items—chips and salsa, salad, and a smoky cheddar cheese fondue—are among the appetizers.

Dairy does double duty at City Cheese—oops, make that ❺ **City Jazz**. The Take 5 cheese platter lays out baby gouda, smoked cheddar, port salut, pepper boursin, and baby brie with crackers and grapes; the A-Train is a baby brie round glazed with honey and served with toasted walnuts and dried fruit; the Big Band is breaded, fried three-cheese ravioli topped with fresh tomato, basil, and aioli. If you're vegan or eating light, you may want to skip the snacks and focus on the fabulous music here.

Cheese takes a bow at the ❻ **Latin Quarter**, too, where only two items on the menu—both appetizers—are meatless. Recent rave reviews about the restaurant's Nuevo Latin cuisine make us even sadder that the only things available for vegetarians are nachos and quesadillas, the sort of thing we can find on the menu at Mexican restaurants across America.

A refreshing lack of cute theme-y names is in evidence on the menu at ❿ **NBA City**, the most recently opened CityWalk establishment at press time. You won't find a lot of memorabilia here either—no game balls or sweat-stained jerseys—but you will find a surprisingly decent amount of vegetarian food. Mediterranean classics like bruschetta, fresh mozzarella and tomato salad, penne primavera, and a couple of brick oven pizzas are all possibilities for folks who eat dairy. Ask for the primavera without cheese and it's a vegan feast, too. There's also a veggie sandwich made with fire-roasted zucchini, yellow squash, and red peppers, topped with fresh mozzarella, spinach, red onion, cucumber, tomatoes, and basil and served open-face on a ciabatta bun.

At dessert, NBA City Chef Marianne scores a three-pointer with her "Cinnamon Berries:" fresh strawberries fried in a non-alcoholic beer batter, dusted with cinnamon sugar and served with a side of ice cream. With 24 hours' notice, Marianne will make a vegan version of the batter, and serve it up without dairy. *Swish!*

# Chapter 15

# Resorts at Universal Orlando

**Universal Orlando Main Number:** *(407) 363-8000*
**The Portofino Bay Hotel:** *(407) 503-9000*
*Call Portofino Bay directly to speak with*
*hotel chefs and arrange special meals.*

ne of the most important lessons that Universal Studios seems to have learned from Cousin Mickey is that the best way to make money from your theme park guests is to keep them overnight. Universal has partnered with the Loews Corporation to develop five self-contained resorts, the first three of which—the Portofino Bay Hotel, the Hard Rock Hotel, and the Royal Pacific Resort—should all be in place by the end of 2001. As at Walt Disney World, guests of Universal's on-site resorts enjoy exclusive theme park benefits, like early admission, park-wide charging privileges, and complimentary transportation (via water taxi) to CityWalk, the two theme parks, and other on-site resorts.

The first Universal resort—and the only one open at press time—is the 750-room Portofino Bay Hotel. A masterpiece of resort theming, the hotel has been built around a lake and expertly aged and patina'ed to look like the Italian seaside town of Portofino. All of the guest rooms at Portofino are "smart"—they automatically adjust the room temperature to the most comfortable setting, report any room malfunctions to maintenance, monitor whether the mini-bar is dangerously close to empty, and alert housekeeping when the room is vacant. We're not sure how the ACLU feels about smart rooms, but we find the concept a little eerie. Still, there are advantages to Universal's whiz-bang new hotel

## At-a-Glance Grid

# Portofino Bay Hotel: Best of the Best

**Key to Categories and Abbreviations**

**O/L, V: Ovo-lacto and vegan selections**

• - Always available   + - Available upon request   A - Request in advance

**Es: Type of establishment**

T - Table Service   C - Counter service   S - Snack stand or cart

**$: Average price for a single vegetarian entree**

1 - under $10      3 - $16 - $20      5 - $31 - $40
2 - $10 - $15      4 - $21 - $30      6 - over $40

**Meals:**

B - Breakfast      L - Lunch      D - Dinner      S - Snacks

| Portofino Bay Hotel | O/L | V | Es | $ | Meals |
|---|---|---|---|---|---|
| Delfino Riviera | • | A | T | 3 | D |
| Sal's Market Deli | • | • | C | 1 | B, L, D, S |
| Splendido Pizzeria | • | + | C | 1 | L, D |

system. A guest room key card functions as a credit card for use anywhere on Universal property, and kids can have their own cards, mercifully equipped with pre-set spending limits. And for those lucky guests staying in a villa room or suite, personal butler service is available to make all arrangements for theme park tickets, dinner, spa appointments, laundry service, and so on.

Best of all, the food at the Portofino Bay Hotel is great for vegetarians, as one might expect at a Mediterranean resort. From poolside pizzas to upscale northern Italian dining, people with the most restrictive diets can be accommodated with a minimum of fuss. In short, this is a state-of-the art hotel, as worthy of its top-dollar price tag as the best Disney hotel. *Buon Appetito!*

## Best of the Best at the Portofino Bay Hotel

**Delfino Riviera**
**Vegebility: Fair**
**Price: Expensive**
Upscale Italian
Table Service
D
The Portofino Bay Hotel
Universal Orlando
(407) 503-9000
MC/V/AE/Discover

Located above the Harbor Piazza with a view over Portofino Bay, Delfino Riviera is the resort's fine dining establishment. Elegant and delicious Italian food is prepared in classical Ligurian style, with an emphasis on seasonal availability and freshness. Strolling musicians, dinner jackets, and outstanding service conspire to make Delfino an ideal place for a quiet, romantic dinner for two—even two vegetarians!

Those who eat dairy will have no problem ordering directly from Delfino's menu, which offers a number of ovo-lacto, but still meatless, choices. For the first course, there's Carciofini Riviera: baby artichokes with pearl onions, chanterelles, polenta, and black truffle shavings. Mmmm... The polenta is ordinarily made with parmesan cheese, but with a few days' advance notice, Chef Giorgio Albanese is more than happy to make a vegan version. Mixed baby lettuce salads are also available. For soup, vegetarians can sample the Minestrone Genovese: a traditional Ligurian vegetable soup made with pesto. Traditional pesto contains a generous amount of Pecorino Romano cheese, but again, the kitchen is happy to prepare a vegan soup with ample notice.

As a main course, meatless diners can choose between Pansooti alle Erbe—a house-made herb and ricotta ravioli, finished with a unique and delicious walnut sauce—or Trenette con Pesto alla Genovese: trenette pasta with potatoes, green beans, and pesto. Another delicious dish that is easily altered for guests who eat eggs but do not eat fish is the Lasagnette alle Olive con Pescatrice. House made black olive pasta is shaped into 3" wide individual lasagnettes, topped with a delicious ragú of artichokes, white wine, parsley, and a little extra virgin olive oil. Be sure to request your lasganette without fish. For other main course options, ask to speak with Chef Albanese when making your reservation.

*Dolci* at Delfini, as at most upscale Italian establishments, are divine. One tempting option is

*Facts for foodies*

An uncommon pasta in the U.S., **trenette** *("tray-NAYT-tay") is a narrower, thicker version of* tagliatelle *(tagliatelle is better known in this country as* fettucine, *the noodle's northern Italian name). Long strips of* trenette, *made from water and semolina flour but no egg, are dried and imported directly from Italy to the Portofino Bay Resort's Delfino Riviera. Vegans beware, however: Fresh trenette will almost always contain egg.*

the Zabaglione al Frutti di Bosco: mixed berries, chilled zabaglione (a light, creamy custard made with egg yolks, wine, and sugar), and orange sorbet. Leave off the custard for a sweet but light vegan ending to a wonderful meal.

---

**Sal's Market Deli**
**Vegebility: Excellent**
**Price: Moderate**
Recommended
Casual American
Counter Service/Deli
B, L, D
The Portofino Bay Hotel
Universal Orlando
(407) 503-9000
MC/V/AE/Discover

---

Grab a quick vegetarian meal—or a sandwich to go—from Sal's Deli, located in Portofino Bay's Piazza. Modeled after Peck's deli in Milan, Sal's offers a cornucopia of options for vegetarians, from breakfast breads and fruit to prepared salads, sandwiches, and pizzas.

The deli opens at 6 AM, so it's a great place to pick up a continental breakfast or fruit salad on your way to the park. If you don't do dairy, be sure to ask which muffins and danishes are vegan (believe it or not, there are a few!). You can also pack a lunch of Sal's prepared salads to enjoy at the park.

Fusilli with onions, peppers, and broccoli; marinated mushrooms; grilled vegetables; and a refreshing tomato, cucumber, and onion salad are all 100% vegan. Other standouts in the deli case are penne pasta tossed with sundried tomatoes, and a fine assortment of green and fruit salads.

Want something more substantial? Sal's also offers a hearty vegetarian sandwich. The San Franciscan features portobello mushrooms, roasted red peppers, and goat's cheese on your choice of focaccia, kaiser roll, rye, wheat, or white bread. And all breads at the market are purportedly made without egg or dairy. Ask for the sandwich without cheese for yet another vegan option.

After a long day of theme-parking, take one of Sal's pizzas back to your room and collapse in front of the TV—or in a nice warm bath. The deli's pizza crust and sauce are both strictly vegetarian—no stocks, dairy, or eggs—and can be topped with a wide assortment of vegetables and cheeses.

---

**Splendido Pizzeria**
**Vegebility: Good**
**Price: Moderate**
Casual Italian
Counter Service
L, D

---

$\mathcal{F}$or a comprehensive guide to our ratings system, see page xviii.

The Portofino Bay Hotel
Universal Orlando
(407) 503-9000
MC/V/AE/Discover

This little counter service venue is a great place to get a pool-side lunch, dinner, or snack… especially if you're vegetarian! Nearly half of the menu's offerings are meatless, including three vegan choices. Lighter meals include a salad of seasonal grilled vegetables and mixed greens, topped with extra virgin olive oil and balsamic vinegar. On a hot day, tuck into an iced fruit coupe, including sliced fruit, berries, and—a great touch—mint.

Perfect for a quick "launch lunch" on the boat to the theme parks is the Caesar Salad wrap: romaine lettuce and parmesan rolled in a vegan flat bread. And here's the good news: the Caesar dressing does not contain anchovies. If you're in the mood for a thick, chewy sandwich, try a roasted portobello panino, topped with Roma tomatoes, arugula, and mozzarella, and accompanied by fresh basil aioli.

For a yummy lunch or dinner "on the beach," sample Splendido's pizza. The crust here—as at all Portofino locations—is completely egg- and dairy-free. The Pizza Giardiniera, topped with zucchini, tomatoes, olives, and garlic, can be ordered cheeseless for a 100% vegan pie. Ovo-lacto choices include Pizza Quattro Formaggi e Pesto—garlicky pesto on a chewy crust, smothered in Asiago, fontina, mozzarella, and Parmesan cheeses—or the classic Margherita: tomato, basil, and mozzarella. An assortment of imported and domestic beers and mixed drinks is also available.

## Worth a Mention at Portofino Bay

The most popular restaurant at the resort is **Trattoria del Porto**, billed as "an Italian version of T.G.I. Fridays." Open for breakfast, lunch, and dinner, this casual family-friendly establishment is heavy on the meat and cheese, but has a decent selection for vegetarians who eat eggs and dairy. One breakfast favorite is the frittata primavera: a pie-like open-faced omelet filled with roasted peppers, mushrooms, onions, tomatoes, zucchini, and mozzarella cheese. French toast, Belgian waffles, and banana pecan pancakes are other ovo-lacto choices. A large fruit plate and home fries are available for folks who avoid all animal products.

At both lunch and dinner, the Trattoria features a selection of salads and traditional pasta dishes. Vegans might want to wait 'til dinnertime and try the outstanding roasted vegetable platter—featuring peppers, fennel bulbs, zucchini, squash, and portobello mushrooms, all drizzled with balsamic

# Veggie Kids

*Vegetarian children's meals at Portofino Bay are usually light on inspiration and heavy on cheese. Your kids' best bet for a healthful repast and a full tummy is to share your salad wrap or roasted portobello panino.*

## Vegetarian Kids' Meals at Table Service Restaurants

**Trattoria Del Porto:**

Breakfast: Waffles; pancakes; french toast; cereals

Lunch and Dinner: Macaroni and cheese; grilled cheese sandwich; cheese pizza; peanut butter and jelly sandwich

## Kid-Friendly Veggie Offerings at Counter Service Restaurants

**Splendido Pizzeria:**

Pizzas (request without cheese if vegan); salad wraps; roasted portobello panino

**Sal's Market Deli:**

Breakfast breads; fruit; veggie sandwiches; prepared salads; cheese or vegetable pizza (vegans can special order a vegetable pizza without cheese)

## Healthful Snacks

**Gelateria Coffee House:**

Mango, raspberry, and lemon sorbets

and roasted under a wood fire. Brick oven pizzas made with the resort's vegan crust are available at both meals, as well. One warning: nearly all soups at Trattoria del Porto and at Mama Della's Ristorante are made with pancetta.

**Mama Della's** is a family-style Italian eatery, where entrées like Rigatoni with Italian Sausage or Penne with Grilled Chicken are served in large platters for everyone at the table to share. Unfortunately, the only entrée on the menu for Mama's vegetarian bambini is cheese tortellini with pesto. The Risotto al Funghi—arborio rice with porcini mushrooms and peas—is cooked in a chicken broth, but with advance notice, a vegetable stock can be substituted. True., 100% vegan sorbetto is available for dessert, along with other Italian classics like gelato, tiramisu, and zabaglione.

If you're just in the mood for a true sorbet without the monster meal, head over to the resort's **Gelateria Coffee House**. In addition to mango, raspberry, and lemon sorbetti, the café serves freshly brewed espresso and cappuccino, homemade gelato, and a selection of Italian pastries and cordials.

# Outside the Gates:
# Touring Greater Orlando

**Orlando/Orange County CVB:**
*(800) 551-0181; http://www.go2orlando.com*
**Orlando Weekly:** *http://www.orlandoweekly.com/*
**Orlando Sentinel:** *http://www.orlandosentinel.com/*
Check out these Orlando area websites for ideas about
how to spend the day and up-to-date dining reviews.

# Chapter 16

# Greater Orlando

**Orlando/Orange County CVB:**
*(800) 551-0181; http://www.go2orlando.com*
**Orlando Weekly:** *http://www.orlandoweekly.com/*
**Orlando Sentinel:** *http://www.orlandosentinel.com/*
*Check out these Orlando area websites for ideas about
how to spend the day and up-to-date dining reviews.*

*P*ity the poor Orlandoites, for upon them descends each year, all the days of the year, a plague worse than locusts, or frogs, or even Beanie Babies. The creatures are known by many names—tourists, vacationers, "guests"—but they all have one thing in common. They are drawn, as if by a giant magnet, to the sun-drenched temples of pleasure to the south and west, spoken of in hushed tones by Those Who Have Been There And Seen: Walt Disney World. Universal Orlando. Pirate's Cove Adventure Golf.

A fairly predictable lot, these guests. They come, they deplane, they point their rental cars toward The World, they take the wrong exit and cause a 15-car pileup trying to back down the ramp. All in a day's visit. Safely ensconced in their hotel rooms, they don Bermuda shorts and fanny packs and begin tramping from attraction to attraction in search of ever more extravagant corporate pleasure. Four days later, overstimulated and burned out, they point their rental cars back to Orlando International and leave—without ever having thought to venture into the city they are supposedly visiting.

Don't let this happen to you.

Just beyond La-La Land lies the real Orlando, shining like a beacon to those desperately in need of a reality fix—or a lunch that doesn't cost $30.00. Don't be fooled by the proliferation of grocery stores boasting slogans like "The Beef People," and billboards offering "Free Steaks with Windshield Replacement." The constant flow of tourists from an array of cultural backgrounds ensures that plenty of Orlando restaurateurs are able to provide vegetarians with enticing options. Armed with the right info, vegetarians can eat quite well in the shadow of The Mouse.

# Chapter 17

# Southern Orlando

**Orlando/Orange County CVB:**
*(800) 551-0181; http://www.go2orlando.com*
**Orlando Weekly:** *http://www.orlandoweekly.com/*
**Orlando Sentinel:** *http://www.orlandosentinel.com/*
*Check out these Orlando area websites for ideas about
how to spend the day and up-to-date dining reviews.*

*A* hodge podge of neighborhoods and commercial districts, the southern half of Orlando is dominated by the two mega parks that bring tourists here from around the globe. With almost 50,000 hotel rooms on offer, Walt Disney World and its younger sibling Universal Orlando are host to a gajillion vacationers. 99.99999% of vacationers to Orlando who don't stay inside the parks sack out in one of the hotels and resorts located in southern Orlando, and often grab a meal—usually breakfast or dinner—in one of the countless fast fooderies lining the area's main thoroughfares.

After a long day on your feet, it's tempting to stop at the first place advertising a salad bar, but vegetarians can do a heck of a lot better than that. There are fabulous restaurants just a few minutes' drive beyond the entrance to the parks, offering a wider variety of delicious vegetarian fare than many American cities of comparable size.

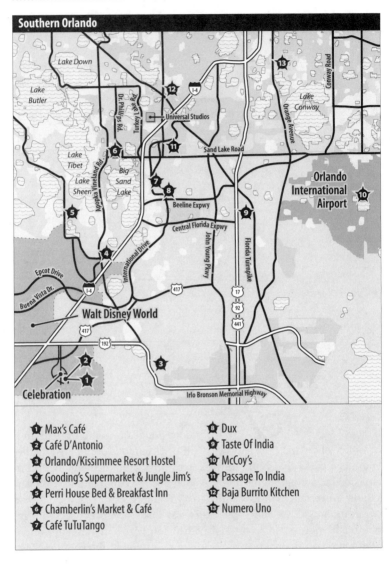

**Southern Orlando**

1. Max's Café
2. Café D'Antonio
3. Orlando/Kissimmee Resort Hostel
4. Gooding's Supermarket & Jungle Jim's
5. Perri House Bed & Breakfast Inn
6. Chamberlin's Market & Café
7. Café TuTuTango
8. Dux
9. Taste Of India
10. McCoy's
11. Passage To India
12. Baja Burrito Kitchen
13. Numero Uno

## Celebration, Florida

Picture if you will a perfect town, a cozy burg with cute houses and safe streets. Imagine passing a lazy summer day on your veranda, a glass of iced tea by your side, the excited shouts of happy children ringing off in the distance. Your new neighbor from down the

**At-a-Glance Grid**

# Southern Orlando: Best of the Best

**Key to Categories and Abbreviations**

**O/L, V: Ovo-lacto and vegan selections**

• - Always available    + - Available upon request    A - Request in advance

**Es: Type of establishment**

T - Table Service    C - Counter service    S - Snack stand or cart

**$: Average price for a single vegetarian entrée**

| | | |
|---|---|---|
| 1 - under $10 | 3 - $16 - $20 | 5 - $31 - $40 |
| 2 - $10 - $15 | 4 - $21 - $30 | 6 - over $40 |

**Meals:**

B - Breakfast    L - Lunch    D - Dinner    S - Snacks

| Celebration | O/L | V | Es | $ | Meals |
|---|---|---|---|---|---|
| **2** Cafe D'Antonio | • | + | T | 2 | L, D |
| **1** Max's Café | • | • | T | 1 | B,* L, D |
| **I-4 Exit 27** | | | | | |
| **4** Jungle Jim's | • | + | T | 1 | L, D |
| **I-Drive and U.S. 192** | | | | | |
| **7** Café Tu Tu Tango | • | • | T | 1 | L, D |
| **8** Dux | • | A | T | 5 | D |
| **11** Passage to India | • | + | T | 2 | L, D |
| **Elsewhere in Southern Orlando** | | | | | |
| **12** Baja Burrito Kitchen | • | + | C | 1 | L, D |
| **10** McCoy's | • | • | T | 1 | L, D |
| **13** Numero Uno | • | • | T | 1 | L, D |
| **9** Taste of India | • | A | T | 1 | L, D |

*Breakfast served only on weekends

street strolls by and you chat for a moment about your houses, comparing your stately Victorian home with her charming Mediterranean villa. You invite her to a "welcome to the neighborhood" dinner this evening at the one of the terrific restaurants downtown, just a short walk away. She wanders off to continue her errands. Alone again, you sit back, relax, and try to remember what life was like before you moved to Celebration.

Sidewalks with unsightly cracks, ugly houses with loud paint jobs and icky curtains, seedy bars, and noisy cars—in other words, reality—has no place in Disney's planned community just a few miles from the Walt Disney World complex. Virtually every detail of life, from where you park your car to what color you can paint your front door, is carefully controlled by a rigid homeowner's covenant—and, ultimately, by Disney. This isn't necessarily a bad thing: there's virtually no crime in Celebration, for example, and every home is wired for high-speed Internet access. And the town's school system is as progressive as any you're likely to find. But some residents complain of a certain corporate blandness to life here.

Dining options are a mixed bag in Celebration, too. All the restaurants in town are privately owned, but hand picked by Disney. Unfortunately, though, vegetarian diners in Celebration don't benefit from the obsessively inclusive menu planning of Dieter Hannig and his team at Walt Disney World. As a result, a decidedly veg-friendly hot spot like Max's Café sits almost caddy-corner to the downright hostile Cuban chain restaurant, Columbia. In this respect, Celebration resembles late twentieth-century America very closely, indeed.

*Realists, take heart!*

# Places to Eat

## Best of the Best in Celebration

❷ **Cafe D'Antonio**
**Vegebility: Good**
**Price: Moderate**
Casual Italian
Table Service
L, D
691 Front Street, Suite 110
Celebration, FL 34747
(407) 566-CAFÉ (2233)
http://www.antoniosonline.com/cafe.htm
All major credit cards accepted

In the heart of Celebration's dining sector, Cafe D'Antonio sits like a beacon to all who love authentic Italian cuisine. Owner Greg Gentile has logged many a frequent-flier mile to the Old Country in search of the best products Italy can provide. The results are simply delicious.

Served in a candle-lit room (or outside overlooking the lake and downtown Celebration), each course—from antipasti to dolci—offers a number of vegetarian options. Begin your meal with fresh mozzarella, made in-house with your choice of cow's milk or imported water buffalo milk, and served with tomato slices, fresh basil, and a drizzling of olive oil. Or tuck into bruschetta alla Romana:

*F*or a comprehensive guide to our ratings system, see page xviii.

freshly toasted homemade bread brushed with olive oil and topped with diced tomatoes, onions, and fresh basil. It's totally vegan, and absolutely divine.

The pasta course includes Penne Pomodoro—perfectly al dente penne pasta, served with a fresh tomato basil sauce—which can be made vegan by omitting the parmesan cheese topping. Another menu standout is the Orecchiette Siciliana: "little ear" pasta tossed with olive oil, garlic, fresh basil, sun-dried tomatoes, and broccoli. Mmm mmm good—but be sure to request this dish without chicken stock. In fact, many of the Cafe's best pasta dishes contain chicken or beef stock, but can be made without. Just ask your server about the contents of your favorite dish before ordering, and make you use the V-word early and often. All of Cafe D'Antonio's house pastas are eggless, though, and vegans are as easily and happily accommodated as vegetarians who eat eggs and dairy.

Meatless diners love the café for its pizzas. Classics like the Margherita and Bianca are joined by less well-known combinations like the Impanata, a pie stuffed with olives, mushrooms, broccoli, cheese, and tomato sauce. Vegans can tuck into a cheeseless Mediterraneo, brushed with olive oil and topped with grilled vegetables. All of the Café's pizza shells

are egg- and dairy-free. A selection of calzones and nightly risotto specials are also available. And for dessert, don't miss the limone and tangerine *sorbetti*: true dairy-free sorbets imported from Italy.

---

☆ **Max's Café**
**Vegebility: Good**
**Price: Moderate–Expensive**
Casual American
Table Service
B (weekends only), L, D
701 Front Street, Suite 160
Celebration, FL 34747
(407) 566-1144
MC/V/AE

At Max's Café, vegetarians are not just tolerated, they're considered! One of the original restaurants in the town of Celebration, this 5,000-square-foot "diner" specializes in American comfort food, including some great vegetarian dishes. Among the best veggie selections is a grilled portobello mushroom melt with tomatoes, lettuce, asiago cheese, and sun-dried tomato vinaigrette on a toasted onion focaccia bun. Fresh confetti-colored salads, innovative pasta dishes, and other delicious sandwiches, including Chef Jeff Adema's fabulous veggie burger, spill from the menu. The burger is made from chick peas, mushrooms, onions, garlic, parsley, spinach, carrots, and a tangy oriental pepper sauce. And watch out: It's

# A Vegetarian Tour of Southern Orlando

*Spend a fun-filled day right outside the gates to the parks on one of our tried-and-true itineraries. Be sure to make advance reservations at the restaurant of your choosing.*

**Itinerary One**

**9 AM:** Tuck into a breakfast of vegan baked goods from Chamberlin's Market and Café at the Marketplace on Dr. Phillips Boulevard.

**10 AM:** Cross under I-4 and make your way over to International Drive for a weird and wacky morning at Ripley's Believe It or Not! Museum.

**1 PM:** Lunch at Passage to India or at Café Tu Tu Tango, both on International Drive.

**3 PM:** Shop 'til you drop (or at least all afternoon) at Belz Factory Outlet Mall, right up I-Drive from Café of India.

**7 PM:** Head north on I-4 to exit 34 and Numero Uno, a great Cuban restaurant with some good meatless fare.

**Or:**

**7 PM:** Drive north on U.S. 435 (Kirkman Road) for a quick but delicious Mexican meal at Baja Burrito Kitchen. Go home and get plenty of rest before another day jam-packed full of fun.

**Itinerary Two**

**8 AM:** Feast on a delicious continental breakfast under the trees at PerriHouse, your bed and breakfast inn. If you're *not* lodging at the Disney-area bird sanctuary, grab a quick breakfast at Chamberlin's Market and Café.

**9:30 AM:** Head west on U.S. 192 to World of Orchids, the world's largest indoor permanent display of the botanical beauties, or—if you're not suffering from theme park burnout—to Splendid China, just a few minutes further west.

**1 PM:** Lunch at Max's Café or Cafe D'Antonio in Celebration. Spend the afternoon exploring the shops or taking in a movie in Disney's planned community.

**6 PM:** Load up your plate with veggie delicacies at Taste of India's all-you-can eat, all-veg dinner buffet. Spend the rest of the evening digesting.

**Or:**

**6 PM:** Enjoy an Original Gardenburger® one of a zillion ways at Jungle Jim's in the Crossroads of Lake Buena Vista shopping plaza. After dinner, hack your way through 18 holes of challenging miniature golf at Pirates Cove Adventure Golf, located right next door.

huge! In fact, all the portions at Max's are large enough to share with a friend.

A formidable "healthy choices" section of the menu showcases three vegetarian items (two of which are vegan), and simply removing the meat from other dishes provides vegetarian diners with oodles of additional options. That's because Adema—whose background includes stints in upstate New York and southern Florida—uses house-made vegan stocks, sauces, and dressings as a base for his meals. Meat-free stocks, Adema says, amplify but don't overwhelm the Café's hearty fare, allowing the true flavors of the foods to come through.

Although the majority of desserts are ovo-lacto, fresh seasonal fruit is available for diners in search of a light ending to their meal. A small wine and beer list accompanies the menu. —*Thanks to gardenia for her help with this review.*

## I-4 Exit 27

We like to think of Exit 27 as the side door to Walt Disney World. As you turn right off the exit, you run into the Crossroads of Lake Buena Vista, a convenient and comparatively inexpensive shopping complex located directly across from the Hotel Plaza Boulevard entrance to the World. Although still officially on Disney property, the shops and restaurants here are more grounded in late 20<sup>th</sup> century American reality than the synergistic corporate ventures you'll find in the parks. There are upscale and casual shops—catering to Disney tourists and the sun-and-fun set— an upscale grocery store, and a handful of national chain restaurants, including **Pizzeria Uno**, **Red Lobster**, **TGI Fridays**, and **Chevy's Mexican Restaurant**. There's also **Pebbles**: a popular local restaurant dishing out California cuisine to rave reviews.

Almost all of the eateries at the Crossroads are able to provide something for vegetarians, but a warning about Pebbles: many of the meatless menu items are made with a beef demi-glace. Order the Perciatelli Piedmontese (a delicious pasta dish that's 100% vegetarian), or ask your server if the kitchen will substitute a different sauce for the demi-glace (good luck!). After dinner, don't miss the opportunity to experience Pirate's Cove Adventure Golf: an 18-hole shrine to the "sport" and one of the most elaborate putt putt courses on earth.

Just a few miles further off of I-4 are great places to stay and to shop. You'll hardly know you're ten minutes from the entrance to Epcot!

## Places to Eat

### Best of the Best off I-4 Exit 27

✿ **Jungle Jim's Lake Buena Vista**
**Price: Moderate**
**Vegebility: Fair**
Casual American
Table Service
L, D
Crossroads Plaza
12501 S.R. 535
Lake Buena Vista, FL 32830
(407) 827-1257
V/MC/AE/Discover

If you just can't get enough of the Original Gardenburger®, it's worth making a trek to Jungle Jim's, located right outside Walt Disney World property in Crossroads Plaza. Even

Gardenburger creator Chef Paul Wenner would be amazed to see the permutations his patty can take at this jungle-themed fast foodery. There's "The Backdraft": a Gardenburger topped with hot pepper cheese and cracked pepper, jalapeño slices, lettuce, tomato, and bleu cheese sauce. Or how about "Teriyaki Pineapple": a Gardenburger basted in teriyaki sauce, topped with grilled pineapple rings, melted cheddar, iceberg lettuce, and tomato? Why not try the Philly Dilly: a Gardenburger smothered with sautéed onions and mushrooms, cream cheese, lettuce, tomato, dill chips, and mayo, served on a butter-grilled "funny bun?" Altogether there are 22 different ways to prepare your burger at Jungle Jims'. But—thanks to the cheese lurking inside the Original Gardenburger—none of them are vegan.

Nor, for that matter, are any of the pastas. Even the spicy crushed tomato sauce sits atop linguine made with egg. The rice contains chicken stock, and there's only butter, sour cream, and cheese available for the oversized baked potatoes. Ask for a side of salsa or bring your own packets of margarine if you're vegan and you're not in the mood for a dry spud.

All is not lost, however: any of Jungle Jim's salads can be made without meat, including a tasty oriental salad of lettuce, crispy noodles, mandarin oranges, green onions, sesame seeds, and a few almonds, served with a coconut bread. Still, some vegetarians have wondered why a chain restaurant would go to such pains to offer so many dishes to vegetarians and virtually none to vegans.

By the way, grease-aholics and the clinically insane will not want to miss the Monte Cristo style Peanut Butter and Jelly sandwich: a PB&J dipped in egg batter, grilled in oil, and coated with confectioner's sugar. *Egads!* What will they think of next? —*Thanks to Nadine Thomas for her help with this review.*

# Places to Stay

## Best of the Best off I-4 Exit 27

✿ **PerriHouse Bed & Breakfast Inn**
**Vegebility: Fair**
**Price: Moderate**
10417 Centurion Court
Lake Buena Vista, FL 32836
Reservations: (800) 780-4830
(407) 876-4830
http://www.perrihouse.com

Three nights' lodging at a romantic bed and breakfast inn is the kind of thing one associates with a vacation in New England or on the Chesapeake Bay, not within shouting distance of Walt Disney World. Thanks to hosts Nick and Angi Perretti, however, a relaxing, natural, and romantic vacation in Orlando is within your reach. When you step onto the grounds of PerriHouse—the Perretti's estate and bird sanctuary—you suddenly find yourself amidst 16 acres of oak trees, grassy fields, and an abundance of wildlife, including a huge number of wild birds. The quiet tranquility of PerriHouse belies its location: just three minutes' drive from Downtown Disney, and under five minutes from the entrance to Epcot.

The main house is a spacious 5,400-sqaure-foot residence decorated in a romantic country style, and built entirely by the Perrettis themselves. Each of eight guest rooms is furnished with a large comfortable king- or queen-sized bed, private bath and outdoor entrance, cable television, central a/c, and ceiling fans. If you're pooped after a day at the parks, you can relax in the hot tub or pool, or enjoy a glass of champagne, beer, or wine (an extensive list is kept on the premises), or both. Children are welcome, and cribs are available.

In the summer of 2000, the Inn will open four "birdhouse" cottages, ideal for honeymooners. And with the addition of a quaint "BirdHouse Wedding Chapel"— perfect for outdoor ceremonies and spur-of-the-moment vow renewals—PerriHouse is destined to become a wonderful spot for romance near (but not too near) the parks.

The best thing about PerriHouse for vegetarian travelers is the continental breakfast buffet, offering more than sixty items. Two sumptuous fresh fruit platters are augmented by giant muffins, breads, pastries, hot and cold cereals, juices, coffee, and tea. Take your breakfast under the trees (basket and blanket courtesy of PerriHouse) to commune with nature in a corner of the world that all too often seems super-natural. The Inn happily lends binoculars and field glasses to aid in bird watching on the estate grounds. On the way back to your room, don't forget to stop in the library to record your morning's findings in the birder's journal.

Guests with special diets are given 24-hour access to the Inn's kitchen, where they can store and prepare food during their stay. The kitchen has a range and microwave, and PerriHouse is located just a few minutes from Goodings Supermarket at the Crossroads of Lake Buena Vista (see review page 210) and ten minutes from the nearest Chamberlin's (Orlando's chain of natural foods markets, also reviewed on page 210).

To top it all off, the folks at PerriHouse will even help you plan your Orlando getaway long before you come to stay. Just ask, and you'll find all of your theme park and entertainment tickets waiting for you upon your arrival. It seems that, at PerriHouse, you can have it all!

# Places to Shop

## Best of the Best off I-4 Exit 27

⊛ **Chamberlin's Market and Café**
**Deli/To Go: Excellent**
**Produce: Good (95% organic)**
**Prepackaged Natural Foods:**
**Excellent**
**Non-Food Items: Excellent**
The Market Place
7600 Dr. Phillips Blvd.
Orlando, FL 32819
(407) 352-2130
Celebrate Health Hotline:
(407) 644-9821 ext. 269

Stock your hamper with plenty of good eats from Chamberlin's Market—the homegrown Orlando health food chain with locations throughout the greater metro area. Chamberlin's has been supplying natural foods to the community since 1935, making the venerable institution one of the oldest such stores in America. It's also one of the very first natural supermarket *chains* in the country, with seven stores and plans to expand.

The Chamberlin's closest to Walt Disney World and Universal Orlando is in the Market Place shopping center on Dr. Phillips Boulevard. A small full service nat-ural foods market, it offers wholesome baked goods (many of which are sugar- and dairy-free), fresh organic produce, natural supplements and remedies, cruelty-free and all-natural personal hygiene items, and a selection of healthful snacks—perfect for a quick pick-me-up between rides. There's also a small assortment of organic wines.

As at all Chamberlin's locations, the Dr. Phillips market offers outstanding vegetarian and vegan café items designed by Chamberlin's Executive Chef John Procacci. Hot and cold prepared foods, like Procacci's Arame Rice Patties or Butternut Squash Lasagna, are totally meatless and—for the most part—vegan. Menu items change frequently, and are complemented by a large selection of sandwiches, freshly baked cookies and breads, and a massive salad bar.

⊘ **Goodings Supermarket**
**Deli/To Go: Good**
**Produce: Fair**
**Prepackaged Natural Foods: Fair**
**Non-Food Items: Fair**
S.R. 535 & I-4
Lake Buena Vista, FL 32830
(407) 827-1200

Although it's not the best place for a vegetarian to shop in Orlando, Goodings is the closest supermarket to Walt Disney World, and—considering tourists are its main clientele—it could be a heck of a lot worse. A small health food section features rice and soy milks, natural juices and sodas, and a selection of healthful snacks. If you're staying in a self-catering villa or suite, stock up on frozen entrées, including a wide variety of Morningstar Farms products, Wolfgang Puck's all natural vegan pasta wrap, or Wolfie's grilled vegetable cheeseless pizza (a warning: the crust of Puck's cheeseless pizza does contain honey). For the under-one set, two kinds of organic baby food are available, as is a modest selection of cruelty-free beauty and bath products for the whole family.

"Goodings to Go" offers a cornucopia of hot and cold pre-packaged meals and snacks, including a number of vegan and ovo-lacto choices. Carrot and cucumber sushi, tossed, prepared and fruit-salads, individual quiches, and pre-packaged main courses—like vegetable lo mein or veggie lasagna—can be picked up for less than $5 apiece on your way to the parks. An espresso bar provides a wide variety of caffeinated beverages, and an assortment of smoothies is available for those with a natural sweet tooth.

The real disappointment at this Goodings location is the produce. The quality and selection are generally lacking, and—on the day we canvassed the store—not a single organic fruit or vegetable could be found (although we were told that some organics—lettuce and carrots, at least—are usually available). If good produce is what you're after, save your pennies for gasoline and head elsewhere.

# I-Drive and U.S. 192

In the early '70s, old fogeys like yours truly journeyed to Orlando to see the new park that Mickey built. Back then southwestern Orlando was still largely open land. Driving down International drive toward the Mouse's new House, one could almost imagine the orange groves and ranches that once dominated Central Florida. It was, from a marketing perspective, a wasteland.

Fortunately for real estate developers, the tourist industry abhors a vacuum. Almost overnight, the rivers of humanity making their way to Walt Disney World spawned an incredible assortment of businesses, legitimate or otherwise, with one simple goal: to siphon a little bit of cash from every vacationer's pocket. Nowadays hotel chains, fast food restaurants, schlocky dinner shows, and souvenir emporiums are everywhere, but especially along International Drive (known as I-Drive) and Irlo Bronson Memorial Highway (U.S. Route 192).

The thirst to shop is most extravagantly slaked at Belz Factory Outlets: 45 designer outlets all offering 30 to 60% off regular prices. Tourists in the grip of theme park fever are treated at Pirate's Cove Adventure Golf, the most elaborate putt putt course on earth, located on I-Drive and at the Crossroads of Lake Buena Vista. And there are enough temples to the weird—like Ripley's Believe It or Not Museum on I-Drive or Splendid China, a miniaturized tribute to the People's Republic off of 192—to send the most jaded kitschaholic into a giggling fit.

But even in the midst of this wacky, overdeveloped landscape, it is still possible to find beauty of a natural sort. Gardeners will love World of Orchids—a celebration of ferns, lush tropical foliage, and thousands of orchids—just west of Walt Disney World on 192. Don't get us wrong: World of Orchids isn't exactly a national park. But being surrounded by all those plants is a refreshingly naturalistic experience in comparison with the surrounding area.

## Places to Eat

### Best of the Best on I-Drive and U.S. 192

☫ **Passage to India**
**Vegebility: Excellent**
**Price: Moderate**

Casual Indian
Table Service
L, D
5532 International Drive
Orlando, FL 32819
(407) 351-3456
All major credit cards accepted

Depending on how you feel about strip malls, a journey up and down International Drive can feel like your own personal shopping paradise—or a private hell. After a while the neon signs begin to blur together, and no one could blame you if you drove right past yet another anonymous storefront with red neon letters proclaiming "Indian Restaurant" from on high.

And what a tragedy that would be. For below that unpretentious sign, in one cozy, eclectically appointed room, is one of the best Indian restaurants you're likely to encounter—but don't take our word for it. Ask Elton John, or Shaquille O' Neil, or Robert Smith of the Cure, or international cricket star Imrat Khan—all fans. Or just ask any of the Indian families who crowd into the restaurant's funky red vinyl booths every night to enjoy owner Uday Kadam's totally authentic Indian cuisine. You could even solicit the opinion of one of the restaurant's many vegetarian patrons, who love the fact that Passage to India's menu contains a profusion of veggie dishes, all of which are cooked using separate utensils and pans. And here's the icing on the cake: since virtually everything is made fresh *à la minute*, the vast majority of veggie selections can be easily adapted for vegans (be sure to ask that no *ghee* be used in the preparation of your meal).

All this veg-friendliness is well and good. But the secret to the restaurant's magic is Kadam's insistence on the freshest possible ingredients, including dried whole cloves, cardamom pods, and other spices instead of the aged, powdered concoctions many restaurants settle for.

For appetizers, don't miss the vegetable samosa, whose flaky, greaseless crust is a revelation to American tongues used to oily steam table fare. It's wonderful with mint sauce or with sweet and slightly spicy tamarind sauce, made with real tamarind pods instead of the more common—and less complex—tamarind extract. A great complement is Passage to India's lentil soup, redolent of cilantro and seasoned to perfection with just a touch of heat.

And someone in your party should definitely try the vegetable korma, one of the best you're likely to enjoy in this lifetime. The vegetables are crisp, the sauce is creamy, and the whole spices will transport you to a rare place in the culinary landscape where you realize that cooking isn't about com-

plicated techniques or the latest gadgets or whether your sauté pan is stainless or teflon. Bite into a crunchy green bean, catch a whiff of whole cardamom, and you'll realize that cooking is about attention, ingredients, freshness, *food.*

And that's no small achievement for a funky little hole in the wall on I-Drive.

*Facts for foodies*

A French phrase meaning "to the minute," **à la minute** signifies that a dish is made freshly to order rather than being prepared ahead of time and stored. Some fine restaurants carry this philosophy to its extreme, serving plates of freshly made cookies *à la minute!*

⭐ **Café Tu Tu Tango**
**Vegebility: Fair**
**Price: Expensive**
Casual International/Eclectic
Table Service
L, D
8625 International Drive
Orlando, FL 32819
(407) 248-2222
All major credit cards accepted

The concept restaurants (Rainforest Cafe, Planet Hollywood, Hard Rock

Cafe) which took the country by storm in the late eighties and early nineties are ubiquitous in Orlando, Land of the Impressionable Visitor. Indeed, the genre's fullest flowering is embodied by Universal Orlando's new CityWalk entertainment district. The trend appears to be on the wane nationwide, however, as diners discover that a megabuck investment in décor and theming often results in nickel-and-dime food and service. Café Tu Tu Tango may well be the exception that proves the rule, offering a much-better-than-average menu based on tapas: a selection of appetizer-sized dishes.

The Café's setting is a faux Mediterranean artist's loft where real, live artists paint as guests dine. Beautiful hand-painted tiles and eclectic canvases cover nearly every inch of wall space. The meal is punctuated by staged surrealistic events, like the appearance of a tarot card reader or a strolling minstrel. Unlike traditional Spanish tapas, which focus on finger foods exclusively, the International Drive restaurant offers a wildly eclectic menu featuring pint-sized treats like mushroom skewers and sun dried tomato pizza, but also salads and sandwiches made to order. A small tower of plates stands at the center of each table—along with plenty of forks, knives, and spoons—for sharing creative and delicious dishes with fellow diners.

There are only a few legitimate vegetarian items on the menu, but most dishes are easily adapted thanks to the kitchen's reliance on largely vegetarian stocks, rice, and dressings. The wild mushroom soup is made with four types of mushrooms—steeped in a soy-mushroom broth—and soba noodles. A succulent couscous made with tomatoes, cucumbers, olives, and fresh herbs is also a delight. And two desserts that are made on premises deserve mention: the first is a melt-in-your-mouth rich amaretto and almond flan; the second is a luscious guava cheesecake served with a strawberry puree. Both are terrific.

When you stop to admire the non-edible art of Tu Tu Tango, know that everything is for sale. The owners expect to have sold $90,000 worth of art by the end of 1999. Actually, our only complaint about the restaurant is financial, as well: to really fill up on the teeny tiny portions of Café Tu Tu Tango's admittedly delicious tapas, you could easily find yourself spending $15 or $20 for three or four small dishes.

So much for the starving artist!

*—Thanks to gardenia for her help with this review.*

---

 **Dux**
**Vegebility: Fair**
**Price: Very Expensive**
Elegant International

Table Service
D
9801 International Drive
Orlando, FL 32819
(407) 352-4000
All major credit cards accepted

Stereotypes die hard. Twenty-five years ago, a vegetarian—and least in the minds of many Americans— was someone who baked her own bread, wore flares and a head-band, and dined exclusively at cafes where the menu was written on a chalkboard. Today, artisanal bread-making is all the rage and flares are hot (*sans* headband, of course), but a heck of a lot of vegetarians have more sophisticated tastes than they used to. Sadly, many fine restau-rants still assume that they can get away with charging $40 for a "vegetarian plate" of pasta and veggies. Of course, most restau-rants don't have Scott Hoyland designing their menus.

At Dux, Hoyland offers a three-course vegetarian tasting menu that changes with the seasons, according to the availability of fresh ingredients. A typical dinner might start out with a salad of red and green pears, Roquefort cheese, and Belgian endive, fol-lowed by a terrine of fresh field mushrooms, braised endive, and Yukon potatoes, and finished with a financier topped with kiln-dried cherries and Balkan ice cream in a warm kirsch sauce. While the

above menu is suitable for ovo-lacto vegetarians, Hoyland is ready to alter menu selections on the spot to accommodate vegans.

Give him 24 hours' notice, how-ever, and Hoyland will create a custom-made vegan menu that is out of this world. Look forward to treats like warm and creamy avocado soup, a perfect dairy-free overture to the main course: sea-sonal mushrooms in phyllo dough, bathed in a rich vegetable sauce and decorated with leeks, toma-toes, and fingerling potatoes. And while presentation is important for most chefs, Hoyland goes to the extreme to make sure his fabu-lous food looks equally wonderful. Witness the couscous-stuffed pur-ple onion, served with tiny broc-coli, zucchini, and garlic accents: another vegan beauty!

Dux also offers scrumptious vegan desserts. Pistachio wheels embrace fresh orange sorbet, driz-zled with raspberry sauce. Or how about a double-crusted macaroon crème brulee, served with fresh seasonal fruits? Irresistible.

Some diners find Dux too pric-ey. But at $59.00 with wine pair-ings, his three-course vegetarian tasting menu is reasonable, con-sidering the quality of the food, the beauty of the setting, and the mas-terful wine selections by maitre d'hotel Marcelo Napolitiello. All conspire to create an evening even the most discerning vegetarian gastronome will savor. —*Thanks to gardenia for her help with this review.*

## Places to Stay

### Best of the Best on I-Drive and U.S. 192

**✪ Orlando/Kissimmee Resort Hostel**
**Vegebility: Fair**
**Price: Way Cheap**
4840 West Irlo Bronson Highway
Kissimmee, FL 34746
Reservations: (800) 909-4776, ext. 33
(407) 396-8282
http://www.hiayh.org/ushostel/sereg/
orland2.htm
V/MC

If Walt Disney World is your destination and discount lodging your preference, the Kissimmee Hostel is the place for you. With the Main Gate just five miles away, you'll have no problem extinguishing that monetary inferno in your pocket, but—at less than $20 for dorm rooms and around $40 for private rooms—at least your accommodations will be reasonable. Formerly a motel, this AYH-affiliated hostel has amenities that others lack, including a pool, lots of private rooms, and paddleboats. Dorm rooms have six beds each and private rooms are simply unconverted motel rooms, most of which contain kitchens. And when we say kitchens, we mean real

## Pasta and a Show

Orlando offers a profusion of glitzy dinner shows to satiate the chronically under-entertained nighttime denizens of I-Drive and Route 192. All of the major diversions offer some sort of ovo-lacto vegetarian meal—usually Stouffer's veggie lasagna, accompanied by limp salad from a bag. Vegans are pretty much out of luck. Furthermore, many vegetarians will be none too happy to hear that at least two of the area's more popular suppertime diversions—Arabian Nights and Medieval Times, both on Route 192 in Kissimmee—make extensive use of horses.

If you've caught the dinnertime fun bug, though, keep in mind that the less popular shows, or those that simply have fewer seats, tend to offer better food than the gargantuan 3000-seaters. For example, Sleuth Mystery Dinner Theater on International Drive presents a somewhat entertaining murder-mystery, accompanied by—yep—lasagna. But this dinner has a few nice touches the others are missing, such as a version of the ubiquitous entrée which appears actually to have been fashioned by human hands.

King Henry's Feast on International Drive takes the frozen lasagna route, but also offers a vegan potato-leek soup that's worth a try. King Henry's is heavy on the British humor (since most of the guests are, indeed, from Great Britain—a huge vegetarian market), but is still very amusing for Americans. —*Thanks to gardenia for sitting through hours of Orlando dinner shows and eating lasagna more often than anyone should ever have to!*

kitchens; no microwaves and paper plates here. Each fully-equipped—albeit small—kitchen features a stove, oven, refrigerator, full sink, coffemaker, toaster, and a wide assortment of pots, pans, and plates: everything you'll need to whip up a meatless feast.

If you need a bit more space in which to create your culinary masterpieces, the hostel's communal kitchen has been recently renovated and is completely handicap accessible. The Publix supermarket across the street should do nicely where raw materials are concerned, if you're content with conventional (non-organic) produce and mass-market tofu. Otherwise, jump in your rental car and head north to the nearest Chamberlin's natural grocery on Dr. Phillips Boulevard (see review, page 210). Even if you're not cooking, Publix can serve as your pantry, with a large in-store delicatessen featuring prepared salads and veggie sandwiches. Or take your pick from the myriad restaurants and fast fooderies along Rte. 192.

There's no curfew at the Kissimmee hostel, and the office is open 24 hours to assist you after you've lost your keys on some dance floor at Pleasure Island. Note, however, that the communal kitchen is closed from midnight until 6 AM. Unfortunately, no public transportation is available to Disney World, but for $6 a private shuttle will transport you right to Mickey's front door.

Sound like the best deal in town? A lot of budget travelers agree, making this one of the toughest places in town to get a room. Vegetarians in the know book their stay at the Orlando/Kissimmee Resort Hostel at least six months in advance. —*Thanks to Tiffany Shumaker for her help with this review.*

# Elsewhere in S. Orlando

There are plenty more opportunities to get lost in the southern reaches of Orlando—or in the Orlando International Airport, for that matter. Keep one eye on the road and the other on the maps included in this chapter to find these veg-friendly gems, or call the restaurant for detailed directions.

# Places to Eat

### Best of the Best
### Elsewhere in Southern Orlando

**Baja Burrito Kitchen**
**Vegebility: Good**
**Price: Inexpensive**
Casual Cal-Mex
Table Service
L, D
4642 Kirkman Road
Orlando, FL 32811
(407) 299-5001
V/MC/AE/Discover

With two other locations—one in Central Orlando, the other further north in Altamonte Springs—this bastion of fresh Cal-Mex cuisine gets our vote as the best place for a veggie to worship at the Temple of the Pepper. And this one is just a short drive north of Universal Orlando on Florida Route 435.

Baja Burrito Kitchen distinguishes itself from the competition in a few ways. At many Mexican restaurants, a server slaps down a loosely filled bowl of broken chips and a pathetic little ramekin of salsa, only to disappear for the next hour or so while you peruse the menu and long for more salsa and chips. Baja Burrito Kitchen dispenses with this ritual, with the help of its well-stocked salsa bar. With a dinner entrée you get all the chips you can dip into six different salsas, ranging from the comfortingly familiar Salsa Fresca to the uncomfortably incendiary Habanero Sauce.

Secondly, BBK prides itself on its food being vegetarian-friendly. There's no chicken stock in the rice, and no lard in the beans—or, for that matter, anywhere else in the restaurant. Meat is used primarily as a garnish for already delicious base ingredients, rather than being the main flavor component. As a result, about a third of the restaurant's regular menu items are satisfying vegetarian fare, from the standard bean and cheese burrito to the fantastic soft vegetarian tacos and the super fresh, crispy tostada salad.

Even though BBK is a chain, it's a small one, and it's local. That means you can still feel good about helping a local business fly. In addition, it means the personal touch is still there, at least where freshness and preparation are concerned. In fact, freshness is something of a religion at Baja Burrito Kitchen: menus boast that none of the branches owns a freezer, or even a can opener! While the bit about the can opener is a tad unlikely, Baja Burrito Kitchen most definitely is a great alternative to the limp, greasy Tex-Mex fare that you'll find throughout Orlando— or any other American city, for that matter.

---

**Taste of India**
**Vegebility:**
    **O/L: Excellent; Vegan: Poor**
**Price: Inexpensive**
Casual IndianVegetarian
Buffet/To Go
L, D
9251 S. Orange Blossom Trail
Orlando, FL 32837
(407) 855-4622
V/MC/AE

Occasionally in the world of vegetarian restaurants, you come upon a nondescript café quietly offering up an all-vegetarian menu with very little fanfare and even less press. These restaurants exist everywhere, but finding them is not so easy; usually a friend of a friend was curious about the odd little sign and discovered, behind it, some pretty good food. Taste of India is just such a place. As we were wrapping up research in late 1999, our intrepid reporters in the field discovered this all-vegetarian gem in southern Orlando, a teeny-weeny place with zero advertising and practically no word-of-mouth publicity (except maybe in Orlando's South Asian community).

Open since early Autumn, 1998, Taste of India is South Asian to the core. The meals are traditional "Indian vegetarian," meaning eggs are not used in preparation, but *ghee* (clarified butter) and *paneer* (fresh, unripened cheese) are. Vegans beware: despite persistent questioning, re-phrasing, and the use of simple pictograms, we were unable to determine whether any of the items on the menu were, or could be, cooked without dairy. Your best bet is to call and speak with management directly, and keep your fingers crossed that you find someone with more than rudimentary English skills.

If your diet does include dairy, Taste of India is one of the best bargains in Orlando. It's not the place for a romantic meal—the dining room is small and over-lit by fluorescents—but at less than $7 for an all-you-can-eat dinner

buffet, it's an unbeatable deal. Dal soup, fried pakoras, vegetable curries, and spicy rice concoctions are featured on the predominantly North Indian spread, which changes daily but always includes at least one traditional dessert. Alcohol is not available, but delicious mango lassis are, as is a take-out menu.

---

⑫  **Numero Uno**
   **Vegebility: Fair**
   **Price: Moderate**
   Casual Cuban
   Table Service
   L, D
   2499 S. Orange Ave
   Orlando, FL 32801
   (407) 841-3840
   All major credit cards accepted

Meatless Cuban food is about as easy to find as a rockin' public radio station, and many a vegetarian has had to settle for rice cooked in chicken stock, pick the pork out of their black beans, and pretend their plantains weren't fried in lard—while their carnivorous companions munch happily away on beef pastelles and spicy picadillo.

But for a charming taste of Cuban culture that you can actually enjoy, go south to Numero Uno: a small home style restaurant whose diverse and obviously loyal clientele shouts "best-kept secret" from the very rooftops. Families with small children and young

# Veggie Kids in Southern Orlando

*Most children's menus—in Orlando, or anywhere—feature meals some kids like to eat, but not necessarily the kind of healthful meals we'd like to serve. If your attempts to get your ornery tyke to eat something good for him end in disaster, here are the children's options at our favorite veg-friendly restaurants in areas south of Orlando.*

## Vegetarian Kids' Meals at Table Service Restaurants

**Baja Burrito Kitchen:**

Cheese quesadilla; veggie wrap (open-faced tortilla topped with beans, rice and cheese); tortilla chips and melted cheese

**Cafe D'Antonio:**

Cheese or vegetable pizza; pasta with tomato sauce; potatoes; side orders of vegetables

**Café Tu Tu Tango:**

Spaghetti with tomato sauce

**Jungle Jim's:**

Grilled cheese sandwich; peanut butter and jelly sandwich

**Max's Café:**

Grilled cheese sandwich; macaroni and cheese; linguine with marinara sauce

**McCoy's, Hyatt Regency (Orlando International Airport):**

Grilled cheese sandwich; macaroni and cheese; peanut butter and jelly sandwich

**Numero Uno:**

Half portions of adult vegetarian menu items are available upon request

## Healthful Snacks

**Chamberlin's Market**

Vegan, sugar-free baked goods; organic fresh whole fruit

---

couples dressed to impress crowd into the small dining area, along with a live keyboardist, on the weekends. The restaurant offers vegetarians just a couple of options, but they're very tasty—if not exactly low-fat! Those seeking a fantastic (and vegan) introduction to the flavors and textures of Caribbean cooking could do a lot worse than Numero Uno's vegetarian plate, replete with rice, garlicky steamed vegetables, oily fried plantains, sweet corn fritters, and downright knockout red beans. And the pressed spicy bean burger is definitely worth trying if you'd like something hearty, delicious—and bad for you.

Okay, okay, the burger is a little greasy. And yes, it is true that the bread is too soft, and so white it may actually sap the nutrients from your body. But there's something so comfortable, friendly, and quintessentially Cuban about this great little place—the teeny dining room, the keyboardist winking at little kids, and of course, the strong, spicy food—that Numero Uno is one of our favorite dining destinations in Orlando.

## ⚤ McCoy's

**Vegebility: Excellent**
**Price: Inexpensive—Moderate**
Casual American
Table Service
L, D
Hyatt Regency Orlando
International Airport
9300 Airport Blvd.
Orlando, FL 32827
(407) 825-1234
All major credit cards accepted

It's 6:30 PM Orlando time. You arrive at the airport just in time to catch your 7:15 flight, check your bags curbside and rush to the gate (*whew*). Surprise! Your flight has been delayed until 9 o'clock. Great. You're starving, and here you are stuck in a maze of fast food vendors where the only meatless items available are cold french fries and microwaved cheese pizzas.

Or so you think. Luckily, you've been stranded at Orlando International, one of the few airports in the country to feature a Hyatt Regency hotel right inside the main terminal. About ten years ago, Hyatt instituted a corporate-wide "Cuisine Naturelle" menu—nutritious, low-calorie gourmet cuisine made with simple, natural ingredients—and mandated that at least one restaurant in every Hyatt provide the menu to guests.

In the Orlando Airport Hyatt, the menu is served at McCoy's, a casual bar and grill on the 4th

floor, open for lunch, dinner, and snacks. Menu standouts include a hearty red lentil chili, Israeli couscous topped with crisp sautéed asparagus and tomatoes, Garden Pasta—penne pasta tossed with tomatoes and peppers—or, our favorite, the vegetarian pizza: tomatoes, garlic-sautéed spinach, and feta cheese on a whole wheat tortilla. The couscous and the pasta are both normally made with a chicken stock, but chefs are happy to substitute a vegetarian base with no advance notice, making both dishes 100% vegan.

Kudos go to the Airport Hyatt's Executive Chef David Didzunas for making McCoy's regular menu wonderfully vegetarian-friendly, too. Developed in house, the menu features four vegetarian entrées, including a massive fruit plate that's absolutely the best deal on the menu. Two people can feast on one platter, with wedges of cantaloupe, honey dew, and gold pineapple, kiwi and orange slices, grapes, strawberries, and a selection of seasonal berries, served with your choice of yogurt or cottage cheese. One of McCoy's best sellers is the Grilled Vegetable Focaccia: a delicious vegan focaccia made by a local artisan bakery, and topped with chèvre and a mix of eggplant, zucchini, yellow squash, red onion, and roasted red peppers, tossed in a basil marinade and grilled. The sandwich is served pressed, panini-style, with garlic aioli and a side of mesclun greens in a fresh lemon juice vinaigrette. Leave off the aioli and the goat cheese, and it's strictly vegan.

For dessert, there are plenty of sinful goodies from which to choose, but true sorbets are always kept in the back—just in case something lighter is called for. And, of course, there's always that fruit plate. So, next time you find yourself stuck at Orlando International, thank your lucky stars. After all, you could be eating that tasteless airline meal instead! —*Thanks to the Luteran family for their help with this review.*

# Chapter 18

# Downtown Orlando

**Orlando/Orange County CVB:**
*(800) 551-0181; http://www.go2orlando.com*
**Orlando Weekly:** *http://www.orlandoweekly.com/*
**Orlando Sentinel:** *http://www.orlandosentinel.com/*
*Check out these Orlando area websites for ideas about
how to spend the day and up-to-date dining reviews.*

From glitzy tourist centers like Church Street Station to gentrified communities like Thornton Park to thriving Asian and Latin American enclaves, Orlando is a study in diversity. Gritty and urban in some places, serene and bucolic in others, the city has grown, and continues to grow, at a dizzying pace.

After a few days spent within the city's seemingly endless—and often ugly—urban sprawl, it seems almost impossible to imagine Orlando in the days B.D.†, when citrus groves, light industry, cattle ranches, and visiting aristocrats were the city's lifeblood. Fortunately, you can escape the strip malls and stoplights for a time by visiting the Harry P. Leu Gardens. Formerly the estate of a successful industrialist, the man-

---

† Before Disney

**Downtown Orlando**

1 Church St. Station,
   Church St. Marketplace,
   and the Orlando Farmer's Market
2 Dexter's of Thornton Park
3 Garden Café
4 Dong-A Market
5 Baja Burrito Kitchen

6 Chamberlin's Market & Café
7 White Wolf Café
8 Florida Hospital & Cafeteria
9 Chapter's Bread & books Café
10 Café Allegre
11 The Eco-Store

icured lakeside grounds of this 50-acre botanical garden include the largest camellia collection in North America, extensive plantings of ferns, bromeliads, orchids, and palms, and a seasonally changing herb garden.

Across Lake Rowena, through the swaying moss hanging from the branches of the Gardens' live oaks, you can see the dome of the Orlando Science Museum. One of three museums in Loch Haven Park, it's a great place to spend an afternoon. On a beautiful spring day, take a swan-shaped pedal boat out for a spin on Lake Eola, right in the heart of downtown—and a hop, skip and a jump from Dexter's of Thornton Park. Or poke around the shops in the city's small but vibrant antiques district. Walk slowly, browse to your heart's content, and linger over a delicious lunch at White Wolf Cafe. Whatever you do, do it slowly, and

# Downtown Orlando: Best of the Best

**Key to Categories and Abbreviations**

**O/L, V: Ovo-lacto and vegan selections**

• - Always available    + - Available upon request    A - Request in advance

**Es: Type of establishment**

T - Table Service        C - Counter service        S - Snack stand or cart

**$: Average price for a single vegetarian entrée**

1 - under $10        3 - $16 - $20        5 - $31 - $40
2 - $10 - $15        4 - $21 - $30        6 - over $40

**Meals:**

B - Breakfast        L - Lunch        D - Dinner        S - Snacks

| Downtown Orlando | O/L | V | Es | $ | Meals |
|---|---|---|---|---|---|
| ⑤ Baja Burrito Kitchen | • | + | C | 1 | L, D |
| ⑩ Café Allègre | • | A | T | 2 | D |
| ⑨ Chapter's Bread & Books Cafe | • | • | T | 1 | B,* L, D |
| ② Dexter's of Thornton Park | • | • | T | 1 | L, D |
| ⑧ Florida Hospital Cafeteria | • | • | C | 1 | B, L, D |
| ③ Garden Cafe | • | • | T | 1 | L, D |
| ⑦ White Wolf Cafe | • | • | T | 2 | L, D |

*Brunch served on Sundays

enjoy the relaxed southern pace of the real Orlando.

# Places to Eat

## Best of the Best in Downtown Orlando

② **Dexter's of Thornton Park**
**Vegebility: Good**
**Price: Moderate**
Casual American
Table Service
L, D
808 E. Washington St.

Orlando, FL 32801
(407) 648-0620
All major credit cards accepted

The younger sibling of Dexter's in Winter Park, this Dex sits in a sleepy neighborhood near Lake Eola—a sparsely furnished urban hangout for an upscale but casual neighborhood crowd. If you want to hang with the coolest of Orlando hipsters, Dexter's is the place to go. Locals flock to the Thornton Park location for art shows, a booming retail wine business, and periodic wine tastings. They also come in search of great food.

While by no means a vegetarian restaurant, both Dexter's make a point of catering to the wishes of their stylish, health-conscious clientele. The result is a diverse menu featuring a wide range of ingredients and influences, from Cuba to Spain to Thailand and back to America. Tempting appetizer specials at Dexter's Thornton Park location include grilled asparagus, marinated in sweet balsamic garlic oil, topped with gazpacho salsa and served with a warm hunk of rosemary ciabatta bread: a rustic vegan treat.

Vegetarian entrée specials, as in most restaurants, are fewer and farther between. But Dexter's of Thornton Park delivers with a wild mushroom ragout cooked in a port reduction sauce and served over crusty French bread, or fried green tomato pecan cakes, layered with pesto and topped with sliced buffalo mozzarella. Regular menu items include a wide range of salads, pastas (don't miss the fabulous Veggie Peanut Pasta, with housemade noodles), and the incredibly hearty Eggplant Napoleon. Toss in a great selection of sandwich fixins, and you've got a mainstream restaurant that (finally) allows vegans to put together a really satisfy-

ing sandwich, too. Wait 5 extra minutes, and you can enjoy your masterpiece heated and pressed, "Cuban-style." Fantastic!

---

❷ **Garden Cafe**
**Vegebility: Excellent**
**Price: Inexpensive**
Casual Chinese and International
Vegetarian
Table Service
L, D
810 East Colonial Drive
Orlando, FL 32803
(407) 999-9799
V/MC/Discover

The mock meats at the Garden Cafe may—or may not—fool some meat eaters. But no matter: the food at Garden Cafe is not to be missed. Owner and Chef David Chen (assisted by his wife Ming) does his best to ensure that vegetarians and carnivores alike can enjoy his cooking, which employs the best organic and natural ingredients combined in creative ways. The Chens' commitment to vegetarian cooking is an expression of their non-violent Taoist ethic, making the Garden Cafe's kitchen a place not only of creativity, but of meditation. Diners are clearly pleased: Garden Cafe snagged not only Orlando's Best Vegetarian Restaurant Award (Orlando Week-

---

## Stir Fry Fixin's

After dinner at the Garden Café, take a quick trip around the corner and up North Mills Avenue to Dong-A Market. Voted the Best Asian Market in Orlando Weekly's 1999 Reader's Poll, Dong-A is the best place to pick up lemon grass, wood-ear mushrooms, and cellophane noodles for a self-catered Eastern feast.

**❹  Dong-A Market**
816 N. Mills Avenue
Orlando, FL 32803
(407) 898-3807

---

ly Readers' Poll, 1999), but the Best New Restaurant award as well, leaving its more meaty competition in the dust.

Chen spends hours mixing ingredients that look and feel like fish, beef, chicken, pork, and lamb, even if they don't taste quite the same. The textures are so similar to the real thing that a common refrain—at least among vegetarians—is, "Are you sure this isn't meat?" Real carnivores assure us that they aren't as easily duped, however, so veggie patrons looking to impress their meat-eating friends should probably stick to the dishes that are most successful: the excellent sweet-and-sour "chicken," for example. Its soft, chewy, and flavorful chunks of batter-fried tofu won't leave anyone longing for the real thing.

While most of the restaurant's dishes have an Asian flavor, Garden Cafe also serves a number of International vegetarian standbys, including a portobello mushroom sandwich, a selection of grilled veggie burgers, and a number of curry dishes. A deliciously light penne pasta—tossed in a light broth with asparagus, tomatoes, basil, carrots, and zucchini—is also available.
—*Thanks to gardenia for her help with this review.*

---

**❺  Baja Burrito Kitchen**
**Vegebility: Good**
**Price: Inexpensive**
Casual Cal-Mex
Table Service
L, D
2716 E. Colonial Drive
Orlando, FL 32803
(407) 895-6112
V/MC/AE/Discover

With two other locations—one just north of Universal Orlando, the other in Altamonte Springs—this bastion of fresh Cal-Mex cuisine gets our vote as the best place for a veggie to worship at the Temple of the Pepper. Baja Burrito Kitchen distinguishes itself from the competition in a few ways.

At many Mexican restaurants, a server slaps down a loosely filled bowl of broken chips and a pathetic little ramekin of salsa, only to disappear for the next hour or so while you peruse the menu and long for more salsa and chips. Baja Burrito Kitchen dispenses with this ritual, with the help of its well-stocked salsa bar. With a dinner entrée you get all the chips you can dip into six different salsas, ranging from the comfortingly familiar Salsa Fresca to the uncomfortably incendiary Habanero Sauce.

Secondly, BBK prides itself on its food being vegetarian-friendly. There's no chicken stock in the rice, and no lard in the beans—or, for that matter, anywhere else in the restaurant. Meat is used primarily as a garnish for already delicious base ingredients, rather than being the main flavor component. As a result, about a third of the restaurant's regular menu items are satisfying vegetarian fare, from the standard bean and cheese burrito to the fantastic soft vegetarian tacos and the super fresh, crispy tostada salad.

Even though BBK is a chain, it's a small one, and it's local. That means you can still feel good about helping a local business fly. In addition, it means the personal touch is still there, at least where freshness and preparation are concerned. In fact, freshness is something of a religion at Baja Burrito Kitchen: menus boast that none of the branches owns a freezer, or even a can opener! While the bit about the can opener is a tad unlikely, Baja Burrito Kitchen most definitely is a great alternative to

the limp, greasy Tex-Mex fare that you'll find throughout Orlando—or any other American city, for that matter.

---

⭐ **White Wolf Cafe**
**Vegebility: Excellent**
**Price: Moderate**
Casual American
Table Service
L, D
1829 N. Orange Ave
Orlando, FL 32804
(407) 895-9911
MC/V/AE

A great place to discover the "other" Orlando is the small but happening Antiques District, an area which invites one to indulge in a pastime all too rare in car-afflicted Orlando: walking. Park your ride on the 1800 block of North Orange Avenue and wander from shop to shop, but save your appetite for a visit to White Wolf Cafe. This funky hangout began as a corner of Michael Hennessey's antiques store in September 1991, and quickly expanded to include coffee, then ice cream, and (within six *very* busy months) sandwiches and salads.

Some antiques are still there, but Chef Robert Tresnor's food is what's attracting national attention these days. The lunch menu of salads and sandwiches features interesting twists on Mediterranean fare. The Vegetarian Plate sports

# Michael and Anne Marie Hennessey

How does an antiques dealer get into the restaurant profession? For Michael Hennessey, it was a natural progression.

Hennessey was a waiter for much of his life before opening the antique shop, but always secretly dreamed of running his own café. Without knowing exactly what would come of it, Hennessey started offering ice cream to shoppers in his store. After the ice cream came coffee, then sandwiches, and eventually the Cafe's current ambitious menu. "We were just tenacious enough, ignorant enough, and fortunate enough to believe that we could do it!" he chuckles.

When Hennessey says "we," he's referring to himself and Casper, a gregarious white German shepherd after whom the café was named and with whom he shared many years of companionship. The two of them opened shop in August 1991, with Casper naturally falling into the role of maitre d'. "I could see people change as they interacted with him. He won their hearts over with his gentle spirit."

Casper passed away in March of 1993, and today Michael is joined at the café by his business and life partner, Anne Marie. Although Anne Marie is much more skilled at bar and business management than Casper ever was, she's just as focused on what's important: the café's diverse and loyal clientele. "People are the most significant part of our business," she says. Not only are diners considered at White Wolf, they drive the decision making process. "The café menu really has grown from peoples' suggestions," Anne Marie points out. "They wanted items that were different, and not available elsewhere, including a large selection of vegetarian items."

Thanks to the clientele, and the Hennesseys' own interest in lighter fare, the café menu is expanding to include an even wider selection of vegan and vegetarian dishes, focusing on upscale cuisine and a fine dining experience. "Vegetarianism is a natural progression of what we do," Michael elaborates. "This kind of innovation is exactly what Orlando has needed." For our part, we can't help but appreciate the fact that this extremely vegetarian-friendly cafe is named for an animal with a fierce reputation and a gentle manner—a good example for us all.

two hummuses—garlicky traditional and enticing black bean—as well as a unique and delicious mango-almond "tabbouleh." Other salads are augmented by excellent sandwiches like the Cool Cuke, a delicious and deceptively simple blend of cream cheese, cucumbers, sprouts, and tomato on whole wheat.

Tresnor's personal commitment to eating a meatless diet helps to explain the menu's focus on veggies and grains. At dinner, tuck into no fewer than thirteen meatless entrées, complimented by an all-vegetarian appetizer list and Greek and garden salads. Most of the hot entrées tip their hats to Italian cuisine, including the Spinach and Eggplant Rolatini: breaded eggplant stuffed with three cheeses, topped with a fresh vegetable ratatouile, and smothered in yellow pepper marinara—a luscious dish, and great if you're trying to put on a few pounds! Stop in on a Tuesday night for selected wine flights, or sample an entire bottle for just $1.00 over cost with the purchase of an entrée.

Michael and his partner—both professional and personal—Anne Marie Hennessey have plans to expand. The first step will be to install a large display kitchen, including a brick pizza oven. The expanded café will resemble a beautiful old wine cellar and will focus on what the Hennesys call "fine healthful dining," including a broader selection of upscale vegan and vegetarian items than any other restaurant in Orlando.

---

❦ **Chapter's Bread & Books Cafe**
**Vegebility: Good**
**Price: Moderate**
Casual International
Table Service
B (Sunday), L, D
717 W. Smith St.
Orlando, FL 32804
(407) 246-1546
V/MC/AE

So many used bookstores are overflowing with mustiness and dust mites. Chapters Bread & Books Cafe & Bookshop overflows with delicious aromas and inspiring passions. Marty and Jan Cummins have worked hard to create a place that welcomes new friends and encourages bibliophiles. Tables are scattered throughout the bookshop, so you may very well find yourself having Sunday brunch with architect Christopher Alexander or novelist Leon Uris.

Head Chef Eric Nissen offers "casual gourmet" fare, with an emphasis on healthful, low fat preparation. Veggie diners will feel right at home with the extensive menu, which features lots of wraps, salads, sandwiches, pasta, and pizzas. Try the Portobello Wrap, with grilled, marinated mushroom slices added to sprouts, caramelized onions, diced tomato, lettuce, cukes, and herbed cream cheese.

*Phun Phacts*

Wondering what happened to the walls of the old Orlando city hall, blown up for the finale of Lethal Weapon 2? The beautiful hunks of red mountain granite have a new life as tables at the White Wolf Cafe.

# Downtown Orlando: Veggie Itineraries

*Eat your way around the real Orlando at our favorite vegetarian and veg-friendly restaurants. Be sure to call and make advance reservations at the restaurant of your choosing.*

## Itinerary One

**9 AM:** Save your early morning appetite for Chef Dan Bartel's superlative biscuits and "sausage" gravy at the massive all-vegetarian Florida Hospital Cafeteria, right downtown.

**10 AM:** Leave your car in the hospital garage and wander over to Loch Haven Park. Spend the morning exploring three of Orlando's best public museums: the Orlando Science Center, the Orange County Historical Museum, and the Orlando Museum of Art.

**1:30 PM:** Head south on U.S. 17/92 to the Garden Cafe, one of Orlando's three all-vegetarian restaurants, for a combination platter lunch. If you've got a kitchen where you're staying, pop in at Dong-A Market afterwards to pick up some hard-to-find Asian ingredients to use in your stir fried feasts. A selection of traditional vegetarian items can be found further east on Colonial at Chamberlin's Market and Cafe.

**3:30 PM:** Paddle your own Swan boat on Lake Eola, and enjoy the leisurely pace of a real old-fashioned Florida vacation. The kids will love the playground, and if you're traveling with a four-legged canine companion, don't forget the frisbee or tennis ball for a game of catch. The view of the fountain at dusk, with its lights aglow and the sunset behind, is spectacular.

**7 PM:** Enjoy a casual dinner at Dexter's of Thornton Park, a few blocks west of Lake Eola.

**9 PM:** If you have the stamina and the inclination, hit Church Street Station for a night of "old tyme" entertainment.

-OR-

**6 PM:** Head back to your lodgings to start chopping the ingredients for that stir fry, courtesy of Dong-A and Chamberlin's Markets.

## Itinerary Two

**9 AM:** If it's Saturday, make your way to the Orlando Farmer's Market on Church Street for an alfresco breakfast. Otherwise, head over to Chamberlin's on East Colonial to sample some healthful breakfast breads. While you're there, stock your picnic hamper with natural beverages and a selection of vegetarian prepared salads.

**11 AM:** Tour the beautifully maintained grounds of the Harry P. Leu Gardens, former estate of a local citrus czar, at your leisure. The estate's collection of camellias (one of the largest on the East coast) is in bloom October through March.

**1 PM:** Unpack your picnic lunch under one of Leu Gardens' ancient and massive live oaks. Afterwards, surrender to a nap.

**3 PM:** Head west on Virginia to North Orange Avenue for an afternoon of antiquing.

**6 PM:** Dinner (and perhaps some live entertainment) at White Wolf Cafe.

-OR-

**3 PM:** Linger at Leu Gardens before heading north to Edgewater Drive and the ECO-Store, a great place to pick up environmentally conscious gifts for your loved ones back home.

**6 PM:** Dinner at the superlative Café Allègre.

The whole mess is neatly wrapped in a gargantuan spinach tortilla. The two-alarm veggie chili is always made with a meatless stock, but the soup of the day may not be—ask your server to be certain.

Chapters' menu becomes more ambitious at dinnertime, with the addition of a rich Sundried Tomato Alfredo Penne and the occasional veggie special. The three-cheese and wild mushroom pizza is also an evening treat. An Indian flatbread crust is spread with garlicky pesto and topped with chevre, pesto, parmesan, and sautéed mushrooms. Creative uses of fruits and vegetables are found throughout the lunch and dinner options, but fortunately, not everything's healthful: the dessert menu boasts a Snickers Cheesecake, a Peach Blueberry Pie, and a Three-Layer Chocolate Cake.

When the Cumminses learned that Jack Kerouac, the '50s Beat writer who inspired a generation, had lived around the corner, they sprang into action. They immediately purchased the building and founded the Jack Kerouac Writers in Residence Project of Orlando. The project hopes to build a large enough endowment to grant aspiring authors time (and money) to concentrate on their writing, without worrying about bills and day jobs. Writers will live in the very same house Kerouac did when he wrote such classics as *The Dharma Bums* and *The Beat Generation*. Supporters include such diverse Kerouac fans as Jeffrey Cole of Pearle Vision and Sears Optical and David Amram, musician, composer, and conductor. —*Thanks to gardenia for her help with this review.*

---

**Florida Hospital Cafeteria**
**Vegebility: Excellent**
**Price: Inexpensive**
Casual American Vegetarian
Counter Service
B, L, D, S
601 E. Rollins St.
Orlando, FL 32803
(407) 897-1793
No checks or credit cards accepted

---

Near Lake Estelle, the Florida Hospital is a gem in the necklace of the Seventh-Day Adventist Health Care System. In keeping with the vegetarian ethic of the Christian denomination, the hospital's cafeteria serves over 8,000 completely meatless meals each day, making this the largest all-vegetarian cafeteria in North America, if not the world. Many of Chef Dan Bartel's recipes are incredibly faithful reproductions of classic meat-based dishes, formulated for patients who can't have the fat, sodium, or sugar content of the originals. Bartel spends hours next door in the hospital's Food Production Center, striving to simulate the perfect vegetarian corn dog or "sausage" gravy.

This is not to say, mind you, that the Florida Hospital Cafeteria is likely to give Chez Panisse a run for its money any time soon. Despite copious research and endless striving, there appears to be no way to make low-sodium, fat-free, cheeseless macaroni and cheese taste like anything but fat-free, low-sodium, cheeseless macaroni and cheese. But Chef Bartel's creations occasionally score a massive hit, as with the amazingly realistic sausage gravy he developed with the aid of one of his employees. "I'd keep coming back to her with a new version," Bartel says, "and she'd taste it and say, 'Oh, Chef Dan, that's terrible! What'd you put in there?' Eventually I got it right!" Another terrific veg version of a classic is the cafeteria's low-sodium mock chicken noodle soup. It's guaranteed to bring back the school cafeteria lunches of your childhood—for better or worse!

In addition to being one of the only completely vegetarian restaurants in the area, the Florida Hospital Cafeteria is quite inexpensive. It's possible to put together a hearty lumberjack breakfast, complete with juice and coffee, for under $5.00. The hospital's Food Production Center across the street boasts a baked goods shop with a stock that turns over daily, offering some of the freshest—and best—healthful breads and desserts in the area.

# Green Gifts

If you find yourself on the waiting list for a table at Café Allègre, walk a few doors down Edgewater to the ECO-Store. Featuring earth- and animal-friendly products, the shop grew out of founder and environmental activist Beth Hollenbeck's efforts to learn about minimum-impact consumer products, and to share that information with the Orlando community. Since its launch in 1991, the store has expanded to include a large selection of "green" products, including office supplies, baby and pet items, and household products.

A special feature is the ECO-Store's offering of Fair Trade ethnic folk arts from Brazil, Haiti, Bangladesh, and elsewhere. Sales of beautifully detailed *arpillera* tapestries from Peru, Zulu eyeglass chains, and brightly-painted Russian ornaments directly benefit the indigenous artisans who made them and help preserve the traditions behind their work.

**⓫   The ECO-Store**
     2441 Edgewater Drive
     Orlando, FL 32804
     (407) 426-9949

🏛   **Café Allègre**
     **Vegebility: Fair**
     **Price: Expensive**
     Casual International
     Table Service
     D
     2401 Edgewater Drive
     Orlando, FL 32804
     (407) 872-2332
     All major credit cards accepted

"Water, water everywhere, nor any drop to drink." Sometimes a diner in Orlando can feel like Coleridge's ancient mariner, awash in a sea of corporate dining options, with nowhere real to hang out, get to know someone, or celebrate. Café Allègre owner Maria Bonomo-do Pico emigrated from her native New York City to Orlando and found she was missing more than just the crowds; she was missing the flavor of New York's unique eateries.

Her masterstroke was the hiring of CIA-trained Chef Kevin Fonzo, who introduced café patrons to a cuisine that is both complex and approachable. Fonzo's menu changes with the seasons and with the availability of ingredients, allowing only the finest food to grace diner's tables—something you wouldn't entirely expect from a neighborhood café. Another thing you wouldn't expect: Café Allègre was named the Orlando area's "Most Consistently Superior Restaurant" for 1999 by Orlando Weekly. The paper's editors cited the café's "exquisite menu, attentive service and outstanding wine list." Not bad for a neighborhood where restaurants have consistently failed in the past.

Though the menu shows just a few (admittedly tantalizing) veggie options, a quick talk with Fonzo opens up a whole new bottle of truffle oil. Most soups and stocks are made vegan, allowing a wealth of vegan and vegetarian entrées to be prepared with little notice. Of special note is a dish with few ingredients, but a surplus of flavor: White Beans with Garlic and White Truffle Oil. Vegan desserts include Poached Pear with a Vanilla Glaze and a beautiful Raspberry Sorbet with Fruit Compote.

To ensure a really special meal, let the folks at Café Allègre know about your dietary needs when you make your reservation, especially if you plan to visit on Friday or Saturday night. Most evenings, though, you can just walk right in and ask to speak with the chef. Then, have a seat and relax. Something delicious is sure to happen! —*Thanks to gardenia for her help with this review.*

# Church Street Station

Downtown Orlando's biggest tourist destination is ❶ **Church Street Station**, a cobblestoned city block lined with turn-of-the-century buildings and swamped with foot traffic. Street musicians, jugglers, and balloon-benders do their best to enliven the crowds on Friday and Saturday evenings, and more than 50 specialty shops beckon to Orlando visitors in danger of going home giftless.

The main draw at Church Street is a series of nightclubs, packing in locals and tourists alike into the wee hours. It's worth a visit

## Farmer's Market

If you linger on Church Street a bit too late—okay, *way* too late—of a Friday evening, you may just find yourself at the ❶ **Orlando Farmer's Market**, held each Saturday from 7:00 AM to 1:00 PM. Fresh local produce (much of it organic), baked goods, flowers, and more are available for purchase under I-4 at Church Street Walk. In 1999, the Farmer's Market celebrated its 10th anniversary by launching the Arts Market, a once-a-month showcase for over 30 area artists. For more information, call (407) 246-3039.

just to check out the authentic antiques and gorgeous interiors in schlocky old-time hot spots like **Rosie O' Grady's Good-Time Emporium**, but you won't find a whole lot of vegetarian food on the menu. The most veg-friendly table service restaurant at Church Street Station is **Lili Marlene's Aviator's Pub & Restaurant**, where steamed vegetable plates and pasta primavera are the order of the day.

Upstairs in Church Street Exchange's International Food Court, **Burgers 4 U** offers a Gardenburger®, thawed in the microwave, then fried on its own section of the grill. **The Chinese Cafe** dishes out a combination plate of vegetable lo mein, vegetable fried rice, and mixed veggies—all prepared using a vegetarian base—for less than $5. At **The Greek Place**, choose

between the Vegetarian Trio (hummus, falafel, and tabbouleh), a vegetarian gyro sandwich, or a spinach pie, also for under a five spot. And spaghetti with tomato sauce, eggplant parmigiana, cheese pizza slices, and spinach calzones are on the menu at **Corrado's Pizza**.

For dessert, cross the street to **Wm. J. Sweet's Ice Cream**. Two true sorbets are always on the menu, and typically showcase interesting flavors like passion fruit or watermelon.

The best vegetarian meals are half a block east at ❶ **Church Street Marketplace**, where a selection of local and national chain restaurants beckon with fast, focus group-approved fare. Cappellini Pomodoro—angel hair pasta tossed with Roma tomatoes, garlic, basil, and a touch of balsamic—is a light, cheap and filling repast at the **Olive Garden**, as is the Roman Garden Pizza, with spinach and artichoke heart toppings. An added bonus: all Olive Garden pastas are eggless. If you're in the mood for sushi, make your way to **Amura Sushi Bar**, where four vegetable nori rolls are on the menu. Middle Eastern vegetarian specialties can be had at **Martini's Bar & Grill**. For an appetizer, try a Hummus Pizza: hummus, cucumbers, tabbouleh, and Roma tomatoes atop fresh pita bread, and drizzled with a curry crème frâiche. Three pasta dishes and vegetable moussaka are among the entrées.

# Veggie Kids in Downtown Orlando

*The meatless options offered to kids at most restaurants are less than desirable, if you want your children to eat well. Our advice: skip the kiddie menu and share your adult meal with the kids at the table. If your li'l shaver has his or her heart set on a pint-sized meal, here's what to expect in downtown Orlando.*

## Vegetarian Kids' Meals at Table Service Restaurants

**Baja Burrito Kitchen:**

Cheese quesadilla; veggie wrap (a rolled tortilla filled with beans, rice, and cheese); tortilla chips and melted cheese

**Café Allègre:**

Children's portions of the café's vegetarian meals are available upon request

**Chapters Bread & Books:**

Grilled cheese sandwich; macaroni and cheese; pasta with tomato or butter sauce

**Dexter's of Thornton Park:**

Grilled cheese sandwich; small order of parmesan cheese shells with marinara sauce; fruit platter

**Jungle Jim's:**

Grilled cheese sandwich; peanut butter and jelly sandwich

**White Wolf Cafe:**

Lunch: Toasted cheese sandwich; peanut butter and jelly sandwich

Dinner: Same as lunch, plus kids' pizza (cheese and marinara sauce on homemade focaccia bread)

## Healthful Snacks

**Chamberlin's Market**

Vegan, sugar-free baked goods; organic fresh whole fruit

---

At **Jungle Jim's**, you can have your Gardenburger prepared one of 20-odd ways, but if you're vegan you can forget it: the venerable patties contain dairy. Vegans should also avoid Jim's pasta, all of which is made with egg (for more information about Jungle Jim's, see our review on page 207). **Pizzeria Uno** makes its own veggie burger from a blend of seven vegetables, and serves it just one way: with salsa on the side. But it's the deep dish Chicago-style pies that separate Uno from the rest of the pizza pack, including our favorite, the Spinoccoli: spinach, fresh broccoli, a blend of cheese, lotsa garlic, and specially seasoned tomatoes.

# Places to Shop

## Best of the Best in Downtown Orlando

⚘ **Chamberlin's Market and Café**
**Deli/To Go: Excellent**
**Produce: Good (90% organic)**
**Prepackaged Natural Foods: Excellent**
**Non-Food Items: Excellent**
Herndon Village Shoppes

4960 E. Colonial Drive
Orlando, FL 32803
(407) 894-8452
Celebrate Health Hotline:
(407) 644-9821 ext. 269
http://www.chamberlinsmarket.com

If you find yourself in need of healthful supplies while downtown, head east on Colonial to Chamberlin's Market in Herndon Village. Although this branch of the Orlando-wide health food chain is not as impressive as its Winter Park sister, you'll find more—and better—natural products here than at the vast majority of Orlando markets. Natural cruel-ty-free health and beauty products, organic baby food, and a selection of domestic and imported organic wines are in stock everyday at Chamberlin's, along with wheat-free pastas, tofu, and an assortment of vegan frozen foods.

There's no deli case at the East Colonial location, but a sandwich and juice bar offer quick, healthful meals with seating at the counter. Freshly baked breads, a selection of healthful snacks, and a wide assortment of organic produce make this Chamberlin's a great source for snacks and sandwich fixin's.

# Chapter 19

# Winter Park and
# Northern Orlando

**Winter Park Chamber of Commerce:**
*(407) 644-8281; http://www.winterparkcc.org*
**Orlando Weekly:** *http://www.orlandoweekly.com*
**Orlando Sentinel:** *http://www.orlandosentinel.com*
*Check out these area websites for ideas about how
to spend the day and up-to-date dining reviews.*

*J*ust north of downtown lies quiet, gentrified Winter Park, once a wilderness outpost in the midst of dense pine forest. Designer boutiques and glorious turn of the century homes have supplanted the trading post, but much of the greenery is still here: Winter Park boasts more than 70 parks and public greenspaces. It's easy to slip away into reveries of another time by taking an hour-long boat tour around the city's ring of natural lakes, or by enjoying a picnic on the spacious green of Central Park.

In the heart of old Winter Park is the recently renovated Charles Hosmer Morse Museum, one of the world's largest repositories of pieces by Louis Comfort Tiffany. Work in the autumn and winter of 1998 added a new wing, a shop, and four new galleries to this already stunning collection of furniture, ceramics, prints, and drawings by Tiffany and his contemporaries.

In addition to their many other blessings, residents of this tony Orlando suburb enjoy a wealth of dining options. What's our favorite

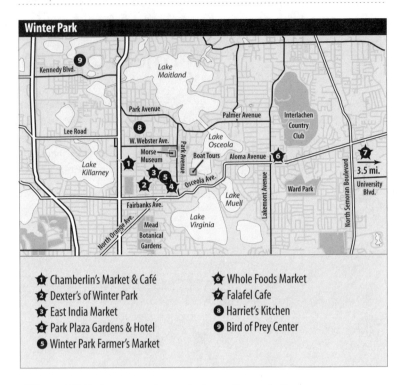

**Winter Park**

1 Chamberlin's Market & Café
2 Dexter's of Winter Park
3 East India Market
4 Park Plaza Gardens & Hotel
5 Winter Park Farmer's Market
6 Whole Foods Market
7 Falafel Cafe
8 Harriet's Kitchen
9 Bird of Prey Center

thing to do? Grab a vegetarian pack lunch at Chamberlin's or Whole Foods Market, and take a canoe out on one of the town's many magnificent lakes. Nothing could be more relaxing—or refreshingly real—after a day spent in Orlando's theme parks.

## Places to Eat

### Best of the Best in N. Orlando

1 **Chamberlin's Café**
**Vegebility: Excellent**
**Price: Inexpensive—Moderate**
Casual American

Counter Service
B, L, D
Chamberlin's Market
Winter Park Mall
430 N. Orlando Avenue
Winter Park, FL 32789
(407) 647-6661
MC/V/AE/Discover

Last time we checked out the café at the Winter Park Chamberlin's, 21 out of the 26 dishes in the deli case were vegan. That's a whopping 80%—more vegan dishes than any right-thinking individual could possibly devour in one sitting. And they're not just vegan,

## At-a-Glance Grid

# Northern Orlando: Best of the Best

**Key to Categories and Abbreviations**

**O/L, V: Ovo-lacto and vegan selections**

• - Always available    + - Available upon request    A - Request in advance

**Es: Type of establishment**

T - Table Service     C - Counter service     S - Snack stand or cart

**$: Average price for a single vegetarian entrée**

1 - under $10      3 - $16 - $20      5 - $31 - $40
2 - $10 - $15      4 - $21 - $30      6 - over $40

**Meals:**

B - Breakfast     L - Lunch     D - Dinner     S - Snacks

| Winter Park | O/L | V | Es | $ | Meals |
|---|---|---|---|---|---|
| ❶ Chamberlin's Café | • | • | C | 1 | B, L, D, S |
| ❷ Dexter's of Winter Park | • | • | T | 1 | L, D |
| ❸ East India Market* | • | • | T | 1 | B, L, D |
| ❹ Park Plaza Gardens | • | • | T | 3 | L, D |
| **Elsewhere in Northern Orlando** | | | | | |
| ❼ Falafel Cafe | • | • | T | 1 | L, D |

*Restaurant temporarily closed at press date

they're often delicious, thanks to Executive Chef John Procacci's hard work and expertise. The Shepherd's Pie—made with tempeh, carrots, corn, and peas—is heaven for anyone who loves comfort food. But, Chef Procacci warns, it's not vegan: the rice milk used in the mashed potatoes contains casein. Now *there's* a chef that knows his ingredients—and how important that is to his clientele!

If you find yourself at Chamberlin's during the breakfast hour, don't miss the California Breakfast Rice. At lunch or dinner, plant yourself in the café's large, atrium-like seating area and sample one of Procacci's signature dishes, like "Vegetarian Chicken," a tofu meatball sub, or a "Zulu Burger"—a delicious concoction made fresh in-house from brown rice, miso, and fresh vegetables. Or grab a specialty pizza: vegan whole wheat and sundried tomato shells topped with vegetarian pepperoni or sausage, rice milk cheese, pineapple chunks, or artichokes.

Chamberlin's bakery offers a vast selection of desserts and cookies that are dairy- and egg-free, and every item has an ingredient list to prove it. After lunch, tuck into a vegan elephant ear, or an impossibly moist and delicious vegan carrot cake, accompanied by a cappuccino from the all-organic coffee bar. For something lighter, grab a freshly-squeezed juice from the in-store smoothie bar.

The dishes served in the café are made with expensive ingredients—over 70% of the items are organic, all dairy products are hormone-free, and all eggs are fertile, organic, and free-range. But somehow Chamberlin's manages to keep prices lower than many fast food joints along I-Drive, with sandwiches for less than $4 and dinners for less than $5. One warning, though: Chamberlin's is not an entirely vegetarian café: one chicken or fish entrée is always on the menu. But policies for the separation of meat items from vegetarian—in the cooking and preparation areas, and in the deli case—are strictly enforced.

---

**❷ Dexter's of Winter Park**
**Vegebility: Good**
**Price: Moderate**
Casual American
Table Service
L, D
558 W. New England Ave.

Winter Park, FL 32789
(407) 629-1150
All major credit cards accepted

A great way to shed your tourist skin and experience Orlando's hipper side is to head over to Dexter's. The original Winter Park Dexter's was so popular it both spawned a superb offshoot (see Dexter's of Thornton Park, page 225), and recently moved to its own larger location. Locals flock to the Winter Park Dex for art shows, free live jazz music (Thursday nights), and periodic wine tastings, selected by Dex's in-house sommelier. They also come in search of the monthly café specials offered by both restaurants.

While by no means a vegetarian restaurant, Dexter's makes a point of catering to the wishes of its stylish, health-conscious clientele. Appetizer specials at the Winter Park Dex might include a sun-dried tomato risotto cake, topped with baby vegetables and gourmet greens, and drizzled with caramelized balsamic vinegar. Those who eat dairy (and aren't watching their weight) should try the baked asiago artichoke dip, served with blue corn chips.

Vegetarian entrée specials, as in most restaurants, are fewer and farther between. But Dexter's regular menu comes to the rescue

---

*F*or a comprehensive guide to our ratings system, see page xviii.

# A Vegetarian Tour of Northern Orlando

*For a wonderful introduction to the genteel life of turn-of-the-century Orlando, head north to our favorite part of town, Winter Park. Just be sure to eat at some of the very veg-friendly restaurants mentioned below, and to make reservations by calling a few days in advance.*

### Itinerary One

**9 AM:** Just thinking about the California Breakfast Rice at the Winter Park Chamberlins makes us jump right out of bed. A bowl of the deliciously sweet and cinnamon-rich grains and one of the in-store bakery's fabulous vegan pastries stick to the ribs, and should tide you over until lunch time.

**10 AM:** Park your car in tony downtown Winter Park and wander over to Lake Osceola in time to catch the Scenic Boat Tour, a great introduction to the town's history.

**12 PM:** Enjoy a delicious macrobiotic lunch at Park Plaza Gardens. Don't forget to sample one of the restaurant's delicious desserts!

**2 PM:** Spend the rest of the afternoon viewing the world's largest collection of work by Louis Comfort Tiffany—and other Art Nouveau and Arts and Crafts masterpieces—at the Charles Hosmer Morse Museum, just a few blocks north on Park Avenue. Or, better yet, hop in the car and head to the Audubon Society's Bird of Prey Center to marvel at the beauty and majesty of nature's masterpieces, and to help support the center's conservation efforts.

**6 PM:** Dinner at Dexter's of Winter Park. Plan your visit to Winter Park for a Thursday, when Dexter's features free live jazz ensembles.

### Or:

**6 PM:** If you happen to be in town on a Friday or Saturday, head over to East India Market. On weekend evenings in season, Chef Mike Vogler stokes up the oak-fired grill in the garden, and prepares delicious blackened veggie burgers and roasted veggies on their own side of the grill. Call in advance to be sure the fire will be hot.

### Itinerary Two

**9 AM:** If you're staying at the Park Plaza Hotel, there's nothing better than taking a leisurely breakfast on the verandah overlooking the green oasis of Central Park. On Saturday, you'll notice a lot of commotion down at the old train station. That's the Winter Park Farmer's Market. After breakfast, wander down to the market to pick up some goodies for your lunch basket (and if you're not staying at the Park Plaza Hotel, you can grab coffee and breakfast at the Farmer's Market, too). Any other day of the week, take your rental car to Whole Foods Market to fill your lunchtime hamper with veggie sushi and prepared salads.

**11 AM:** Rent a canoe and spend the entire day exploring the town's lakes and waterways on your own.

**1 PM:** Spread your picnic blanket on the banks of one of Winter Park's quiet lakes, and drift into reveries of a gentler, less commercialized time in Central Florida.

**5 PM:** Paddle back to the docks and meander back to your room for a shower and a nap.

**7:30 PM:** Savor a vegan, macrobiotic dinner downstairs at Park Plaza Gardens.

with a wide range of salads, pastas (don't miss the fabulous Veggie Peanut Pasta, with house-made noodles), and the incredibly hearty Eggplant Napoleon. Toss in a great selection of sandwich fixin's, and you've got a mainstream restaurant that allows vegans to put together a really satisfying sandwich, too. All in all, the huge variety of fare makes either Dexter's a good bet for hungry vegetarians.

---

✿ **East India Market**
**Vegebility: Good**
**Price: Moderate**
Casual American
Table Service
B, L, D
610 W. Morse Blvd.
Winter Park, FL 32789
(407) 647-7520
V/MC/AE/Diner's

John Spang is a Winter Park legend, having been involved in the town's commercial district for nearly 30 years. From clothing boutiques to ice cream shoppes to resort hotels, Spang has run just about every kind of business imaginable in Winter Park, often to rave reviews. The ice cream business was a huge success, and Spang's 250 homemade varieties were, by all accounts, superb. Stimulated by his passion for coffee (and perhaps a bit too much caffeine), Spang's most recent project is East India Market, where he and daughter Mindy Spang roast a variety of beans to perfection daily amid shelves lined with gourmet deli items, cigars, and produce for sale. An indoor coffee bar offers nine caffeinated concoctions and fresh-squeezed orange juice. A special "humidor room" is available for sampling fine cigars.

But for us the primary draw is the Market's bistro menu, preferably sampled in the lush outdoor dining area. Plants both potted and permanent, cedar tables with green umbrellas, and a massive oak-fired grill make a wonderful setting for great vegetarian soups, vegan breads, and cheeseless wood-fired pizzas with thin, cracker-like crusts. Tempting flatbread combinations include roasted market vegetables; portobella mushrooms, Fontina and arugula; spinach, caramelized onions, and goat cheese; and roasted tomatoes, fresh basil, and buffalo Mozzarella.

The biggest seller on the regular menu is the Market Veggie Wrap: a vegan medley of hummus, quinoa tabbouleh, marinated tomato and red onion, and sprouts wrapped in a phenomenal house-made herbed lavosh bread. The restaurant is also known for its wonderful salads, although some locals—who, true to the neighborhood, roll into the parking lot in Jags, BMWs, and Lexi—have complained that these are not always as fresh as they could be.

# Harriet McNear

All Harriet McNear wanted in life was to find "the perfect path." In her search—and after years of eating lots of rich, fatty foods—Harriet came across macrobiotics in a book by Michio Kushi, founder of Boston's Kushi Institute.

"Was I ready!" Harriet confessed. "Suddenly a whole new world opened up for me. It was just what I had been looking for. And, of course, I started feeling better immediately."

That was the beginning of a quiet revolution in Central Florida, with Harriet at its center. In 1987, she founded Harriet's Kitchen, a whole foods cooking school. In the years that followed, students joined Harriet and a cadre of professional chefs and educators in the teaching kitchen of her light, peaceful Winter Park home to learn how to eat, cook, and live in a healthful, conscious way. Harriet herself became a recognized authority on the subject, and articles have appeared about and by her in *Vegetarian Times*, *Cook's*, and *Macrobiotics Today*. Her school has become a major resource in the area, with a staff of teachers that includes profes-

sional chefs from Walt Disney World and major Orlando restaurants, and recognized authorities in macrobiotic and whole foods preparation from all over the world. In her capacity as a teacher, she brought macrobiotic cooking to life, presenting it in a way that was fun, easy, and delicious.

Harriet McNear died on June 25, 1999 while vacationing in Italy, no doubt in the process of picking up some wonderful recipes to share with friends and students. As a tribute, her husband Paul and others are developing the Harriet McNear Healing Trust, a scholarship fund for others interested in learning about healthful living. And, thanks her dedicated assistant Tammy Crawford and a collection of talented local chefs, the school Harriet founded continues to offer an ambitious program of courses, with topics like "Scrumptious Fall Desserts," "The Joy of Soy," and even a course in vegetarian "Lunch Box Magic." All of the foods used in the classes are high in fiber, low in fat and salt, and use no dairy products, sugars, or honey. The courses are primarily vegetarian, although some do feature fish.

Call the Kitchen for a brochure describing the courses available during your visit to Orlando. And be sure to remember Harriet, the trailblazer, as you travel your own "perfect path."

❽ **Harriet's Kitchen**
PO Box 1301
Winter Park, FL 322790
(407) 644-2167

On weekend nights Chef Mike Vogler stokes up the oak-fired grill in the garden, roasting vegetables in a balsamic mustard marinade and blackening veggie burgers and portobello sandwiches on their own side of the grill. Be sure to call in advance of your visit, however, just to be sure that the café is open. East India was on temporary hiatus at the time this guide went to press, and the re-opening date had not yet been finalized.

---

☆ **Park Plaza Gardens**
**Vegebility: Good**
**Price: Moderate—Expensive**
Casual/Upscale American
Table Service
L, D
319 Park Avenue South
Winter Park, FL 32789
(407) 645-2475
V/MC/AE/Diner's

Let's face it: It's hard to find a vegetarian-friendly menu at an upscale restaurant. It's even harder to find a macrobiotic-friendly meal at any restaurant—upscale or casual, vegetarian or not.

In fact, the only menu where we've ever seen the phrase "macrobiotic-friendly" is at Park Plaza Gardens, the casually hip dining spot in the Park Plaza Hotel. The ambience alone is reason enough to patronize Park Plaza, with tables scattered amid an elegantly appointed forest of potted plants. A sun-streaked idyll during the day, the room becomes a candle-lit oasis at night. Add to this its remarkable vegan-friendly food, and you have a dining spot worth heading north for.

The restaurant's awareness of macrobiotic cooking is due largely to the efforts of the late Harriet McNear, a local visionary who offered courses in her whole foods cookery school, Harriet's Kitchen (see sidebar on previous page). In a revolutionary move, Park Plaza Gardens chefs developed the menu in consultation with McNear in Fall, 1998, with the encouragement of the restaurant's progressive management. The subsequent hiring of Gardens' Executive Chef Clair Epting added strength to strength: Epting himself is expert in macro cooking, and frequently teaches advanced courses at Harriet's Kitchen.

Epting works with Stettner Farm, a nearby 110-acre, 100% organic farm, to provide the best seasonal produce—including many heirloom vegetables—for his menu. With the guarantee of a steady supply from Stettner, he's able to keep plenty of vegetarian staples on hand to accommodate special requests. But with a menu this veg-friendly to begin with, it's hard to imagine needing to stray too far to find something appealing.

The menu changes seasonally, but routinely includes delicacies like a macrobiotic roast corn, leek, and parsnip soup, sprinkled with smoked dulse. Four other vegan—and three more vegetarian—temptations are among the appetizers. For a main course, tuck into the barley and wild mushroom stew, served with Japanese buckwheat soba noodles and topped with a mixture of Thai herbs. Ovo-lacto vegetarians will find farfalle pasta tossed with basil, roasted garlic, and pine nut pesto.

No matter what you order, be sure to leave room for dessert. The descriptions on the menu alone are enough to make the heart flutter. Take the Chocolate Bread Pudding Sundae, for example: chocolate bread pudding made with crusty french bread, and served with a scoop of chocolate Bourbon molasses ice cream and a warm drizzle of Godiva chocolate sauce. Or how about the Green Apple and Blackberry Crisp, served warm with honey cinnamon gelato? Vegan and macro diners will appreciate—and adore—the sorbet and berry parfait: delicate layers of ripe berries and true sorbet. Reservations are recommended.

---

❂  **Falafel Cafe**
   **Vegebility: Excellent**
   **Price: Inexpensive**
   Casual Middle Eastern
   Table Service
   L, D
   12140 Collegiate Way
   Orlando, FL 32817
   (407) 382-6600
   http://www.falafelcafe.com
   All major credit cards accepted

Hidden behind a strip mall in a nondescript locale is a restaurant well worth looking for. Open for lunch and dinner on weekdays only, tiny Falafel Cafe caters primarily to the college crowd studying across the street at the University of Central Florida. Owner and Chef Hind Dajani moved from Kuwait to Lebanon before settling in Orlando, honing her skills in Middle Eastern cooking along the way. Ten years ago, Dajani finally heeded the advice of friends and family urging her to open a restaurant, and Orlando vegetarians couldn't be happier. Falafel Cafe is a great place to go for a delicious, inexpensive meal.

---

*Facts for foodies*

ucked inside pita bread for a delicious and portable sandwich or eaten alone as an appetizer, **falafel** is a popular Middle Eastern snack made of highly spiced, finely ground chickpeas. The chickpeas (also known as garbanzo beans) are soaked, ground, and seasoned with onions and parsley, then shaped into balls or patties and deep fried. Fresh falafel has a bright green interior, and is incomparably better than the greasy, grainy brown balls many restaurants serve. We think falafel tastes best served warm, accompanied by a yogurt or tahini dipping sauce.

Most meatless diners are familiar with falafel, hummus, and baba ghanoush, since Middle Eastern restaurants are usually quite vegetarian-friendly. The difference from restaurant to restaurant is in freshness, preparation, and care, as anyone who's ever bitten into a greasy falafel ball knows. Everything at Falafel Café—from the delicious baba ghanoush (eggplant spread), to the warm, fresh falafel, to the soft and chewy garlic pita bread—is lovingly fussed over. The food is simple, but it is most definitely not plain.

At lunchtime, vegans can choose from no fewer than nine menu items, with two veggie platters mixing and matching the best the café has to offer. There are, in fact, more vegan than ovo-lacto choices on the lunch or dinner menu, a rarity in any restaurant that serves meat. In the evenings, the best option is the enormous Vegetarian's Delight Feast: a sampler of hummus, baba ghanoush, falafel, spinach pie, tabbouleh, and stuffed grape leaves, all for just $9.99. Take that, Sizzler!
—*Thanks to gardenia for her help with this review.*

# Places to Stay

### Best of the Best in Winter Park

✿ **Park Plaza Hotel**
**Vegebility: Good**
**Price: Inexpensive–Moderate**

307 Park Avenue South
Winter Park, FL 32789
Reservations: (800) 228-7220
(407) 647-1072
http://www.parkplazahotel.com/

No one could blame you if, after a stroll down Park Avenue, you decided to leave your boring digs on International Drive and move into the Park Plaza Hotel. After all, how many Comfort Inns offer Persian rugs, beautiful woodwork, lushly-planted balconies, and a vegetarian macrobiotic menu in the restaurant downstairs?

And here's the kicker: rooms here are practically the same price as an I-Drive Holiday Inn. If you like small, sophisticated hotels with personalized service, and don't mind driving 20 minutes to get to the theme parks, staying at Park Plaza is a no-brainer.

Located in the heart of Winter Park's upscale shopping and dining district, the hotel dates from 1921 and has been lovingly refurbished by owners Sissie and John Spang. No two guest rooms in the Park Plaza are the same, but each is beautifully appointed with antiques, floral bed linens, patchwork quilts, and a full bath. Dark wooden slatted shutters and ceiling fans add an Island ambience, as do a profusion of potted ferns, flowering bouganvilleae, and other tropical plants on the suites' wrought iron balconies—a great place to enjoy the local newspaper and complementary continental breakfast. Both are delivered to your room each morning.

Concierge-like service is available at the desk downstairs in the hotel's beautiful European-style lobby. Transportation to and from the theme parks and Orlando International can be arranged, and for an extra fee guests can use the nearby Winter Park Wellness Center's fitness and spa facilities.

And we can't say enough about the vegetarian offerings at the hotel's dining room, Park Plaza Gardens—but we'll try. For a full review, see page 246.

## Places to Shop

### Best of the Best in Winter Park

🔒 **Chamberlin's Market**
**Deli/To Go: Excellent**
**Produce: Excellent (95% organic)**
**Prepackaged Natural Foods: Excellent**
**Non-Food Items: Excellent**
Winter Park Mall
430 N. Orlando Avenue
Winter Park, FL 32789
(407) 647-6661
Celebrate Health Hotline:
(407) 644-9821 ext. 269
http://www.chamberlinsmarket.com

The original Chamberlin's Market opened its doors on East Church Street in downtown Orlando in

---

## Farmer's Market

Voted the area's Best Farmer's Market in a 1999 Orlando Weekly readers' poll, the ❺ **Winter Park Farmer's Market**—a showcase of produce and local foodstuffs held each Saturday—is a Winter Park tradition. The Farmer's Market celebrated its 20th birthday in 1999, and occupies the town's original train station, a beautifully restored structure dating from the early 1880s. Fresh organic fruits and vegetables, baked goods, gourmet cheeses, and fresh and dried flowers are a few of the reasons to head to the corner of New York and New England Avenues between 7:00 AM and 1:00 PM. Sharing a cool breeze, a cup of coffee, and conversation with a friendly local at an outdoor café table is another. For more information, call (407) 623-3275.

---

1935. No, that's not an 8, it's a 3—Chamberlin's is 65 years old. "We were in it when it wasn't so popular!" chuckles owner Dale Bennet, who bought the store in January of 1972. In fact, Chamberlin's is, by some accounts, the 4th oldest natural food store in the country—a dinosaur in comparison with its primary Winter Park competitor, Whole Foods Markets.

The good news is that, although Chamberlin's is "ancient," its healthful, vegetarian offerings are cutting edge, and it's far more active in the community than most natural markets. There's a busy

# Audubon Society Bird of Prey Center

Just a few minutes' drive from Winter Park near the Eatonville and Maitland border, tucked behind a group of older houses and a stand of trees, sits the Audubon Society's Bird of Prey Center. Here, injured raptors are brought to be treated and tended and—once healed and able to fend for themselves—are released into the wild. Guests to the Center are given guided tours which focus on celebrating the birds' majesty and beauty, and on educating everyone about their species' tenuous place on earth. Humankind, as you might imagine, is these creatures' worst enemy.

A recent expansion will allow for even more guests—about 25,000 at a time—to visit the eagles, hawks, owls, and other birds of prey. The expansion also benefits the birds directly, with enormous new flight cages that will allow the raptors to practice their skills before being released. Those that are not able to handle the rigors of life in the wild become a part of the Center's educational programs. Many of the visitors that pass through here are school children: a ray of hope for the continued well-being of these wondrous animals.

About four of every ten birds that find their way to the Center are strong enough to be released. Since the Center began operating in 1979, the number of eagles in the state of Florida has quadrupled from 250 to 1000, due in no small part to the Center's efforts. —*Thanks to gardenia for this information.*

**❾ Bird of Prey Center**
1101 Audubon Way
Maitland, Florida 32751
*Call (407) 645-3826 for information about hours and special events*
*Admission: $5 for adults,*
*$4 for children*

schedule of classes, lectures, and group meetings. There are weekly series of cooking classes. And there's "Team Chamberlin's": a fitness walking group, led in one location by an exercise physiologist, that's open to anyone. It's totally free, with no membership requirements. "It's just a little something we give back to our customers," says Debby Swoboda, Chamberlins' Marketing Director.

With 15,500 square feet of retail and dining space, the Winter Park Chamberlin's is a vegetarian's dream. Organic produce and wine, healthful frozen and prepared foods, natural groceries, herbs, homeopathics, a wholesome bakery, great books and magazines, the occasional wine tasting or community fair, and a huge in-store café and mostly-vegan deli (see review, page 240) make this the one-stop shopping destination for vegetarians visiting Orlando.

**☆ Whole Foods Market**
**Deli/To Go: Excellent**
**Produce: Excellent (95% organic)**
**Prepackaged Natural Foods:**
**Excellent**

# Veggie Kids in Winter Park

*In an attempt to get filling food into kids with a minimum of fuss and at a low price, children's menus appeal to every parent's dietary aces in the hole: noodles and cheese. It's not exactly inspired, but it does cut down on strife at the dinner table. Here's what you can expect from the kid's menus at our favorite veg-friendly restaurants in Winter Park.*

## Vegetarian Kids' Meals at Table Service Restaurants

**Dexter's of Winter Park:**
Grilled cheese sandwich; angel hair pasta with choice of marinara, butter, or Alfredo sauce

**Park Plaza Gardens:**
Pasta with tomato sauce

## Kid-Friendly Vegetarian Offerings at Counter Service Restaurants

**Chamberlin's Café:**
Shepherd's pie (made with mashed potatoes, tempeh, carrots, corn, and peas); veggie pepperoni and veggie sausage pizza; salads

## Healthful Snacks

**Chamberlin's Market:**
Vegan, sugar-free baked goods; organic fresh whole fruit; fresh juices and smoothies

**Whole Foods Market:**
Potato and cheese knishes; stuffed baked potatoes; organic whole fruit; fresh fruit juices and smoothies

---

**Non-Food Items: Excellent**
1989 Aloma Avenue
Winter Park, FL 32792
(407) 673-8788

Whole Foods Markets have been spreading like wildfire throughout the country, frequently springing up near affluent communities like Winter Park, the tony Orlando suburb that welcomed its first Whole Foods in early 1998. As soon as the new store's construction was announced, fears about the imminent demise of homegrown favorite Chamberlin's Market circulated through the Orlando vegetarian community. But stories of Chamberlin's demise proved to be greatly exaggerated, and the two chains seem to be coexisting nicely, providing slightly different goods and services. Fabulously fresh produce, organic wines, and a strong focus on natural gourmet ingredients have helped the national chain tap into Winter Park's health-conscious, affluent populace.

Whole Foods' deli items are not nearly as veggie-friendly as those at Chamberlin's, where a much greater emphasis is placed on vegan and vegetarian dishes. But there are still plenty of delicious choices, including Chinese grilled tofu, Mediterranean couscous, and tabbouleh—all of which are vegan. Hot ovo-lacto items include a selection of knishes, stuffed baked potatoes, and tofu croquettes. Vegetarian and vegan deli selections change frequently and are clearly marked, and all ingredients are listed on a card accompanying each dish.

One of the best reasons to visit the Winter Park Whole Foods is the sushi. Two in-store Japanese sushi specialists prepare fresh nori makis all day long, including two vegetarian options. Both are available in pre-packaged assortments to go. A smoothie and juice bar offers nutritious libations to accompany your meal, and the bakery sells a selection of delicious freshly-baked cookies, pastries, and breads.

If you're looking for ingredients to make a meal at home, Whole Foods offers a wide variety of top-of-the-line (and top-dollar) products. The produce at the Winter Park store has no match in the Orlando area. All fresh vegetables are organic, as are the majority of fruits, including delicious and hard-to-find items like Mission figs and Jamaican ugli fruit. A wide variety of standard and exotic greens, fresh herbs, and gourmet mushrooms—fresh and dried— are all on hand to help you put together a fabulous meal.

Elsewhere in the store you'll find free range eggs, organic milk, and a nice selection of gourmet domestic and imported cheeses—a few of which are made without animal rennet. A rather large section of the store is devoted to organic wines, including vintages from France, California, and Washington state, and domestic and imported microbrews. Bulk items, natural health and beauty products, nutritional supplements, baby and pet supplies, freshly-cut flowers, and an assortment of suitably wholesome cards and gifts are available, as well.

# Appendices

# Index of Recommended Dining Establishments

### Great Places to Eat, Catagorized for Rapid Retrieval

*Italic numbers indicate the page(s)
where a restaurant is reviewed in depth.*

## Restaurants By Vegebility

## Restaurants By Price

# General Index

Every Establishment Included,
Organized Alphabetically

*Italic numbers indicate the page(s)
where each is reviewed in depth.*

## Lodgings

## Markets

## Other Establishments

## Restaurants

# Advertisements

*V*egetarian *Walt Disney World and Greater Orlando* was made possible in part by the generous sponsorship of *Vegetarian Times* magazine and its partners in the promotion of healthful living.

Additional research and production costs for this edition were partially underwritten by a select group of advertisers in the Orlando area. All research had been concluded and reviews written before local establishments were approached by an independent advertising representative, and only those that were highly recommended by the authors were asked if they wished to participate. The result is a group of advertising partners whose products Vegetarian World Guides can endorse without hesitation.

*Vegetarian Times* is the premier magazine for those looking to improve their overall health. From advice on creating a gourmet meatless meal to **VEGETARIAN** *times* commentary on the latest research to assessments of alternative health care, *Vegetarian Times* is the leading authority on all things natural. Good Health, Great Food, Smart Living...this is *Vegetarian Times*.

**CHAMBERLIN'S MARKET & CAFE**
your natural food center

$6$ **Locations to Serve You**

**Your Vacationing Source for Natural Groceries, Fresh Organic Produce, Complete Line of Supplements and Herbs, Fresh Bakery, Organic Wines**

### 1 South West Orlando
The Market Place • 407-352-2130
Minutes from major attractions
(1 mile west of I-4 at Sand Lake Rd on
Dr Phillips Blvd)

### 2 East Orlando
Herndon Village Shoppes • 407-894-8452
(1/2 mile east of Fashion Sq on E Colonial Dr
[same center as Pier 1])

### 3 Casselberry
Lake Howell Square • 407-678-3100
(Semoran Blvd [Hwy 436] 1 mile north of
Howell Branch Road)

### 4 Oviedo
Oviedo Marketplace Super Store • 407-359-7028
(New Oviedo Mall-Red Bug Rd & The Greenway
[Hwy 417]) Entrance outside, next to
Bed, Bath & Beyond

### 5 Altamonte Springs
Goodings Plaza • 407-774-8866
(2 miles west of I-4 on Hwy 434
at Montgomery Rd.)

### 6 Winter Park
Winter Park Village Super Store • 407-647-6661
(1/4 mile south of Lee Rd on 17/92)

**Orlando's Natural Resource Since 1935**

**Our Cafe Offers:**
Homemade Soups
Famous Vegetarian Chili
Sandwiches & Salads
Fresh Fruit Smoothies
Organic Carrot Juice
Fresh Sushi at Super Stores

Open 7 Days for Your Convenience
www.chamberlins.com

# Don't keep it to yourself!

*Vegetarian Walt Disney World and Greater Orlando*

*Including Universal Studios Escape*

*The essential guide for the discriminating traveler*

*By Susan Shumaker and Than Saffel*

*Foreword by Paul McCartney*

*A Vegetarian World Guide*

Now you can give the gift of a delicious, healthful vacation to someone you know—and save money, at the same time. Send in the coupon below with your check, money order, or credit card number, and we'll take $2 off the cover price of each book.

## Shipping and Billing Information

Name (Print) _____

Address _____

City, State, Zip _____

Country _____ Day Phone _____

Email _____

Quantity _____ x $12.95    Subtotal _____

Sales Tax (WV residents add 6%) _____

Shipping ($3.95 first book; $1 ea. add'l book) _____

Total _____

## Payment Information

☐ Check / Money Order (Payable to Vegetarian World Guides)

☐ Visa  ☐ Mastercard  ☐ American Express

Card No. _____

Expiration (MM / YY) _____

Signature _____

Return this order form with payment to:

**Vegetarian World Guides**

**PO Box 3533, Morgantown, WV 26503-3533**

VWDW + GO

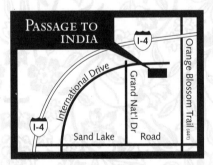

# AUTHENTICALLY ORGANIC FOOD

The three most important aspects of your diet are water, air, and salt quality. The fourth most important is the vitality of the soil.

We do our best for you. **EDEN FOODS**

Each EDEN® brand food is selected and prepared by Eden Foods as if it were for our children.

The EDEN® brand means: no irradiation, no preservatives, no chemical additives, no food colorings, no refined sugars, no genetically engineered ingredients; the safest, most nutritious, certified organically grown food that can possibly be offered.

Write or call 888 424-EDEN for FREE product information, recipes, and coupons.

Ⓚ parve

*Please support certified organic farmers, society's greatest hope for positive change.*

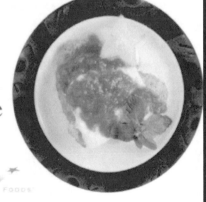

# About the Authors

**The Idealist**　　　**The Crank**

Susan Shumaker and Than Saffel have lived and traveled on four continents, and are looking forward to tackling the other three. They have worked together since 1993 as co-owners of Stone Circle Productions, a multimedia design company which has produced award-winning CD-ROMs for the education market.

For the past three years the two have focused their energies primarily on vegetarian journalism, writing a number of articles for *Vegetarian Times* magazine and launching the *Vegetarian World Guides* series. The experience of developing the guidebooks has forced them to improve their already existing skills in research, writing, editing, and graphic design, and to develop skills in areas where they weren't already proficient, such as marketing, book distribution, and patience.

They currently reside on a farm in Morgantown, West Virginia with their two dogs, Morgan and Hannah, and their 1-year-old daughter, Rhowyn. Both are actively involved in efforts to support vegetarianism and community-supported agriculture in the Morgantown area.

**Restaurant**                                          **Date Visited**

**Address** *(Street, City, State, Zip)*

**Phone**                          **Web Site**

**Dress Code**   ☐ Casual  ☐ Upscale  ☐ Jacket Required

**Type of Service**   ☐ Snack Stand  ☐ Counter  ☐ Buffet  ☐ Table Service

**Meals Served**   ☐ Snacks  ☐ Breakfast  ☐ Lunch  ☐ Dinner

**Payment**   ☐ MC  ☐ Visa  ☐ AE  ☐ Disc  ☐ Diners  ☐ Check  ☐ Cash only

**Vegability**

**Ovo-lacto selections are available:**
☐ Always    ☐ Upon request    ☐ With advance notice

ovo-lacto selections are listed on the regular menu

**Vegan selections are available:**
☐ Always    ☐ Upon request    ☐ With advance notice

vegan selections are listed on the regular menu

**Your Meal**

**Appetizers**

**Entrées**

**Desserts**

**Beverages**

*over* ▶

**Your Meal** *(continued)*

**Your comments** *(please be as specific and descriptive as possible)*

**Your Name**

**Address (Street, City, State, Zip)**

**Day Phone**                    **E-mail**

☐  I am willing to be quoted on the Vegetarian World Guides' Web site, and in future editions of this and other Vegetarian World Guides.

**Signature**

Please send this completed review form to: **Vegetarian World Guide Reader Reviews, P.O. Box 3533, Morgantown, WV 26503-3533.** Feel free to attach menus, more notes, and any other relevant materials. Vegetarian World Guides cannot return these items, but we look forward to hearing from you!

**Restaurant**                                    **Date Visited**

**Address** *(Street, City, State, Zip)*

**Phone**                        **Web Site**

**Dress Code**    ☐ Casual ☐ Upscale ☐ Jacket Required

**Type of Service**    ☐ Snack Stand ☐ Counter ☐ Buffet ☐ Table Service

**Meals Served**    ☐ Snacks ☐ Breakfast ☐ Lunch ☐ Dinner

**Payment**    ☐ MC ☐ Visa ☐ AE ☐ Disc ☐ Diners ☐ Check ☐ Cash only

**Vegability**
  **Ovo-lacto selections are available:**
    ☐ Always    ☐ Upon request    ☐ With advance notice

           ovo-lacto selections are listed on the regular menu

  **Vegan selections are available:**
    ☐ Always    ☐ Upon request    ☐ With advance notice

           vegan selections are listed on the regular menu

**Your Meal**

**Appetizers**

**Entrées**

**Desserts**

**Beverages**

*over* ➤

**Your Meal** *(continued)*

**Your comments** *(please be as specific and descriptive as possible)*

**Your Name**

**Address (Street, City, State, Zip)**

**Day Phone**                              **E-mail**

☐   I am willing to be quoted on the Vegetarian World Guides' Web site, and in future editions of this and other Vegetarian World Guides.

**Signature**

Please send this completed review form to: **Vegetarian World Guide Reader Reviews, P.O. Box 3533, Morgantown, WV 26503-3533.** Feel free to attach menus, more notes, and any other relevant materials. Vegetarian World Guides cannot return these items, but we look forward to hearing from you!